MEISTER ECKHART

THE MYSTIC
AS THEOLOGIAN

AN EXPERIMENT IN METHODOLOGY

MEISTER ECKHART

THE MYSTIC AS THEOLOGIAN

AN EXPERIMENT IN METHODOLOGY

Robert K. C. Forman
City University of New York
Hunter College

ELEMENT

Rockport, Massachusetts • Shaftesbury, Dorset

© Robert K. C. Forman 1991

Published in the U.S.A. in 1991 by
Element Inc
42 Broadway, Rockport, MA 01966

Published in Great Britain in 1991 by
Element Books Limited
Longmead, Shaftesbury, Dorset

Cover illustration from a window of the Cathedral at Sens, France.
Photograph courtesy Richard J. Payne.
Cover design by Max Fairbrother.
Typeset by Poole Typesetting (Wessex) Limited.
Printed and bound in the U.S.A. by
Edwards Brothers Inc

Library of Congress data available.

British Library Cataloguing-in-Publication Data.
A catalogue record for this book is available from the British Library.

ISBN 1-85230-249-6

For Yvonne

The perfected soul cannot remain bound up in anything,
But must burst forth out of and over all things
To get to divine freedom,
In which she takes great delight.

(W 2:127)

Contents

Preface

The idea for this book came out of a suggestion made by Herb Richardson. I was delivering a paper to a regional conference of the American Academy of Religion on the place (or rather the lack of a place) of mystical experience in Kant's *Critique of Pure Reason*. I got to chatting with Herb about my paper and associated ideas about mysticism and philosophy. Herb is a good listener and an encouraging man. He was nearly as excited by my ideas as I was and suggested that I write a book on Meister Eckhart.

That suggestion was rather strange, considering my background. I have done work in Hinduism, mysticism and the philosophy of religion as it relates to mysticism. Though I had done some work at that point on Eckhart, I had no pretensions of being in any way an expert. I am not a linguist nor an expert on medieval Christianity or medieval philosophy.

Why, then, did Herb suggest that I should write a book on Meister Eckhart? Even more importantly, why would anyone want to read such a book? I think there is an overarching reason why Richardson's suggestion was a good one, and there are three specific contributions this book has to make to Eckhart scholarship, the study of mysticism, and the study of religion in general.

My academic work has been all about mysticism. I sometimes call myself a "mysticist," If there were an academic specialty called "the Philosophy of Mysticism," that would be my field. I have read and studied mystics from a variety of traditions. I have read and am pretty well current on the philosophical debates raging around mysticism.

In this field I have a rather unusual vantage point. Most of the debates on the philosophical nature of mysticism are an attempt to place mysticism in some sort of larger philosophical context; e.g., attempts to analyze mysticism in Wittgenstein's terms, in terms of the language of the tradition in which it stands, or in a Hegelian framework, etc. These attempts are laudable. However, such frameworks were constructed to explain our "ordinary" experience, and only applied later to mysticism. Mysticism is thus the "far-out" tail of the dog of ordinary sensory experience and the "ordinary" modes of knowledge. I have always thought this viewpoint was the wrong way to look at it. Mystics tend to distinguish that which they speak of *from* their ordinary experience. While their accounts of how the two are distinguished differ from one to another, the consistent claim is that mystical experience is unlike ordinary experience in significant ways. If we take such assertions as correct, as I do, then to analyze *mystical* experience in terms of systems built to explain *ordinary* experience is to misjudge or mis-describe the mystical.

What I attempt to do herein is to evaluate Eckhart's mysticism in its own terms, not in terms of a philosophical system it gives rise to, or in the language used to describe it, etc. I take the experiences Eckhart describes, not the more abstract doctrines of man, God, person, etc., as *the* starting point for my evaluation and analysis. I am attempting to build his system from the ground floor of experience on up.

This lead me to the first specific contribution I have to make. Methodologically, this book is quite novel. I see scholars of Eckhart—and of spiritual writers in general—as falling into two categories. On the one hand is the historian of ideas. He looks at Eckhart (or Bonaventure, or Shankara) and examines the intellectual trends to which he was heir. Eckhart has been seen as heir to the Biblical frame, the Neo-Platonist doctrines, the Scholastic heritage, or even the Celtic heritage! The second sort of analyst is the "spiritual historian," e.g., a Jean Leclercq or a Ewert Cousins. Such men look at the sort of "spiritual" history to which Eckhart was heir, appealing in an abstract way to his doctrines of God and the relationships that a man might have to Him.

I see myself as doing neither of these. Rather, if I might coin another term, I would call myself an "experientialist." I am attempting to portray as clearly and as precisely as I can Eckhart's phenomenological portraits of mystical or personal experience. I ask rather simple questions of him and of the other people I study: If I were a disciple of yours, if all goes as you say, what kind of experience might I expect to undergo? A vision perhaps? A blank awareness? A change in personality? Nothing special? What will it look like? Feel like? Then, and only then, having discerned answers to such questions, I will turn to my figure's more abstract doctrines, asking about his philosophy and theology only on the basis of the experiences I perceive him to be describing. I ask about the place of those experiences in that philosophical system. Finally, I interpret the system as a whole in terms of the experiences. Thus the method begins from the opposite end of the usual starting place.

The second contribution I see myself making here concerns the typology of mystical experience. Most students of mysticism find a single experience described in a system. Zaehner, for example, describes Zen mystics as "nature mystics." Stace finds one mystic advocating "introvertive" mysticism, and another advocating "extrovertive mysticism." James finds all mystics describing pretty much the same transient experiences. Typologies generally describe mystics in pretty static terms.

But as I read the texts, I notice that mystics speak consistently of a growth and a development. The journey image is common. The birds in the *Conference of the Birds* go through one stage after another. Maharishi Mahesh Yogi speaks of Transcendental Consciousness, which is generally followed by Cosmic Consciousness, which may be followed by Unity Consciousness. The stages are progressive and developmental. Eckhart speaks of a series of experiences, too, as we will see. The growth that any individual mystic may undergo is, it seems to me, the critical factor in the creation of any typology, not the distinctions between "types" of mysticism advocated by a tradition. Such growth moves towards a vertical as opposed to a horizontal typology. This study is the first of what I hope will be a series attempting to detail such development stages. Thus the second contribution of this book is a new and more detailed picture of the experiences a mystic may undergo, in particular the experiences described by Eckhart.

The third contribution concerns philosophy and theology. Studies of God, for example, have in general been looking for proofs of his existence "out there." A few, notably Schleiermacher's, have looked for God within an aspect of one's ordinary experience. No one, to my knowledge, has suggested what I suggest in chapters six, seven and eight: that God, although not found within one's ordinary experience, can become—in mystical experience—the "oceanic" whole from *within* which one perceives. This contention suggests that the critical change in mystical experience is not change in some object and is not an emotion in any common sense of the term, but rather involves a change in one's vantage point, as it were. One comes to experience from within the divine, as it were. This change of vantage point is not something the mystic philosophizes about in the abstract. It is, as I understand it, the most matter-of-fact feature of his or her everyday experience. Ontology should be seen as an expression of this aspect of the novel epistemological structure to which the mystical journey gives rise. What this God is, and why He should be thus, become the subject matter of much of the book, especially the last chapter.

The contributions of this book should be, and I expect will be, seen in two lights. First, it is a study of Eckhart in particular. Certainly I spend the bulk of my time and energy on him. Second, it is, more broadly, a study of mysticism. The reader will note that frequently in the early chapters, at critical junctures in Part I and often in Part III, I make reference to mystics other than Eckhart himself. Furthermore, though I do not dwell on this, it is a study of the nature of mysticism in general, i.e., mystical experience and how we might construe it as relating to mystical doctrine and texts. In this sense the book is a study of "mysticism" with Eckhart being, if you will, the case study. If my reader concludes that this book makes a valuable contribution, it should be apparent that it will be applicable to other mystics— even from other traditions—and perhaps to religious experiences in general and the religious life as well. I will not, however, draw out these implications in any detail. There is, after all, only so much a single book should attempt, and I fear I have attempted too much already.

My special thanks goes to Ewert Cousins, whose constant encouragement and excellent suggestions have been of significant help at nearly every step. It takes a big man to understand and sincerely encourage another whose vantage point is different from his own. Thanks also to Wayne Proudfoot, whose pointed questions and lively discussion helped me see the crux of many of the issues I discuss. Many persons have read sections of the manuscript and made excellent suggestions: Robert Kraus, Denise Denniston, Linda Hess, Jonas Barciauskas, John Tabor. My heartfelt thanks to each. My long-overdue thanks go to my parents, whose care and support made a graduate career possible. Yvonne Kraus Conrad Forman's mind, heart, time, and love permeate every corner of this work, and all my work: "one life, one being, and one work," as Eckhart put it. And my final appreciation goes to Meister Eckhart himself. In both my academic work and my personal life, his constant one-pointed attention on the single absolute truth has uplifted, inspired, and served as a constant reminder to me. Through the deepest of the valleys every writer (and person) traverses, he has unflaggingly helped me forward. I hope that my reading does justice to him and serves to bring alive to others the wisdom I have found in him.

This book was researched and written during 1983–84. Much to my disappointment, due to circumstances beyond my control it has taken 6 years to get it into print. In the intervening years the discussions of some of the issues broached herein have progressed, and I have had the good fortune of editing and publishing *The Problem of Pure Consciousness* with Oxford University Press. That book advances the philosophical grounding for certain of the claims made and approaches taken herein, and the philosophically sophisticated reader is encouraged to turn to it. Unfortunately however I have not been able to substantially revise this book in the light of recent discussion of Eckhart, Mysticism, or *the Problem of Pure Consciousness*.

My thanks are due to Richard Payne, for his long sustained support, and the staffs at both Amity House Press and Element Books.

Abbreviations

Aside from the standard abbreviations, the following abbreviations are used in this book:

Caputo — Caputo, John D. *The Mystical Element in Heidegger's Thought.* Oberlin: Oberlin Printing Co., 1978.

Clark — Clark, James M. *Meister Eckhart: An Introduction to the Study of his works with an Anthology of his Sermons.* Edinburgh: Thomas Nelson and Sons, 1957.

Clark and Skinner — Clark, James M. and John V. Skinner, eds., and trans. *Meister Eckhart: Selected Treatises and Sermons.* London: Faber and Faber, 1958.

Colledge and McGinn — Colledge, Edmond and McGinn, Bernard. *Meister Eckhart: The Essential Sermons, Commentaries, Treatises and Defense.* New York: Paulist Press, 1981.

DW — *Meister Eckhart Die deutsche Werke Herausgegeben im Auftrage der Deutschen Forschungsgemeinschaft,* edited by Josef Quint et al. 5 vols. Stuttgart and Berlin: W. Kohlhammer Verlag, 1936.

Fingarette — Fingarette, Herbert. *The Self in Transformation: Psychoanalysis, Philosophy, and the Life of the Spirit.* New York: Harper and Row.

Kieckhefer — Kieckhefer, Richard. "Meister Eckhart's Conception of Union with God." *Harvard Theological Review* 71 (1978): 203–225.

Ludwig   Ludwig, Arnold. "Altered States of Consciousness." In *Altered States of Consciousness,* ed. Charles Tart, pp. 225–34. New York: John Wiley and Sons, 1969. This is a reprint of an article which first appeared in *Archives of General Psychiatry* 15:225–34.

LW   *Meister Eckhart Die latinische Werke Herausgegeben Auftrage der Deutschen Forschungsgemeinschaft,* edited by Josef Koch et. al. Stuttgart and Berlin: W. Kohlhammer Verlag, 1936.

McGinn in Szérnach   McGinn, Bernard. "Meister Eckhart: An Introduction." In *Introduction to the Medieval Mystics of Europe.* Edited by Paul Szernach, pp. 237–58. Binghamton: SUNY Press.

Maurer   Maurer, A., ed. and trans. *Parisian Questions and Prologues.* Toronto: Pontifical Institute of Mediaeval Studies, 1970.

Pfeiffer   Pfeiffer, Franz, ed. and trans. *Meister Eckhart.* Gottingen: Vandenhoeck and Ruprecht, 1924.

Quint   Quint, Josef. *Meister Eckhart: Deutsche Predigen und Traktate.* Munchen: Carl Hanser, 1955.

Schurmann   Schurmann, Reiner. *Meister Eckhart: Mystic and Philosopher.* Bloomington, Ind.: Indiana University Press, 1978.

Tobin   Tobin, Frank. "Eckhart's Mystical Use of Language: The Contexts of *eigenschaft.*" *Seminar* 8:159–68.

Ueda   Ueda, Schizuteru. *Die Gottesgeburt in der Seele und der Durchbruch zur Gottheit: Die mystische Anthropologie Meister Eckharts und ihre Konfrontation mit der Mystik des Zen Buddhismus.* Gutersloher: Gerd Mohn, 1965.

W   Walshe, M. *Meister Eckhart: German Sermons and Treatises.* 2 vols. London: Watkins, 1979, 1981.

PART I

Introduction

CHAPTER ONE

Introduction

Scholarly advances often come from asking unconventional questions. My questions came after I had acquainted myself moderately well with the secondary literature on the great thirteenth-to-fourteenth-century mystic Meister Eckhart.[1] One finds excellent studies of Eckhart's intellectual forbears,[2] of his doctrines of God,[3] Christology,[4] epistemology,[5] analogy,[6] etc. These are undeniably useful and important. But these philosophical, theological, and linguistic studies did not seem to elucidate Eckhart but to distract attention away from the Meister's principal emphasis.

Eckhart was a Dominican prior, provincial, and vicar his entire adult life. Though at times he served as a professor in Paris and probably in Cologne, the bulk of his energies were devoted to preaching and directing the monks and nuns in his charge. Above everything else, the Meister Eckhart who has come down to us was a preacher and a spiritual master. Whatever his philosophical and theological presuppositions, his primary role in the sermons and the tractates, which taken together are the writings for which he is renowned, is that of a leader of souls.[7] He led, he cajoled, he taught, and he exhorted his listeners towards what he knew as the ultimate salvific experiences.

In virtually every sermon and tractate Eckhart hammers away at one point: that some interior transformation—called variously the Birth of the Son (or Word) of God in the Soul, the Breakthrough of the Soul to the Godhead, and other names—should happen within the individual.

> What does it avail to me that this birth is always happening, if it does not *happen to me?* That it should happen in me is what matters.[8]

That a Birth is happening in me may admit to a merely theoretical interpretation that God is present in the Soul ontologically and/or through grace. Such is commonly asserted by Christian theologians and is not necessarily mystical. But Eckhart was not content with such theoretical assertions of God's nearness. He stressed a consciousness of God's presence. For example, in DW 68 and W 69 Eckhart notes that God is within a stone and a log of wood but they have no awareness of His presence. If they were as conscious of God's presence as is the highest angel, they would be as blessed as the angel.[9] It is only in proportion to my conscious awareness of God's presence that I am blessed.[10] Just as being a king requires that the individual (and the populace) believe and be consciously aware that he is king, the nearness of God to the soul becomes valuable if and only if the individual is consciously aware of that fact.[11] Eckhart notes that while the soul may not be aware of God's coming and going, "she can sense when He is with her."[12] As a result of such awareness of God's presence, the soul will *know* and therefore have no need of sermons or teaching.

> . . .in whatever soul God's kingdom dawns, which knows God's kingdom to be near her, is in no need of sermons or teaching: she is instructed by it and assured of eternal life: for she knows and is aware how near God's kingdom is, and she can say with Jacob: " 'God is in this place, and I knew it not'—but *now* I know it."[13]

The direct experiences Eckhart advocates occur not only in some distant future or at the Day of Judgment, but are able to be experienced here and now.

> But I say yet more:. . .there is not one of you who is so coarse-grained, so feeble of understanding or so remote but he may find this joy within himself, in truth, as it is, with joy and understanding, before you leave this church today . . . Be sure of this for it is true, and Truth herself declares it.[14]

One may—indeed one must, according to Eckhart—come to discover "this joy" in this life.

That some direct encounter with the divine should happen to

or within the individual is Eckhart's constant emphasis. "Follow the first step and continue: you will get to the right place, and all is well."[15] "That our Lord will invite us, too, to enter in and dwell with him eternally, and he with us, may God help us."[16] He emphasizes repeatedly that he is talking of the transformed man, of the man who has discovered the Birth or the Breakthrough of which he speaks, and of the man who has gained union with God.

Though the meaning of the formula Eckhart uses to conclude his sermons is often overlooked, it is very important, for in it he shows the real point of his remarks. Virtually every sermon concludes with a prayer that something "should happen in me": may we be "be born in him again as God" (W 1:12): "may we be . . . freed" (W 1:47): "may we become and remain eternally one with him" (W 1:61). That something—some lived transformation or some mystical experience(s)—should happen in me: this is the key to Eckhart.[17]

All of his works should be understood in the light of this possibility:

> For what I say here is to be understood of the good and perfected man . . . not of the natural, undisciplined man, for he is entirely remote from, and totally ignorant of this birth. (W 1:1)

To distinguish the "good and perfected man" from its opposite, "the natural undisciplined man," is to suggest that there is a starting point, a *terminus a quo*, and a point towards which someone may move, a *terminus ad quem*. This must be read in the light of his constant emphasis that one may bring the good with you, releasing one's attachments (see chapter four). Hence, he is making no hard and fast distinction between the natural and perfected man, but rather what he says "here" describes the results of a process which may lead from one to the other.

It is in this light that Eckhart's words should be read. His sermons, tractates, and even his more academic and speculative writings are about people, living people, who have undergone or are undergoing the transformation and experiences that he knew, advocated, and perhaps even himself lived.

If such inner transformations and significant experiences stand as the preoccupation of his sermons, and if one should read a mystic in the light of his or her emphasis, it is as surprising as it is disappointing that the secondary literature leaves one with no clear sense of the transformations and experiences towards which he pointed.[18] Having read the literature, I still found myself wondering about them. What did Eckhart say, I wondered, specifically about the spiritual journey and its resultant, possibly mystical, experiences? My wonderings formed themselves into a single overarching question to which this book addresses itself: *Were I a friar or a nun under your tutelage, Meister Eckhart, what mystical experience(s), if any, might I be expected to undergo, and what significance would it (they) have?*

This question is very different from those most commonly asked by recent Eckhart scholars, who are concerned with Eckhart's mystical anthropology or speculative system.[19] Those authors might attempt to determine the nature of, for example, Eckhart's most abstract doctrines of God, Christ, and/or emanation, and then determine man's theoretical place in this overall scheme of things. With the answer to such a question in hand, and somewhat as an afterthought, such a student of Eckhart's mystical anthropology might then delve into a few mystical experience(s) and show how they express or are interpreted by this system.

James Clark's "Introduction" is typical.[20] Clark devotes some 55 pages to an exposition of Eckhart's theology, beginning with the Meister's notion, of the *via negativa* way of speaking to God and an exposition of the relationship between God and being (*esse*). He then proceeds to a discussion of the two kinds of Grace, the composite nature of man, the definition of Truth, and the nature of virtue and vice. Finally, in the few pages of the chapter entitled "The Mystic," he makes mention of a few passages about *experience*. But even these expositions are so shrouded in discussions of the created or uncreated nature of the spark in the soul and of the various symbols that are used to describe it that it is difficult to see what experiences are being described. I do not wish to fault Clark in particular, for whom I have the greatest respect as an interpreter and translator. Most other Eckhart scholars also place their discussions of experiences, if such discussions are to be found at all, at the end of a doctrinal exposition.[21] From such accounts I find it virtually impossible to guess what it might be like to undergo the experiences that Eckhart stresses.

Nor does the fault lie with Eckhart studies alone, for it is my impression that this is standard methodology in the study of mystics.[22] Unlike such studies, my principal interest is in the character of the experiences as Eckhart describes them. My interest finds resonance in the questions asked by Kieckhefer; i.e., are the experiences advocated by Eckhart temporary or permanent?[23] He argues that Eckhart's main emphasis is on a habitual form of experience, an argument with which I concur. (See chapter five). Yet answering his question is only a first step towards answering mine. If the experiences are permanent (as I believe some are), exactly *what* is habitual? What is the subjective nature of or the felt character of "that" which is enjoyed permanently? Does one habitually experience perhaps a blue light, as Muktananda did,[24] or a sense of being enclosed in some huge oceanlike space? Is it a joyous or sorrowful habit? What happens to one's sense of time? Are there any tactile accompaniments? Does one's feeling about or perception of the world change? With the answer to such questions clearly in mind, I would also like to know about the relationship between the beginning state and the latter one(s) and the nature of the transformation process leading from the one to the other. Finally (and this is a question which other Eckhart scholars have addressed, though they have given different answers than I will) does Eckhart discuss one or several types of experiences? If there are several, what are they like and what is the relationship among them? In short, what I am curious about is the phenomenological descriptions of experiences that the texts present to us. What is it like, to use Thomas Nagel's language, to undergo the phenomenon of which Eckhart writes?

METHODOLOGICAL CONCERNS

I wish I could answer such questions as easily as I can ask them! I wish I could neatly divide the texts into clear-cut piles, and say that over here are autobiographical passages, over there are phenomenological descriptions of that which a friar or nun might undergo; in this pile Eckhart speculates on these descriptions, and the connections are as follows . . .

I wish the texts lent themselves to this sort of analysis. But the truth is that, for a variety of reasons, we have not one shred of an autobiography *à la* Mechthilde's *Flowing Light of the God-head*, St. Teresa's *Life*, or Muktananda's *Play of Consciousness*. It was not common for men of Eckhart's position to leave such autobiographies. Eckhart was no exception. Nor have we phenomenological descriptions of mystical experiences in unambiguous language, *à la The Lives of the Brethren*, the writings of St. John, or perhaps *The Cloud of Unknowing*.[25] Devoid of such "raw data," it goes without saying that the speculative material cannot be readily correlated with any particular description.

The lack of such unambiguous autobiographical or descriptive materials should not be taken to imply that no mystical experiences are being described or evoked. As I have pointed out, some such transformations and lived experiences are of primary concern. They are so much present that the entire system is, as I will show throughout, particularly in chapter eight, shot through with the facts of those experiences. The lack of clear-cut phenomenological reports does, however, make the job of answering my questions much harder.

Is it possible, even in theory, to do what I seek to do? Can one somehow divine what sort of experience stood behind a text, as it were? A related question: when there are no clearly autobiographical passages, can one tease experience-portraits out of a complex text which has an interwoven set of purposes, linguistic uses, and themes?

With reference to the first question, it is in principle impossible to answer a question about what experiences stand behind a text. The experiential or psychological source of any text whose author is deceased cannot in principle be answered with certainty. First of all, it is commonplace in epistemology that we cannot have an experience of someone else's experiences. Two people can share what is public; they cannot share subjective experiences. I may be able to feel myself perceived in a particular way using phenomenological means, but this feeling is not an experience of someone else's experience. Even in this situation certainty is not possible. In the case of a text, however, even this is not possible. We can never get to a shared experience enough to know for certain what psychological episodes might have given rise to the words we have before us. It is possible, for example, that Eckhart describes some experience which he never himself underwent, or that he read of it in some dusty manuscript, or that he heard of it from a trusted friend or nun under his guidance. Although such explanations may be somewhat implausible, any of them is possible.[26] The first question must be left as unanswerable in principle.

This predicament is not true for the second question. For although it may be difficult to tease Eckhart's notions of mystical experiences out of texts which do not directly depict them, doing so seems inherently no more impossible than is the attempt to understand what Eckhart meant by a theological concept that he also does not define point-blank. The processes are similar. Let us say I wanted to characterize how Eckhart presents Moses. First I would work up a concordance of every use of this term, also drawing in related terms and stories, such as the burning bush, the receipt of the Ten Commandments, the parting of the Red Sea, etc. Then I would look for parallel passages from other authors. For example, Eckhart defines "Moses" in two places as "one who was taken out of the water."[27] He derived this definition from Isidore's *Etym* VII, chapter 6, number 46,[28] so I would look there to see whether or in what way Eckhart transformed this definition and use. With such definitions, background, and themes in hand, I would determine the thrust of the Moses image, and show some of the nuances that Eckhart lends to this term. I might finally relate it to what I understood as his larger theme.

I propose to do something parallel, except rather than theological terms, I propose to study experiential terms, and instead of providing a theological significance, I would attempt to point out these terms' more phenomenological uses and significances (though the theology will also be explored, especially in the last chapter). Thus my principal question will be in part addressed by means of these questions: what are the definitions of the experiential terms as Eckhart uses them? With what nuances does he imbue them?

To get as near as possible to purely phenomenological descriptions, I will capitalize on Ninian Smart's well-known distinction between high and low levels of linguistic ramification.[29] Where a concept gains its meaning "in part from a range of statements taken to be true," it is highly ramified, he said.[30] For instance, when Eckhart says, "as long as a man is in a state of grace, all his works are worthy of eternal reward . . . for God does the works in grace" (W 1:129), this utterance gains its meaning at least in part from such highly ramified terms as "state of grace," "eternal reward," and "God." The term *God*, gains its meaning at least in part from such doctrinal statements as "God created the Universe," "Jesus Christ is God," "God has acted in history," etc.[31] We verify the truth or falsity of propositions using these terms "in other ways than by immediate mystical experience," writes Smart.[32] We might check with scripture, scholastic writings, etc.

Conversely, in the following passages Eckhart describes an experience in comparatively low ramified terms.

> If only you could suddenly be unaware of all things, then you could pass into an oblivion of your own body as St. Paul did, when he said, "Whether in the body I cannot tell, or out of the body I cannot tell; God knows it" (2 Cor 12:2). In this case the spirit had so entirely absorbed the powers that it had forgotten the body: memory no longer functioned, nor understanding, nor the senses, nor the powers that should function so as to govern and grace the body, vital warmth and body-heat were suspended, so that the body did not waste during the three days when he neither ate nor drank. (W 1:7)

When Eckhart speaks of being "unaware of all things," of being oblivious to the body, or of the nonfunctioning of the memory, something of the nature of an experience is conveyed without any religious doctrine's being presupposed as true. Propositions using such phrases will not be verified by checking with scripture or philosophical argument, but rather by comparison with the character of the experience itself. Hence low-ramified utterances are nearer to experience descriptions than are higher ones.

Of course even relatively unramified descriptions presuppose a range of statements deriving their meaning from extraexperiential sources. As linguistic philosophers are fond of reminding us, every word derives its meaning from a language and a conceptual system as a whole.[33] This is unavoidable. At best we can hope to asymptotically approach Eckhart's descriptions of experience by concentrating on his simplest language. This concentration will bring us closest to utterances that are guaranteed by the character of the experience itself.

These distinctions between high- and low-ramified language are not sharp and impermeable. I am not attempting to isolate low-ramified language and avoid Eckhart's theoretical talk. Not at all! I will attempt to bring in as much of his thought as possible. But I will emphasize the low- rather than the high-ramified language and attempt to read the latter in terms of the former.

At times I will read an instruction as a description. For example, in one sermon Eckhart quotes Dionysius as follows:

> Dear son Timothy, do you with untroubled mind soar above yourself and all your powers, above ratiocination and reasoning, above works, above all modes and existence, into the secret still darkness, that you may come to the knowledge of the unknown super-divine God.[34] There must be a withdrawal from all things.[35]

This passage is in the form of a command. It first instructs Timothy (and by extension all listeners or readers) to soar above himself. The last sentence, now in Eckhart's own voice, commands that one must withdraw from things. Though these are commands, they also may—and indeed must—be read as a description of both the technical character of the process (soaring above ratiocination and reasoning, above works and modes) and also in some sense as descriptive of the character of that which is gained (like a secret, still darkness).

It is legitimate to read a command as a description, as I have done, given the possibility of fulfilling the command. "Turn off the light!" describes the performance it commands. And indeed Eckhart (as well as many other mystical authors) does tell us that the state of life that he advocates is available in this life, at least as a foretaste. At the very outset of this sermon Eckhart tells us that he is speaking of something that is consummated in the virtuous soul:

> We shall therefore speak of this birth, of how it may take place in us and be consummated in the virtuous soul, whenever God the Father speaks His eternal Word in the perfect soul. For what I say here is to be understood of the good and perfected man *who has walked and is still walking in the ways of* God. . . (W 1:11)

If the perfected man "is still walking" in this form of life, then by following the commands one may come to walk thus. That is, it is possible to fulfill his instructions. Hence the passage in the form of a command is not only evoking or instructing. It is also describing. I shall read such passages, where appropriate, in this light.

To sum up my method, I have used the following procedure. First, I set up a mystical concordance. It is clear from even a cursory reading that a relatively small number of terms denote the key Eckhartian experiences. Through extensive use of the indexes, I attempted to compile a listing of the occurrences of these terms and related terms.

My second task has been to develop definitions of these terms, and to determine their low-ramified nuances. In chapter five, for example, I detail the uses of the term *gezucket* (rapture), studying the less highly ramified passages that apply to it, and detail its significance as Eckhart uses the term.

I sometimes have faced the problem of having to decide which mystical term or experience was being described with a particular low-ramified passage. To solve it I came to rely on the structure of the sermons. Eckhart typically interweaves two threads into any sermon. First, the scriptural passage or phrase on which he preaches becomes the leitmotif, image, or key phrase for that sermon. This is standard medieval homiletic form. Sometimes the phrase determines the queries of the sermon, as in W Sermon 2 (= QT 58), which rhapsodizes on Matthew 2:2, "Where is he who is born King of the Jews?" The question "Where?" evolves and permutes itself in a variety of contexts. It opens the sermons, evolves into the questions "Where in the soul?" "In whom?" and later becomes "Where do you know this from and in what way?" *"In Principio,"* the opening words of Genesis and St. John's Gospel, run like a leitmotif throughout Sermon 53 (= DW 22). It begins virtually every paragraph, and becomes the phrase with which Eckhart expresses and ponders everything.

The second thread in any individual sermon relates to his more general concerns: he investigates some form of mystical encounter and its interpretation. Each sermon is generally devoted to one significant type or stage of the mystical progression, to wit the Birth of the Word in the Soul or the Breakthrough of the Soul to the Godhead. Throughout the sermon he discusses one or the other of these, frequently employing language derived from the opening quotation to do so. Sometimes, of course, he discusses more than one stage in one sermon, as in Sermon 50 (= DW14). When he does so he typically discusses their relationship. In such cases he alerts his listener to the fact that he is discussing a particular stage by introducing its vocabulary.

(See chapter seven.) But in general, the experiential utterances that appear in any individual sermon can be applied to the stage that stands as the principal concern of that sermon.

There are two exceptions to this rule of thumb: first, no sermon is devoted exclusively to rapture. Eckhart does not advocate the pursuit of such, as I will discuss in chapters five and six. Hence no sermon is devoted solely to it. Rather, rapture is generally discussed in the context of the Birth, which, as I will show, Eckhart presents as its fulfillment or completeness. The second exception: because Eckhart is so consistently goal-oriented, no sermon is solely devoted to the mystical transformative process. Discussions of the process he advocates (i.e. of detaching oneself from one's attachments) are found always in the context of the experience towards which that process leads.

The numeration system developed in 1857 by one of the earliest Eckhart scholars, Pfeiffer, in his *Meister Eckhart*, which is followed on the whole in Walshe's recent English translation, can be roughly correlated with this underlying subject matter. The lower numbers typically have rapture and the Birth as their dominant concern, while the higher numbers tend to focus on the Breakthrough. Although there are no neat lines here, the middle-numbered sermons frequently discuss the relationship between the Birth and the Breakthrough. It is tempting to draw the conclusion that, since Pfeiffer attempted to arrange his text roughly chronologically, Eckhart changed his subject over the decade or so during which the sermons were composed, and further that this perhaps resulted from an evolution in his own experience. However since no one has yet authoritatively determined the chronology of the sermons, this must remain but an enticing speculation.

This then is the procedure I followed in writing this book. If Sermon X is generally about, for example, the Birth of the Word in the Soul, then any low-ramified characterization of a mystical experience which I found there was taken as descriptive of that stage. So, too, for the Breakthrough of the Soul to the Godhead. In this way I began to bring together the descriptions of each stage, in effect working up a set of experiential definitions from my concordance.

The final step of my method is that of reassembly, presenting the system as a whole with the now systematized discoveries about mystical experience behind me. This I will do periodically throughout the book, but I consolidate my thoughts in the concluding chapter. There I attempt to outline his speculative system and relate its key points to what he says about experience.

One result of my method is that many of the passages discussed in my text are the passages not responded to by other Eckhart scholars. While they have emphasized the more highly ramified and theologically sophisticated utterances, I have emphasized the less highly ramified and more "on the ground" descriptions of experience. For example, Kertz,[36] Wentzlaff-Eggebert,[37] Ueda,[38] and Caputo[39] all focus on W 2:135, in which Eckhart says,

> the Father gives birth to His Son in the soul in the very same way as he gives birth to him in eternity, and no differently. . . . The Father begets His son unceasingly, and furthermore, I say, He begets me as His Son and the same Son.

This is unquestionably an important passage, not only because it appears in the Papal Bull *In Agro Dominico* condemning Eckhart, but because Eckhart discusses herein the theoretical relationship between Father, Son, and the transformed Soul. I, too, discuss it in chapter six. But what these men neither quote nor discuss is the following passage from the next paragraph, which describes some aspect of an experience.

> . . .whatever is changed into something else becomes one with it. I am converted into Him in such a way that He makes me one with his being, not similar. By the living God it is true that there is no distinction. (W 2:135–6)

It is towards such previously undiscussed or less emphasized passages that I will direct my energies. Hence my work may be viewed as a corrective to an unnoticed intellectual bias seen in the secondary literature.

The book may also be viewed as an attempt to show the reader how I read Eckhart. I am attempting to share a vision. It will strike many as quite novel, I expect. As such I have made it a point to quote Eckhart extensively. In so doing I hope that the reader may him/herself come to read Eckhart in a fresh light.

My work may also be viewed as a methodological experiment which may have applicability not only to Eckhart, but to any mystical author.

Finally, two caveats: from a perusal of my method and from the fact that we have no explicitly autobiographical or unambiguously descriptive passages, the reader should be prepared not to expect certainty. Perhaps the best we can hope for from such a project is a good guess. Eckhart himself is long dead; we cannot check our conclusions with him. Nor does this sort of inquiry lend itself to quantification or to a historian's set of certain facts. As I view my work, I think of it as an exploration into a man's principal emphasis. I have asked the one question which seemed to me the central one, and it was a question I didn't see others asking. This exploration had led me to what seems to be one plausible reading among many. I hope that my modest attempts to explore Eckhart will open readers up to him in new and interesting ways.

The second caveat: it will be clear to the philosophically minded reader that I have assumed the answer to a question which is by no means commonly assumed today. The question is, simply stated, does experience give rise to doctrine or does doctrine give rise to experience? I have assumed throughout this book that mystical experience may be thought to give rise to doctrine in significant ways. This assumption implies that experience is in some sense independent of doctrine. For many of my readers this will not seem obviously true—indeed, it will seem false. I will not attempt to argue my case here in any detail, for I have done so elsewhere. I have begun to argue this case in "The Construction of Mystical Experience" and in *The Problem of Pure Consciousness*. I direct the interested reader to these three works.[40] In a word, I maintain that unlike most experiences which *are* deeply determined by the beliefs, language, and expectations with which one enters them, mystical experience in general results from a process of forgetting, undoing, letting go, and detaching from ordinary (creaturely) concepts, beliefs, and attachments. Such a process leads to a state of complete abandonment of all creaturely images, etc., and is therefore best understood as independent of those concepts. "What" comes then is independent in significant ways from the preexperiential set, and is plausibly understood as placing a demand on the belief system to express and describe "what" comes in a way that makes sense within the intellectual context of the day. When Eckhart teaches that one gains the state he advocates by a process of letting go and forgetting, or when he says that what comes as a result is not the product of the power of reason or of the senses, I see him as laying out factors which correlate with just this notion of mysticism. Because this state is transcendent to the reasoning and intellection process, Eckhart is right to say it is mode- and power-transcending. He denies that God is the result of any intellectual construction. I see myself as taking such assertions with the utmost seriousness, and in a way that my opponents on this issue never can.

A word on texts: the touchstone of any modern study on Eckhart is the critical edition of his works. Begun in 1936 and yet to be completed, four volumes each of Latin and German works have appeared to date, edited respectively by Josef Koch et. al, and Josef Quint et. al. To avoid spurious material I will rely on Quint's and Koch's determination of material which is reliably Eckhart's own. In addition to the DW and LW, I will include any material in Quint's translation into modern German which has not yet appeared in the critical edition.

There are several first-rate translations of the German works which have appeared since the critical edition was published. There is no reason to add to their numbers. For the sake of consistency I will use Walshe's two-volume translation of Eckhart's sermons, making changes only where necessary. It is the only complete work and is excellent. Page references will be to these volumes. For the reader's convenience, sermon numbers will be provided for the DW numeration and Walshe's. Since there is no complete set of translations of the Latin works, I will use Clark's, McGinn's, Maurer's, and my own.

There has been some debate over whether and in what proportion the commentator should rely on Eckhart's Latin or German works. Although the doctrinal teachings are "basically the same in both languages,"[41] the two have very different styles and emphases. In the Latin works Eckhart was very much the philosophical theologian. Writing to his learned colleagues in a close and spare style, he was working within the scholastic mold formed by his predecessor, Thomas Aquinas. In the German works, especially the sermons, Eckhart was acting as a spiritual guide and preacher to religious men and women. There he is more outspoken and straightforward about his (and their) mystical concerns and the nuances of certain experiences than in his

more circumspect Latin ones. I agree to some extent with
McGinn:

> Approaches that would favor the subtle scholastic theologian over
> the extravagant vernacular preacher, or reverse this by champion-
> ing the originality of the German works over the more arid style
> of the Latin treatises and sermons, can never give us the full
> Eckhart.[42]

Hence I will include references to both Latin and German works
throughout. Most of the more explicit experiential material is
found in the German works, especially the sermons, and I will
perforce emphasize them. This is no loss, since, as Schurmann
writes:

> . . .the German works should be recognized as the most significant
> reflection of his thought and of the creative genius of his lan-
> guage. . .When Eckhart addressed himself to the nuns of the
> Rhineland (who preserved these sermons for us) in his mother
> tongue, he was more original and more personal; he spoke to
> them without the confining apparatus of late scholasticism. . . .
> The Latin works mark the road, but the German works invite us
> on the journey.[43]

To this I would add that the German works also mark the
journey in a way that the Latin works could not. His mysticism is
formulated most vividly there. It is largely in German that he
performed his main role of leading his audience towards certain
transformations and experiences, and it is to these works that I
will turn most often for his descriptions of them.

MYSTICISM AND ECKHART

Although I have made every effort to develop my experience
descriptions based on what I found in the Eckhartian corpus itself,
I want to be forthright. There is a great deal of literature with
which I am to some extent conversant—theoretical, classical, and
autobiographical, and from the full panoply of traditions—on the

nature of mystical experiences, and my reading of the Meister has been to some extent informed by it.[44] My reading in this literature had led me to, perhaps, pick up on certain passages more than others. Perhaps I will be accused of reading this material into Eckhart. I do not know how a scholar might avoid bringing his own background of knowledge into the object of his studies—nor indeed whether it would be preferable to attempt to do so. But that is another matter.

In this case, however, there is one reason that makes it appropriate to allow this information to inform my reading of Eckhart. Researchers on States of Consciousness have intentionally studied subjects from many traditions and eras, and have attempted to formulate their definitions in ways that are not limited to any one age or culture. To some extent their findings should apply to any mystic. If Eckhart is indeed a mystic, and I think there is little doubt about this, then this literature should be at least in part relevant.

In part due to my background in this material, I understand mysticism as a much broader phenomenon than most Eckhart scholars, and this is, I suspect, one reason that I have developed a very different appraisal of Eckhart as a mystic.

Most Eckhart scholars write out of a more or less traditional Christian perspective. Although few have defined mysticism clearly, an excellent modern definition of mysticism which is also informed by the traditional view is found in Margaret Smith's article, "The Nature and Meaning of Mysticism."[45] Mysticism, she writes,

is to be described rather as an attitude of mind; an innate tendency of the human soul, which seeks to transcend reason and to attain to a direct experience of God, and which believes that it is possible for the human soul to be united with Ultimate Reality, when "God ceases to be an object and becomes an experience." Mysticism has been defined as "the immediate feeling of the unity of self with God. . .it is the endeavor to fix the immediateness of the life in God as such—in this God-intoxication, in which the self and the world are alike forgotten, the subject knows himself to be in possession of the highest and fullest truth."

The aim of the mystics, then, is to establish a conscious relation with the Absolute, in which they find the personal object of life. . . . That union which they seek is "the supernatural union of

likeness, begotten of life, which is the union of the human will
with the Divine.''[46]

According to Ms. Smith, mysticism is the natural tendency of the
human soul, which seeks to attain a direct experience of God. Her
definition also focuses on the ecstatic moment, in which the self
and the world are forgotten.

The obvious flaw in such a definition as Smith's is that it
eliminates agnostic or atheistic mysticism, such as is found in
Theravada Buddhism or Jainism. This flaw is especially significant in light of the fact that Eckhart has been shown to parallel
Buddhistic thought and has been called with considerable plausibility an agnostic or atheistic mystic.[47] If this appellation is true,
he would be excluded from those mystics covered by Smith's
definition! Nor will it suffice to attempt to replace the term *God*
here with something like *the Transcendent,* as Ninian Smart does
in his article, "Mystical Experience."[48] Such a replacement keeps
the form of the definition constant (the mystic has an experience
of some Godlike X) and thus leaves out Buddhistic and agnostic
mysticism.

A more promising route in defining *mysticism* is that taken by
Smart in his later article, "Interpretation and Mystical Experience."[49] There he defines mysticism as primarily consisting in
"an interior or introvertive quest culminating in certain interior
experiences which are not described in terms of sense experience
or of mental images, etc."[50] Because no mention is made of a
purported object, *mysticism* here can include agnostic or atheistic
mystics. Although "certain critical interior experiences" is left by
Smart intentionally vague, for the purposes of this book it will
suffice as a starting point. It is superior to Smith's in that it will
include both ecstatic and also more permanent or habitual experiences.

Because I understand mysticism as a phenomenon which may
be either ecstatic or habitual, I have come to a different conclusion than many about Eckhart as a mystic. Quite a number of
scholars have claimed that he was no mystic.[51] One of the com-
monest reasons given is that he did not emphasize those "special
states of experience" like rapture which are so commonly
thought to be the *sine qua non* of mysticism.[52] Bernard McGinn,
for example, argues that Eckhart disapproves of visions, locu-

tions, and sensations: these he calls the "sensible variety" of mystical experience. In this I believe that he is right. He also claims that Eckhart disparages ecstatic rapture, which he calls the "introvertive" variety of mystical experience. In this I believe that he is wrong. It is true that Eckhart's "principle" emphasis is not on such ecstatic moments but rather towards something more permanent. It is not true, however, that Eckhart disparages rapture. As I will argue in chapter five, he actually speaks of such experiences relatively frequently and quite sympathetically, especially in his frequent discussions concerning Paul's rapture (see 2 Cor. 12:2). I will argue that what he disparages—and adamantly so—is not rapture but the attachment to rapture which a fascination with it signifies.

However, even if Eckhart were entirely against rapture, according to my definition he could still advocate mysticism. As per Smart's definition, the term *mysticism* should be understood to include more than only ecstatic and quietistic experiences. The kind of permanent or habitual transformation that Kieckhefer points towards, in which the subject enjoys a sense of union with the transcendent even while being active in the world, will still count as mystical. And I will show in chapters six and seven that this viewpoint is what Eckhart advocates. Hence I believe that Eckhart's teachings are best regarded as mystical.

With this definition in mind, I can specify why I believe that Eckhart was himself a mystic. As I have said before, this matter is, in principle, impossible to determine with absolute certainty. At best one may form only an impression, but there are several reasons for believing that Eckhart was indeed himself a mystic.[53]

1. Although Eckhart left us with no unmistakably autobiographical passages wherein he specifies in systematic detail his religious experiences, he has left us with countless asides and utterances that give the impression that he himself had experienced firsthand that of which he spoke. His language is so idiosyncratic, so immediate and compelling, that it is hard to imagine such freedom and such a sense of authority without an immediate experience. A few examples:

For the man who has once for an instant looked into this ground,

a thousand marks of red-minted gold are the same as a brass
farthing. (W 1:117)

If you could naught yourself for an instant, indeed I say less than
an instant, you would possess all that this is in itself. (W 144)

On the basis of such a sense of authority and fluidity of expression
one may believe that here was a man who himself had experienced the revelatory nature of the experience he describes and
hence knew firsthand about how one might evaluate money or
possessions in comparison. In the following passage he describes
himself as convinced beyond even a shadow of doubt:

Whoever has understood this sermon, good luck to him. If no one
had been here I should have had to preach it to this collecting box.
(W 2:82)

Again it is hard to imagine someone so convinced by what he was
saying that he would have said it even to an empty church, were
it not for a personal vision driving that conviction.

2. Despite the absence of systematic autobiographical passages,
there are quite a number of passages that employ the first person
(Ich, mich and *mir)*. These passages may be taken as indicative of a
firsthand experience. In the context of the sermons in which they
appear they are striking indeed, for it is unusual to see any first-
person utterances in medieval sermons written by man of Eckhart's position. A few examples:

The Father begets His son unceasingly, and furthermore, I say, He
begets me as His Son and the same Son. I say even more: not only
does He Beget me as His Son, but He begets me as Himself and
Himself as me, and me as His being and His nature. . . . God and I
are one. Through knowledge I take God into myself, through
love I enter into God. (W 136)

Out of that purity He has been ever begetting me, his only-
begotten son, in the very image of His eternal Fatherhood that I
may be a father and beget him of whom I am begotten.
(W 2:64)

This spirit must transcend number and break through multiplicity, and God will break through him: and just as He breaks
through into me, so I break through in turn into Him (W 1:136).

> Here God's ground is my ground and my ground is God's ground.
> Here I live from my own as God lives from His own. (W 1:117).

When Eckhart speaks paradoxically, as he does in the next statement, one may think that he is doing so out of the paradoxical quality of his own experience.

> For in that essence of God in which God is above being and distinction, there I was myself and knew myself so as to make this man. Therefore I am my own cause according to my essence, which is eternal, and not according to my becoming, which is temporal. (W 2:274–5)

Finally, although this last quotation is not in the first person, the peculiar significance it seems to carry for its author, as well as the idiosyncrasy of its expression, may indicate that it is a third-person description of a firsthand experience. Walshe views it thus.[54]

> It seemed to a man as in a dream—it was a waking dream—that he became pregnant with Nothing like a woman with child, and in that Nothing God was born. He was the fruit of nothing.[55]

Walshe suggests that this story may be a record of a personal event which uses the third person after the style of Paul in Second Corinthians 12:2, in which he, too, spoke obliquely of "a man."

3. Periodically Eckhart makes reference to his own previous works by saying, "a master says." Such a sense of his own authority may indicate something akin to what William James called the authority for the mystic of the mystical experience itself.[56] At times this internal sense of authority seems to outweigh even the authority of the Scriptures.

> Yesterday I sat in a certain place and quoted a text from the Lord's Prayer, which is "Thy will be done." But it would be better to say: "Let my will be thine", for what the Lord's Prayer means is that my will should become His, that I should become He. (W 1:149)

He seems to exude such confidence as to know what the Lord's Prayer should say! As someone once remarked of the great twentieth-century Hindu mystic, Ramana Maharshi, "He knows! He KNOWS!"

4. There are two more speculative items that also may be taken to suggest that Eckhart was indeed a mystic, or at least to give the impression to those who knew him firsthand that he was. The first is a mystical poem with the Latin title *Granum Sinapis* ("The Grain of Mustard Seed"), which has been preserved in several manuscripts.[57] The dialect, in his own native Thuringian, was written about the time the Meister lived, and it is unmistakably in keeping with his system. Some scholars have argued that it is probably by Eckhart's own hand.[58] Even if it were not Eckhart's own, it was composed under his influence, either direct or indirect, for it is a quite remarkable summary of his thought. What makes it especially interesting in the present context is that its more speculative material (i.e. the material that says the creation arose out of its source in God's "modeless" heart) leads directly and concisely into mystical instructions: i.e., that the peak must be climbed by becoming blind and dumb to the self. Taken as a whole, this poem has considerable mystical depth, and it suggests that either Eckhart himself or someone he influenced deeply thought of his works as primarily concerned with an inner experience. Here are excerpts from Walshe's lengthy metrical rendering:

> When all began
> (beyond mind's span)
> the Word aye *is*
> Oh what bliss
> When source at first gave birth to source!
> Oh Father's heart
> From which did start
> that same word:
> yet 'tis averred,
> the Word's still kept
> in womb perforce. . . .
>
> The peak sublime
> deedless climb
> if thou art wise!
> Thy way then lies
> through desert very strange to see,
> so deep, so wide,
> no bound's descried.
> This desert's bare
> of *Then* or *There*
> in modeless singularity. . . .

As a child become,
both blind and dumb.
Thy own self's aught
must turn to naught.
Both aught and naught thou must reject,
without a trace
of image, time or space.
Go quite astray
the pathless way,
the desert thou mayst then detect.

My soul within,
come out, God in!
Sink all my aught
In God's own naught
sink down in bottomless abyss.
Should I flee thee,
thou wilt come to me;
when self is done,
then Thou art won,
thou transcendental highest bliss. (W 1:30)

5. Though we have no biography of Eckhart by someone who knew him firsthand, we do have a vision of the Meister recorded in the autobiography of Eckhart's disciple, Heinrich Suso. The vision of Eckhart was one of several visions that Suso had of people who appeared to him at the time of their death. Here is Suso's brief account:

> Among others there appeared to him the blessed master Eckhart and the saintly friar Johannes der Fuotrer of Strassburg. He was told by the master that he lived in transcendent glory in which his purified soul was deified in God. Then the servant [Suso] wanted to know two things of him; the first was, how those persons stand in God who strove to attain the highest truth by self-abandonment without any falsehood. Then it was shown to him that the absorption of these men into the formless abyss cannot be expressed in words by anyone. Then he asked further, what was the most profitable exercise for a man who would fain achieve this. The master replied: "He should sink away from himself, according to his selfhood, in profound abandonment (*gelassenheit*), and accept all things from God and not from creatures, and establish himself in quiet endurance in the face of all wolfish men."[59]

I make no judgment about whether Suso actually saw Eckhart or whether Eckhart was in any sense the author of the words attributed to him. The point to be noted from this passage is a more mundane one. It seems reasonable to assume that the Eckhart Suso knew would have been at least fairly consistent with the Eckhart presented in this tale. Suso, it seems fair to say, would have asked him in this vision the kinds of ultimate questions he longed to ask the flesh-and-blood Eckhart. Certainly the questions he represented himself as asking would have been like those Suso's readers would have expected, or else Suso would probably have explained his reasons for asking them. Suso was driven to ask two questions: what ultimately happened to someone who strove towards self-abandonment? and, what is the most productive exercise for a man to perform if he wants to attain this ultimate goal? I hardly need point out that such questions of technique and results are the very questions one would be quick to ask an accomplished mystic and spiritual leader who had himself gained the highest goal. At least in the eyes of Suso, who knew him personally, the Meister probably was such a man.[60]

All told, the above reasons cannot be said to make a watertight case for believing that Eckhart was a mystic. But from them one may be left with the impression that here was a man who knew well and firsthand of what he was speaking, who could rely on this as firmly as he could on anything, and who left others with the impression that he knew these things from firsthand experience.

OVERVIEW OF THE BOOK

This book addresses the question "Were I a friar or nun under your tutelage, Meister Eckhart, what might I be expected to experience, and what significance would it have?" The answer to this question will touch on many areas. In the next chapter I will place Eckhart's interest in mysticism in its appropriate cultural milieu. He was not alone in his time and place in this interest.

There was a widespread interest in mysticism during his day and age—evidenced, for example, by the so-called Rhineland Mystical Tradition. I will suggest a few of its causes, and discuss Eckhart's historical relationship to that tradition.

In Part II, the bulk of the book, I will concentrate on the question "What would I be likely to experience?" I will show that Eckhart presents a transitional process (not unlike that which the Eckhart of Suso's vision described) and not one but several different types of mystical experiences. These experiences are more or less progressive and developmental. In each chapter I will investigate one important stage of the mystic's journey and show how it relates to the previous ones. In effect this means that each chapter will be devoted to an analysis of a single term or a few critical terms in my concordance. Since each of these terms has both their theoretical and experiential significations, at times I will investigate Eckhart's more abstract theories about man and his relationship to that which is "higher." However, such analyses will always be made in the service of understanding the nature and nuances of the mystical experience at issue. In Part II experiences will remain our focus.

Although occasionally I will touch on this topic throughout the book, in Part III I will confront the more abstract system directly. Keeping in mind the findings of Part II, in the last section I will address the question "And what significance does it have?" Having briefly characterized the system as a whole, I will show how experiences fit into it and how the system is indebted at critical junctures to those experiences as I have portrayed them. The experiences will be seen to stand at the nub of the whole affair. Their availability makes the system plausible, and they stand as its goal.

It goes without saying that I will be dealing throughout with large and difficult questions. I will touch here on issues of theology, philosophy, psychology, textual criticism, and, of course, mysticism, all in the service of a study of mystical experience. Inevitably I will leave more questions unanswered than answered. This is the danger (and the seminality) of an investigation which touches on so many issues. But inasmuch as I am asking unconventional questions and developing an equally unconventional methodology to answer them, I hope that the reader can bear with my halting attempts, and that he or she finds it at the very least thought-provoking. If there are a few who find the book helpful in understanding the spiritual transformation as Eckhart portrays it, who are drawn to reading Eckhart for themselves, and who find the study of Eckhart useful on their own quest, then my labors will not have gone unrewarded.

CHAPTER TWO

Eckhart's Historical Context

Before I begin my examination of Eckhart, I want to present the historical and biographical facts. The biographical information I can bring to bear is neither especially complete nor interesting. With the exception of his trial for heresy at the end of his life, his story is typical of many Dominican Friars. The history, however, is quite interesting. As we will see, there were thousands, if not hundreds of thousands, of mystically oriented men and women, especially women, who both foreshadowed and followed the famous Meister: the so-called Rhineland Mystical Tradition.[1] His emphasis on an inner transformation and certain mystical experiences may be viewed as both an expression of and a formulator of their spiritual strivings and mystical experiences.[2] Perhaps more than anyone else in his era, Eckhart lent a significance and an intelligibility to the spiritual journey which was at once both plausible and provocative. He made the inner journey seem not only worthwhile but indeed the only worthwhile endeavor.

In this chapter I will describe Eckhart's general historical context and give a few reasons for his period's fascination with mysticism. Then I will introduce two of the religious groups amidst which Eckhart lived and worked, and show Eckhart's connections with each. Finally I will outline Eckhart's biography. I do not pretend to be a professional historian. I offer the following to aid the reader who is either new to the study of the age or of Eckhart.

GENERAL HISTORICAL CONTEXT: CAUSES OF A WIDESPREAD INTEREST IN MYSTICISM

When we look at Eckhart's historical context, the mid-thirteenth through the mid-fourteenth centuries, the first things that strike us are the breadth and the depth of the social transformations and shifts marking the period. The Europe, the Germany, and the Rhineland Valley of Eckhart's birth (*c.* 1260) were deeply and importantly different from those of his old age and death (*c.* 1327). This period straddles the transition from the so-called High Middle Ages to the Late Middle Ages. Although such periodizations are inevitably oversimplifications, there were undeniably economic, institutional, intellectual, and religious collapses and transformations marking the period.

Continent-wide, although the fully developed intellectual and disciplinary system of the high medieval socio-religious system stands as one of the most remarkable achievements of man, in the Late Middle Ages it came under assault from without and within. Externally, the Mongols from the East and the Turks in Asia Minor threatened stability. Even more ominous for the stability of Europe were the internal changes: the collapse of the great empire and the increasingly apparent diminution of papal suzerainty which had been the hallmark of the High Middle Ages. The upheavals of the age are summarized well by Richard Weber:

> Two global wars, the overthrow of the Western and Atlantic political, economic and social order, the erosion of faith in the postulates of liberal and rational Western civilization, the rise of new powers, new ideologies and a half century of violence, war and terrorism . . . [M]edieval civilization was sapped from within, assaulted from without, and a great culture began to die, a marvelous synthesis of faith and learning slowly unraveled and came apart. There were population problems, economic depressions, demands for reforms and a merry dance of hedonists bent upon instant pleasure. It was a time when men and women began to think that the world was coming to an end. They were of course right: a world was coming to an end: the world of the Middle Ages.[3]

One element of the medieval world that was ending was religious: the church-state synthesis that had held Europe together for a thousand years was crumbling. This was most strikingly marked by the period of the "Great Interregnum" (1254–1273), when the great Empire had no Emperor. This period marked the end of the long-cherished ideal of a Europe politically unified under emperor and pope. Replacing this ideal, the spirit of nationalism was waxing. Epitomizing this spirit was the Sicilian Revolt. On Easter Monday, 1282, the people of Palermo rose up in revolt against their French ruler, Charles of Anjou, and massacred French men, women, and children in the famed Sicilian Vespers. The Pope made a last-ditch attempt to control his world by excommunicating the rebels. Yet despite his efforts, by affiliating themselves with the Aragon King, the Sicilians did in fact succeed. Nationalistic fervor found its *cause celebre* in Germany when the same French king defeated and killed Manfred at the Battle of Benevento (1266). Two years later Conradin, the fifteen-year-old grandson of Frederick II, was also defeated in battle and, with the approval of the Pope, Charles of Anjou had him publicly executed. Such wars and executions were the most visible sign of the increasing tensions produced by the growing nationalistic particularism, and the corresponding decrease of ecclesiastical control. The great system uniting a continent under the unified rule of the Universal Lord was crumbling.

In the greater Rhineland Valley of the period, the medieval religious world was coming to an end particularly rapidly. The key to this transformation was the rise of the towns and cities. Not only in the Rhineland, but in many areas of Europe, in the twelfth and thirteenth centuries, great towns were coming into existence, creating new needs and new ways of life.[4] Cologne, for example, home to many of the Rhineland Mystics and home to Eckhart for a decade, more than doubled in a century, growing from about 15,000 in the beginning of the twelfth century to roughly 37,000 by 1320.[5]

R. W. Southern argues that the rise of cities was the most important single fact in changing the complexion of Christianity in the period, for such demographic changes brought religious changes in their wake. By way of explanation he remarks, "there is something about towns which makes their inhabitants restive, rebellious and above all articulate."[6] Although Southern seems right, it is hard to specify exactly what that "something about towns" might be. Perhaps it can be seen in the differences between the social pressures in each setting. Medieval rural life, where a man was encouraged to conform and to keep his eccentricities to himself, is not fertile soil for an outpouring of new ideas. But in a city where people of divergent backgrounds as well as unusually inquisitive people are thrown together *en masse*, men and women are more likely to begin to speak their minds. Compounding this, the money economy and increased mobility of the towns had led to more diversified occupations, the acquisition of new skills and new liberties, further encouraging a more autonomous and inquisitive population. The squalid poverty experienced by many also puts strains on the religious explanations. In sum, certain facts of city life tended to encourage religious experimentation.

Exacerbating this general tendency of city-dwellers to unauthorized thinking, the rapid growth of cities would bring personal upheavals and psychological pressures in its wake, which for many must have been severe. A migration to towns meant that a man or a woman went from agrarian peasant to urban proletariat overnight. He or she would have to cope with a radical shift in behavioral patterns and customs, and would lose his or her long-cherished network of village relationships.[7] Furthermore, the discontent engendered by any such transformation would have been worsened by the effects of overcrowding, the blatant poverty, the capriciousness of unemployment, and periodic famines. Such pressures would have been especially great on single women, of whom there were many in the new towns, since their problems were compounded by a degrading social status.

With such far-reaching changes it is not surprising that the rationalizations which had developed out of and justified the ancient social institutions would come increasingly under fire. The late medieval period witnessed political rebellions (the Jacquerie in France and the Peasants' Rebellion in England), the rise of the belief in witches, and a multi-faceted search for what Richard Weber called "new identity and community." This may be understood in Peter Berger's sociological terms.[8] Without the social order which reinforces it, the individuals of the new community find themselves stripped of a collectively recognized system of meaning and order, a *Weltanschauung*. To fill this

vacuum of meaning, a quest for some new system of rationaliza-
tion naturally arises, one which is independent of the old, now
collapsed, ecclesiastical and institutional structures. Numerous
alternatives will be simultaneously explored. Because mysticism
is a new religious form which is independent of collapsing institutions and structures, yet also provides its adherents with a con-
vincing system of meaning and belief, it becomes one other
obvious alternative.[9]

This search for a novel system of religious order was further
hastened by the decreasing respect in which the Church's representatives were held. At the highest level, the papacy and the ecclesiastical hierarchy were infamous for their corruption, decadence, and
secular greed. The sumptuous palace and finery of the Avignon
papacy, which existed from 1309 onwards, was an infamous mark
of its slide away from spiritual values towards secular and political
interests. Barbara Tuchman summarizes particularly vividly the
depths to which the Church had sunk in the period:

> Avignon became a virtual temporal state of sumptuous pomp, of
> great cultural attraction, and of unlimited simony—that is, the
> selling of offices. . . . [E]very office, every nomination, every
> appointment or preferment, every dispensation of the rules. . .
> everything the Church had or was, from cardinal's hat to pil-
> grim's relic, was for sale. . . . To obtain a conferred benefice, a
> bishop or abbot greased the palms of the Curia. The collection
> and accounting of all these sums, largely handled through Italian
> bankers, made the physical counting of cash a common sight in
> the papal palace. Whenever he entered there, reported Alvar
> Pelayo, a Spanish official of the Curia, "I found brokers and clergy
> engaged in reckoning the money which lay in heaps before
> them."[10]

It comes as no surprise that such movements as the Albigenses and
Waldenses and such reformers as Catherine of Siena and Birgitta
were to lament ecclesiastical decadence. Birgitta is said to have
wailed that "fear of God is thrown away and in its place is a
bottomless bag of money."[11]

The loss of credibility extended to local church officials as well.
Flagrant concubinage, frequent illiteracy of local priests, and a
widespread quest for wealth and political power left the entire
church besmirched. Perhaps most threatening to ecclesiastical
credibility was the notoriety of the dispensation of appointing a

candidate to a benefice for a price. Horror stories abounded concerning candidates who were approved though obviously below even minimal priestly standards: a seven-year-old boy was appointed to a Bohemian parish, priests were unconsecrated, bishops could not read Latin, and eighteen-year-old sons of the wealthy were appointed to archbishoprics. Such guardians of the faith must have shaken the system's credibility at its very core. Tuchman writes:

> The unfit clergy spread dismay, for these were the men supposed to have the souls of the laity in their charge and be the intermediaries between man and God. Writing of "incapable and ignorant men" who could buy any office they wanted from the Curia [Henry of Hereford wrote,] "Look . . . at the dangerous situation of those in their charge, and tremble!"[12]

Indeed, trembling there was—throughout Christian Europe. Devoid of respect for their ecclesiastical leaders, the populace was left with a vacuum of allegiance, open to and eager for some new religiosity that would be unaffiliated with the ecclesiastical structures. In the Rhineland Valley and beyond, a revolutionary millenarianism arose.[13] In France the "Shepherds' Movement" developed in a frenzy of anticlericalism.[14] I have already mentioned the bloody Jacquerie rebellion in France and the Peasants' Rebellion as well as the belief in witches that appeared at this time, all of which had religious overtones.[15] For many—the Beguines and Beghards, the Friends of God, many Dominican nuns, and others—this search for new spiritual satisfaction was increasingly sought within oneself and in one's personal relationship with God, and correspondingly away from external institutions: in mysticism.[16]

I have outlined some of the social forces at work on the society in Eckhart's day and region. To say that there were such forces at work on someone like Eckhart does not imply, however, that Eckhart was explicitly advocating social reform or revolution. Bernard McGinn points out that Eckhart was no political revolutionary:

> Eckhart's writings show no interest in the politics of the day, and surprisingly little in directly social or economic concerns. He was far from being an advocate of social revolution. . . . The Meister's teaching regarding inner transformation has no direct relation to one's social or economic status.[17]

McGinn here is arguing against Matthew Fox, who, in a neo-Marxist interpretation of Eckhart, describes socio-political forces at work in the day and argues that Eckhart advocated social reform.[18] I think Fox is right to point to the socio-political forces at work. But I also feel that McGinn is more correct to say that Eckhart nowhere advocates such reform. Rhineland Mysticism, or any widespread fascination with mysticism—a fascination which is evident throughout Eckhart's works—is one common way of responding to social upheavals. One needn't be a revolutionary *per se* to be part of a revolution.[19]

ECKHART'S RELIGIOUS MILIEU

A. The Rhineland Mystical Tradition

In part because of the social forces described above, a widespread interest in mysticism developed in the greater Rhineland valley of the period: the so-called Rhineland Mystical Tradition. Sometimes Eckhart is said to be the father of this tradition.[20] Such an appellation would be fair only if we restrict the term to the so-called "school of Eckhart," which would include authors like Suso, Tauler, Silesius, and perhaps Ruysbroeck. But it would be misleading to think that Eckhart was the father of Rhineland Mysticism in general, for there was a hearty tradition of mysticism which not only followed him but preceded him as well.[21]

Among the earliest mystics in the area was Hildegard of Bingen (1098–1179), who founded numerous Benedictine convents along the Rhine River.[22] She enjoyed visions from an early age, writing them down in her somber and austere *Scivias*. This was an account of twenty-six visions about the relations between God and man, redemption and the Church. Elizabeth of Schonau, another Benedictine, also has left us books of visions, assembled by her brother. The *St. Trudperter Hohe Lied* (*c.* 1140) is a lyrical and emotional tract in the style of St. Bernard, and was one of the earliest mystical tracts written in vernacular German.[23]

B. The Beguines

In the thirteenth century, the numbers of men and women in the Rhineland Mystical Tradition began to burgeon. The most renowned mystical group of the period was the Beguines. This was a movement of lay women who wore religious habits and formed small quasi-cloistered houses, "Beguinages," which were not affiliated with any traditional order. Such women, and later their male counterparts, could be found all over Northern Europe.[24] Their greatest stronghold, however, was in the greater Rhine Valley. Most famous of these Beguines was Mechthilde of Magdeburg (1207–1282), whose autobiography, *The Flowing Light of the Godhead*, emphasizes an affective, visionary, and ecstatic mysticism.[25] (It is worth noting that Mechthilde's Magdeburg was but 160 miles from Eckhart's Erfurt.) A similar note is struck by St. Mechthilde of Hakenborn's (1241—1299) *Book of Special Grace* and by St. Gertrud the Great's *Messenger of Divine Love*, both written in Latin. Such women, like the Beguines as a whole, emphasized contemplation, devotion to the Eucharist, and mystical visions.

In the Rhineland Valley of Eckhart's day and age, the Beguines were the most visible and possibly most significant religious movement. When the Chronicler Matthew Paris outlined the most notable developments in the German religious scene of 1243, he singled out the Beguines:

> At this time and especially in Germany, certain people—men and women, but especially women—have adopted a religious profession, though it is a light one. They call themselves "religious," and they take a private vow of continence and simplicity of life, though they do not follow the rule of any saint, nor are they as yet confined within a cloister. They have so multiplied within a short time that two thousand have been reported in Cologne and the neighboring cities.[26]

Paris reemphasized their significance a few years later when he summarized the main events of the previous half-century:

> In Germany there has arisen an unnumerable multitude of celibate women who call themselves Beguines: a thousand or more of them live in Cologne alone.[27]

Their cultural significance, and their importance for someone in Eckhart's position, can be seen from the demographics. Let us look at Cologne, for from this city in which Eckhart was active, thirteenth century systematic records have survived.[28] In Cologne the first records of Beguines date from about forty years before Eckhart's birth: in 1223 Sisters Elizabeth and Sophie, said to be Beguines, acquired a house. It was not until Eckhart's day, however, that the Beguines burgeoned. Between 1250 and 1330 (roughly Eckhart's lifetime), no fewer than 110 Beguinages were established in Cologne. By the end of the fourteenth century there were 169 convents in the city, housing about 1500 Beguines: no less than seven percent of the entire population![29] In Strasburg, (today Strasbourg in France) a city of 20,000 in Eckhart's time, there were in excess of 300 Beguines.[30] Eleven years before Eckhart's death Bishop Johannes Durbheim of Strasburg wrote, with perhaps some exaggeration, that there were more than 200,000 Beguines in the area.[31] Whatever the exact numbers, such a movement clearly exerted a considerable influence on the spiritual life of the Rhineland Valley.[32]

Fate drew the Beguines and the Dominicans together. Perhaps because of the encouragement and guidance they received from the friars, or because of economic assistance provided by the Dominicans,[33] Beguines tended to cluster near Dominican and Franciscan priories.[34] Of the 167 Beguinages in Cologne whose address is known between 1263 and 1389, 136 were near Dominican and Franciscan priories.[35] Two-thirds of the Beguinages in Strasburg were located within three blocks of priories.[36] The Beguines were commonly under the directorship of Dominicans.[37] When their orthodoxy came under fire, as it did with increasingly stridency towards the end of the thirteenth century, members of Beguinages often elected to transform their houses wholesale into Dominican nunneries. The Dominican Cloisters at Metz, Adelhousen, St. Catherine in Coblenz, Frankfurt, Engelthal, Gnadenzell, Steinheim, Cologne, and others began as Beguinages.[38] Transformation of other preexisting heretical groups into Dominican nunneries was also common.[39]

In short, the Beguines flourished in the Rhineland Valley during the precise period of Eckhart's activity. Considering that Dominicans were encouraging, guiding, preaching, and listening to Beguines and ex-Beguines, and that Eckhart was a prior, a preacher, and a vicar of houses of nuns in Strasburg and Cologne, he was likely to have had considerable contact with them. Benedict Ashley has observed the important role played by the Dominican friars in fostering the religious life of the Beguines and the Dominican nuns and the symbiotic relationship between them and concludes, "Eckhart during his studies in the Order at Erfurt and Cologne must have been well acquainted with this mysticism before he went to Paris for his University studies and teaching and in later life he became deeply involved in it as preacher and a spiritual director."[40]

Who, then, were these Beguines? Although the name *Beguine* is of uncertain origin,[41] it can be said that unlike most other significant religious movements, the Beguines began as a women's movement. There was a large number of unmarried women in the cities of the period, since they had a wider variety of economic opportunities open to them there than in the rural villages.[42] (A male group, the Beghards, did develop later.) The group was composed of deeply pious, largely lower-class[43] women who desired a quasi-cloistered life devoted to God which was devoid of the complications of ecclesiastical control. Unlike the more formal convents of the traditional orders, they had no definite rule, sought no papal authorization, were burdened by neither constitution nor bureaucracy, were indebted to no patrons, and had no fixed discipline enforced by Church authorities. To enter required neither irreversible commitment to an abbot or rule nor lavish endowment. Rather, a relatively informal statement of intention was all that was necessary. Some women simply "offered themselves to Christ," others declared that they wished to "serve the Lord Jesus Christ in the habit of a Beguine," and then took the habit as a "girl dedicated and offered to God."[44] Typically, as Matthew Paris observed, they renounced marriage and took an oath of chastity.

Rather than structure and discipline, the Beguines emphasized personal piety, devotion to God, and intense religious experience. Dedication to God meant first of all that the Beguines chose voluntary poverty, living on their labor in a hospital or through some modest cottage industry like weaving or embroidery. This poverty had its mystical overtones, being interpreted as an inward, spiritual poverty. Their external poverty was interpreted as mirroring the interior process of stripping attachments from the soul. Grundmann has argued that this interpretation of their poverty foreshadowed the spiritual poverty implied by Eckhart's term *Abegescheidenheit*. He states: "Only in the movement of female piety in Germany did the idea of poverty expand in the direction of its original religious meaning, not into the organization or the dogmatic and not into the polemical, but rather into the mystical—the striving after inward, spiritual poverty."[45]

Along with this interior process of poverty—i.e., stripping off of attachments as well as belongings—came a pursuit of intense, mystical, and frequently visionary forms of religious experience. The Beguines stressed contemplative prayer—sometimes using the charismatic prayer called *iubilus*[46]—and visionary experiences. For example, in Mechthilde of Magdeburg's *The Flowing Light of the Godhead* the contemplative life figures heavily. She depicts herself in long hours of prayer and mass.[47] She "records" a dialogue between her soul and contemplation.[48] She tells us how the spiritual person must "turn his heart from the world."[49]

Growing out of such practices, she undergoes the visions and ecstatic experiences that form the focus of the work:

> Then first was my spirit brought out of my prayer and set between heaven and earth. And I saw with the eyes of my soul the beautiful manhood of Christ.[50]

Elsewhere she saw Paradise and how it was made.[51] Many Beguines experienced visions or rapture, and even the stigmata. Intense, often emotional, spiritual experiences, frequently laced with sexual overtones, became the keynote of this movement. I quote Mechthilde again:

> I would fain die of love if I could, for I have
> seen him whom I love, I have seen with my eyes filled with light him who was
> in my soul . . . Lord, draw me to thyself, Then shall I be pure and lightsome, but if thou leave me to myself, I shall remain weighed down and
> full of darkness.[52]

Or again:

> My body is in great distress.
> My soul is in highest bliss,
> for she has seen and thrown her arms around her Loved One all at once.

Poor thing, she is distressed by him:
he so draws and delights her,
she cannot withhold herself,
and he brings her into himself.

Then the body speaks to the soul:
"Where have you been? I cannot bear it any more."
And the soul says, "Shut up, you fool, I want to be with my
   beloved;
You will never enjoy me any more—I am his joy; he is my
   distress—
Your distress is that you can no longer enjoy me:
You must put up with this distress for it will never leave you."[53]

As have been so many mystics, the Beguines ultimately were charged with heresy, pantheism, and antinomianism, the belief that one is independent of the moral law. They were discouraged and condemned in a series of decrees culminating in a papal condemnation issued in 1312.[54] Marguerite Porete, a well-known French Beguine, was burned as a heretic in 1310.[55]

But the tradition of mysticism in the greater Rhineland Valley did not cease with the demise of the Beguines. As I mentioned, many Beguinages were converted into houses of recognized orders, chiefly Dominican ones.[56] Thus it is not surprising that in the Dominican hagiographies of the thirteenth century, a similar contemplative and visionary note to theirs is sounded. To take just one example, in the *Lives of the (Dominican) Sisters* a (German) Sister Agnes of the Rhineland town of Ochsenstein is described:[57]

> After receiving with her usual purity of mind the most holy sacrament of the altar, at the time appointed by the customs of the monastery, [Sister Agnes] was immediately caught up above herself, and all her bodily senses were entirely put to sleep through the ecstasy of her mind. Then she saw, with the mind's spiritual vision, a luminous crowd of angels surrounding her.[58]

In a *Brautmystik* (Bridal Mysticism) vision similar to Mechthilde's, Sister Agnes is taken by the angels to God himself, where she becomes "engaged to the Lord Jesus Christ in this heavenly vision." There are many such visions reported throughout the *Lives*, as well as in other works.

The women of this tradition were a new source of literary production and a new kind of audience which must have had no small influence on Eckhart.[59] The Beguines were among the first who wrote mystical tracts in the vernacular.[60] The earliest of these were translations from the Latin, but they also refined the genre of the mystical biography and autobiography. Furthermore, they developed the art of writing down vernacular sermons verbatim. It is probable that our transcriptions of Eckhart's sermons are by their hand, or by the hands of Dominican nuns inspired by this skill. Since the last years of Eckhart's life were spent preaching in the vernacular to audiences in which sat numbers of such intensely religious women—nuns and Beguines—as both audience and scribes they must have significantly contributed to the concerns, themes, and spirit of these sermons. As McGinn rightly remarks, "the characteristic themes and modes of expression of these sermons can hardly have been unaffected by this setting."[61]

C. The Dominicans

The Dominican Order in which Eckhart lived and worked his entire adult life unquestionably influenced him. Let us look in some detail at the themes of Dominican life as Eckhart would have encountered them.

The Dominican Order can be viewed as another response to the rise of cities and the changing needs of its inhabitants.[62] As I have already noted, urban dwellers were dissatisfied with the old formulae on which Christianity had rested for a millennium and had turned towards a variety of religious and political experiments: political rebellion, religious innovations, heresies, etc. One of the most common complaints, made by the Albigenses, Waldenses, Beguines, and others, was that the church hierarchy had become too opulent. It was this complaint that stood out in the incident that sparked the birth of the Dominicans. Dominic met three abbots returning from an unsuccessful attempt to convert heretics in Languedoc. He recognized that, trailed by full retinue and dressed in their sumptuous finery, these abbots represented exactly the kind of decadence the heretics rightly criticized.

Dominic determined that what such city-dwellers needed was not some sumptuous, antiquated pomp and old ritualistic answers but something more substantial. He offered them instead a carefully formulated and preached doctrine that would satisfy their more educated and inquisitive minds, taught by friars who lived a more primitive, "apostolic" lifestyle that would appeal to their spirits.

When Dominic and his followers developed the friar's lifestyle, they imbued it with the two-fold character which it maintains even today. The first is its emphasis on preaching. To encourage the mobility necessary to preach wherever the need arose, the friar had to be free of traditional encumbrances: he pledged himself not to a fixed monastery or church, as was traditional, but to his superior;[63] he was burdened by no gold or money;[64] and he was tied down by no large estates that had supported the old monasteries.[65] This spare "apostolic" lifestyle answered to the just complaints that the Church's representatives had become too opulent.

Rather than administering large estates, the focus of the friar's life became preaching. The hours he chanted the office were reduced from the traditional six to roughly three; the traditional manual labor requirement was dropped. The friar filled up his day instead with study. Years were spent learning Latin, liberal arts, scripture, philosophy and theology. A high level of sophistication was frequently attained. Some of the greatest medieval scholastics—Thomas and Albert the Great—were Dominicans. There were other important medieval Dominican scholars as well: William of Moerbeke, who translated Aristotle and other Greek writers, St. Antonius, Raymond of Penofort, and James of Voraigne, author of the beloved and well-read *Golden Legend*, not to mention Eckhart himself. From the Dominicans' intellectual and preacherly vocation came the movement's name, *Ordo Praedicatorum*, the Order of Preachers.

The second characteristic of the Dominican lifestyle was its contemplative spirit. Dominic knew that one cannot lead others to the heights if one has not scaled them oneself. Hence the first soul to be reached was that of the friar himself. The friar was to pursue preaching and teaching, intoned the early constitution, "from the abundance and fullness of contemplation after the example of our most holy father . . ."[66] The contemplative nature of the order was acknowledged by the Curia. Writing to the Dominicans of Paris in 1220, Pope Honorius III petitioned them "who sit at the feet of the Lord with Mary" to pray for him "whom the importunity of Lea almost continuously denies the longed-for embraces of Rachel."[67] (Lea here represents the life of action, the *vita activa*, while Rachel represents the *vita contemplativa*.)

To achieve this contemplative spirit, Dominic preserved in the Dominican routine many of the contemplative habits he had enjoyed as an Augustinian Canon. As a result, the thirteenth-century Dominican friar lived a life fairly similar to the traditional monk. Though the details differed, the fundamentals were the same: the friar entered by making a public profession and showed his allegiance through traditional garb and tonsure. Devoted to his superior, he lived a disciplined, obedient life. He practiced abstinence, sleeping on straw mattresses dressed in tunic and shoes. Many Dominicans practiced ascetic mortifications such as hairshirts[68] and later flagellation.[69] Finally, perhaps to balance the hurly-burly of the towns in which the priories were always established, Dominic and the constitution emphasized and reemphasized the need for silence.[70] (Silence is a key theme in Eckhart, as I will show, although rather than the absence of conversation, it is a mystic's silence.)

This contemplative tone remained a thread running through the fabric of Dominican life until Eckhart's time—and even today.[71] Meditation and silent mental prayer, I should note, played a significant role in the Dominican daily routine as early as the mid-thirteenth century, and probably before. Bl. Humbert de Romans (d. 1277), the fifth Master General of the order, emphasized that the friar was to practice two forms of mental prayer: *orationes secretae*, morning and evening prayers recited in the choir or elsewhere in the Church following the recitation of the Divine Office, and *orationes [secretae] extraordinariae*, which could be performed at any time and place. In the *orationes secretae* one was to meditate on the benefits of God, the Incarnation and Redemption, heaven and hell, on one's exterior and interior state, etc. *Orationes extraordinariae* was inevitably less formulaic. The novice was to be instructed by his master that he should spend his leisure time in *meditation* (preferably in the church, though prayer at any locale was enjoined). Both forms of *orationes* were said to result in not only desirable affections and experiences but also resolutions to practice the virtues and shun the vices. Humbert viewed mental prayer as at least as important as the recitation of the Divine Office: the Office was the institution of the Church, he wrote, while meditation was the institution of God. Jesus practiced mental prayer, but never an Office, he noted. Furthermore, the silent form of prayer was more efficacious, he thought, being mental not vocal. Well established by custom, mental prayers were obligatory. Records survive of similar emphases on mental prayer made by nearly every succeeding Master General, well beyond Eckhart's day.[72]

The emphasis on contemplation and meditation can be seen clearly permeating the late thirteenth century volume, *The Lives of the [Dominican] Brethren*, which was published in 1271, about the time Eckhart entered the order. Many were the brethren, according to this popular *vitae*, who "were so eager for contemplation and so fervent that seldom did they rise from prayer without having first obtained some special grace from God."[73] We read of one fervent brother who,

> on the feast of St. Peter of Verona . . . fell into an ecstasy after matins, when it seemed to him that as he entered the choir he beheld assembled there the choirs of martyrs, confessors, and virgins, with the blessed Virgin standing in the middle besides the holy martyr Peter of Verona, all singing together the canticle of eternal joys with the triple Alleluia, and the antiphon, "Light everlasting shall shine upon thy saints, O Lord."[74]

In *The Lives* are miraculous powers—fires extinguished by prayer alone, rainstorms abating, languages learned miraculously, and even that worldwide mark of mystical powers, levitation.[75] Whatever the accuracy of such stories, they can be taken to reveal a religious ideal that played into the Dominican self-conception.[76]

The emphasis on the contemplative life was even more marked in the houses of the "second order," the Dominican nuns, with whom, it will be recalled, Eckhart had close contact. They had no apostolic ministry. Rather than a preacher's vocation, the nun's main preoccupation was the chanting of the office and prayer. Meditation was particularly encouraged among them.[77] The study appropriate for a preacher's life, though never wholly abolished, was replaced with the more traditional manual labor. The performance of this requirement, generally sewing and cottage industries done in groups, was often accompanied by a reading of spiritual texts.[78] As we saw in the *Lives of the Sisters*, the "Second Order" retained a contemplative orientation.

It seems fair to presume that it was this thread of *contemplatio*, as well as the Dominicans voluntary poverty, which was one of the main reasons the Rhineland Beguines preferred to cluster around the Dominicans, and which in turn led Pope Clement IV in 1267 to single out the Dominicans to guide and council these women. When the Beguines converted, it would have been no great leap to move to a Dominicanism which was near to their own apostolic and contemplative lifestyle.

In sum the Dominican life lived by Eckhart was twofold. On the one hand it was an active life, suited to an urban ministry, in which preaching and teaching played the key roles. Yet it was simultaneously a contemplative one: immersed in hours of silence, the friar or nun chanted the Divine Office and practiced mental prayer dail . St. Thomas appreciated the duality of its professed ideals when he wrote that the life of teaching and preaching proceeds "from the fullness of contemplation." Having a life which proceeds from contemplation, according to Thomas,

> is more excellent than simple contemplation for as it is better to enlighten than merely to shine, so it is better to give to others the fruits of contemplation than merely to contemplate.[79]

From such language the Dominicans took their motto, which epitomizes the twofold spirit of the order, *contemplare et contemplata aliis tradere*, "to contemplate and to give others the fruits of contemplation."

When Eckhart changed the emphasis of the mysticism found in his Rhineland Valley, he did so in a mode that harmonized with this twofold Dominicanism. He redirected the visionary mystic's emphasis away from passing ecstatic episodes and advocated a transformation that is permanent, one that may be enjoyed while living and working in the world. In emphasizing the mystical life, Eckhart represents the contemplative aspect of Dominicanism; and in redirecting it towards the more profound, permanent transformation he is in accord with the Dominican ideal of an entire life lived out of the "fullness of contemplation."

ECKHART'S LIFE

Although a considerable amount of information has been gradually accumulated by scholars, what we know of Eckhart's life remains sketchy. He was born around 1260 in the village of Hocheim in the central German province of Thuringa.[80] We know nothing of his youth. There is no good reason to think, as some have, that he was of noble birth or that he was called John. Of his youth all we can say with certainty is that sometime in his mid-teens he entered the Dominican order at Erfurt. As a typical Dominican novice, he would have spent one year familiarizing himself with the routine, and he would have studied the Divine Office and the Constitution for another two. Following that he might have undergone an eight-year period of advanced study: five years of philosophy and three of theology. As I have noted, he would have spent his day largely in silence, have chanted the Office for three or more hours a day, and have regularly practiced the mental prayer, *Orationes Secretae*.

In 1277 Eckhart went to the Dominican Studium in Paris, associated with the recently founded University of Paris, which was the intellectual center of Europe. There Eckhart certainly became aware of the great debates of scholasticism, the problem of universals, etc. Probably he remained in Paris for only a year or two. There is some evidence he studied personally with Albert the Great,[81] and if so, this would put him in Cologne at the Studium Generale some time before 1280.

The next thirteen years of his life are unfortunately lost in obscurity. Typically a man destined for higher study taught novices at his home monastery; perhaps Eckhart did so at Erfurt. There is a record of him in 1293 in Paris again, where he was lecturing on Peter Lombard's *Sentences*, probably in partial fulfillment of his *magister* requirements.

From this point on our information about his whereabouts becomes uninterrupted. From 1294—1300 he was prior of the Dominican house in Erfurt and concurrently held the elected office of Vicar of the Dominican houses in Thuringa. As Vicar he would have supervised both priories and convents. Dating from this period we have the first of his German works, the *Counsels on Discernment*, a series of twenty-three brief and relatively unsophisticated counsels on the spiritual path which were to be read during mealtimes.[82] In 1298 a General Chapter determined that two offices should not be held simultaneously, so one might suppose that in this year Eckhart once again became a prior only. In 1302 he turned up again in Paris, where he became a *Magister*. ("Meister" is a Germanization of this term.) From this period we can date his *Parisian Disputations*, a not atypical Scholastic disputation that concerns the identity of existence and knowing in God, the meaning of existence (*esse*), and the relationship of Being to the perfections of living and moving.[83]

The following year he was named to be the first provincial of the newly formed Saxonia Province in northern Germany, a post he held until 1311, supervising some forty-seven priories and numerous convents. Administering such a large area necessarily meant being on the road constantly, for the Dominican houses were located all over Northern Germany. Added to these duties in 1307 he was again appointed to be a vicar, now representing the Dominican General, assigned the onerous task of reforming certain disaffected houses in Bohemia. With all these duties, it is no surprise that few writings are attributed to these years.

In 1310 he was elected to be Provincial of Teutonia, which suggests that he was a popular and perhaps charismatic figure. He was not destined to play this role, however, for his order sent him instead to Paris for the fourth and final time. Here he occupied for the second term the chair once held by St. Thomas Aquinas, the Dominican professorship reserved for foreigners, which indicates the considerable academic respect he must have enjoyed. In 1314 he again returned to the Rhineland Valley, where he would remain for the rest of his career as an active preacher and spiritual leader. Also in 1314 he began working with nuns in Strasburg, then a center not only of Dominican nunneries but other houses of religious women as well, such as Beguines.[84] The German sermons that I will be investigating in some detail are thought to stem from this period. The audiences to which these sermons were delivered would have included the kind of religious women I described earlier, and the transcriptions we have are probably from their hand.

In 1323 or later, Eckhart was in Cologne, possibly wearing the robes of a professor to advanced theological students as well as continuing as a guide and advisor to Dominican nuns. In these years he must never have lost his popularity as a preacher. This I can say since it was at this time that the inquisitional proceedings against him were begun; and as Eckhart himself remarked, it was his popularity as a preacher that brought him to the attention of "envious men" who began the trial.[85]

The story of his trial and subsequent condemnation is a long and complex one, and has been exhaustively treated elsewhere.[86] Suffice it to say that in 1326 the Franciscan Henry of Virneburg assembled an inquisitional tribunal, which culled three or more lists of about 150 propositions out of Eckhart's works and attacked their orthodoxy. At issue was the pantheistic and antinomian tenor of some of his remarks, for they seemed to imply the equality of man with God, as well as man's independence of both the moral law and the ecclesiastical authority. Eckhart responded in a lengthy defense. It must have been a painful and disheartening episode for this charismatic leader of souls to defend himself to those he regarded as lesser minds,[87] for, as scholars commonly assert, in his defense Eckhart does not demonstrate his full rhetorical energy and skills. His principal argument was that he did not intend heresy, and so could not himself be a heretic.[88] He repeated on several occasions that he intended no heresy, that he submitted in advance to any correction by papal authority, and that he was ready to recant anything judged to be heretical.[89] Such statements demonstrate that he never lost his papal allegiance and, certain students of Eckhart notwithstanding, he had no revolutionary intention of challenging the Church's authority.[90] Despite his avowals of orthodoxy and fidelity, the Cologne tribunal determined that his remarks were indeed heretical.

As was his legal right, Eckhart appealed to the Pope. In 1327 he set out for the papal palace in Avignon, accompanied by four members of his order.[91] In Avignon the papal commission winnowed the list of 150 down to a more manageable group of twenty-eight taken from both his Latin and German works.[92] The commission concluded that these propositions were heretical as stated (*prout verba sonant*), which allowed Eckhart the ". . . escape hatch he had sought of not being personally condemned as a heretic. The 28 propositions of 1329 so condemning him, *In Agro Dominico*, were divided into two groups." Propositions 1–15 were determined to be openly heretical, while 16–26 were thought to be suspect but capable of a Catholic interpretation. The last two propositions were determined to be heretical, but it was added that Eckhart denied having uttered them. Probably Eckhart never lived to hear this verdict, however, for on April 30, 1328 Pope John XXII, in a letter to Henry of Virneburg, assuring him that the final determination would soon be made, spoke of Eckhart as deceased.

There are several observations that can be made on the basis of this contextual portrait and bittersweet biography. First, one may be inclined to think of Eckhart as a quiet contemplative, a cloistered sage in his cell. But from the meager facts of his biography which have survived, it is clear that here was no reclusive quietist. Eckhart was a busy and responsible man, supervising great numbers of people and houses most of his adult life. He wrote letters assuring towns that a priory would not extend its land holdings further without their permission.[93] He counselled disaffected friars back into the fold. He preached the over eighty-six sermons which survive and almost certainly scores more which do not. He wrote a great deal, both in Latin and German. And he travelled. Administering large regions of houses meant he was constantly on the move. Travel then was on foot, hazardous and arduous; roads were bad, amenities few, and robbers many. Certainly there were no quiet cenobitic cells along the way for a contemplative retreat. During his many years as a vicar and provincial, his life could not have been in the embraces of the contemplative Rachel, but rather caught in the snares of the active and responsible Lea. In itself such activity needn't imply an attitude towards or away from contemplation. But as we will see, such a life does dovetail with his thought that the highest form of religious life is not a *quietistic* but an active life in which one maintains a felt union with God.

Although no firsthand descriptions of him survive, it is clear that Eckhart was held in extremely high esteem. He was a scholar of some eminence. Clark remarks that ". . . [H]e may have been inferior to St. Thomas in the range and extent of his erudition, but after the death of Duns Scotus in 1308 he had no rival in Germany and very few in Europe."[94] But his real talent seems to have been as a spiritual guide, preacher, and leader. He was elected to offices of leadership again and again, even to two offices at a time. His role as a spiritual guide to religious women seems to have been especially significant. Though the early period of leadership included supervision of both male and female houses, his latter years, those of his maturity, in which his fame was great, was passed interacting with and preaching to female religious. The sermons in which his mysticism finds its crescendo derive from this latter period. He was teaching, it is true, but even more importantly he was a spiritual master, leading and guiding souls to the highest as he knew it. Such sermons bear the stamp of this soteriological intent. When he speaks of the Birth or the Breakthrough, he is urging real friars and nuns towards real salvific experiences they will hopefully undergo.

Finally, in his trial as in his life, he remained an active participant in the mystical religious milieu of his day. He was a son as well as a father of the Rhineland Mystical Tradition. It was the resonance that such people as the Dominican nuns and the Beguines must have felt with his teachings that brought him to the popularity he enjoyed—and that thereby brought him to the attention of Henry of Virneburg. As I said at the outset, he gave a shape and a direction to their mystical strivings and experiences. Although he far excelled his compatriots in sophistication, and although the language and details differed, in the concerns, themes, issues, and conclusion that man was capable of living a life infused with the transcendent, he was in complete accord with the Beguines and other mystics in the Rhineland Valley. I am not claiming that he read or spoke with, for example, a Mechthilde of Magdeburg and as a result employed her language. Rather I am suggesting that the fascination with mysticism was "in the air" if you will, and that Eckhart was as inspired by the breeze as anyone. The people with whom he was in daily contact—their needs, their concerns, their fascinations and tales—all must have played a part in leading the Dominican master to his primary interest in the spiritual path and goal. There is a certain poetic justice in the fact that the mystical tradition of the area was in part responsible for his trial and later condemnation. Had it not been for the numerous accusations against the heresy of the Beguines and others from the mid-thirteenth century onwards, the very inquisitorial spirit to which he fell victim would probably not have been present. Nor in all likelihood would the pantheistic overtones of his doctrines have touched so raw a nerve. Whatever the rightness or wrongness of Eckhart's condemnation, it is fitting that just as the Beguines' career started in a garden full of mystical flowerings and dreams and ended with the cold finality of *Ad Nostrum*, which condemned their beliefs as heretical, so, too, Eckhart's career as an eminent member of his Order blossomed into a career full of the fragrance of mystical poesy and then ended with the quashing sounds of *In Agro Dominico*. In more ways than one Richard Weber was right: "Meister Eckhart was at the center of this mystical revolution. He was its greatest figure."[95]

PART II

The Portrait of Experience

And therefore, when a man accommodates himself
barely to God, with love, he is un-formed,
then informed, and then transformed
in the divine uniformity
wherein he is one
with God.

CHAPTER THREE

Eckhart's Stages of Mystical Progression[1]

Were I a friar or a nun under Meister Eckhart's tutelage, what experiences might I expect to undergo?

One logical way to start to answer this question is by looking at Eckhart's divisions or phases of the spiritual journey. Thus we may have an overview of the territory to be covered in this part of the book.

As in so many of the Eckhart studies, there is virtually no agreement in the secondary literature about how or whether Eckhart divides the stages of progress. For example, Jeanne Ancelet-Hustache and Evelyn Underhill seem to suggest that he portrays the purgative, illuminative, and unitive ways, although unfortunately they provide little or no evidence for this claim.[2] James Clark, in his "Introduction," notes that this traditional tripartite division is conspicuous for its nearly total absence.[3] He concludes that Eckhart "does not chart the various stages of the way."[4] The famous Rudolf Otto, in his recently popular *Mysticism East and West*, again points to a three-fold typology, which he calls "stages," but which are not the traditional three found by Underhill and Ancelet-Hustache.[5] Otto's stages are the experiences of: (1) all is one and one is all; (2) the one is superior and prior to the many; and (3) the one is the real above the many.[6] These stages are not to be understood as "separate chronological stages in the history of mystical experience or in the lives of individual mystics," he tells us, but are rather "gradation[s] which seem to lie in the nature of the vision itself."[7] Whatever the merits of his division, he references it more with excerpts from Plotinus than from Eckhart.[8]

John Caputo argues that there are two principal stages of mystical experience.[9] These are the Birth of the Son in the Soul and the Breakthrough of the Soul to the Godhead. Though he calls them "themes in Eckhart's mysticism," he notes that the first "crowns and perfects" the second, "as a fruitfulness perfects virginity."[10] Such a relationship denotes a progressivity. Jonas Barciauskas concurs with this twofold progressivity.[11]

Richard Kieckhefer, in the most thorough English study of Eckhart's mysticism to date, presents a system of four as his archetype of Eckhart's stages, referring to the four steps into God outined in W 2:259.[12] They are as follows:[13]

> First, the soul experiences within itself the growth of fear, hope, and desire—i.e., of natural human emotions. Secondly, these emotions are altogether extinguished from the soul. Thirdly, the soul becomes oblivious to all temporal things. And fourthly, it enters into God as he exists and rules eternally. In this fourth state it never thinks about itself or temporal things, being immersed in God as God is immersed in it; whatever it does, it does in God.[14]

These four, Kieckhefer claims, depict a "moral process" which anticipates the afterlife. He asserts that these four are the archetypical Eckhartian stages, though he makes no mention of the other systems Eckhart mentions, nor does he account for those passages that appear less obviously "moral."[15]

Clearly what is needed is a systematic textual study of Eckhart's references to the mystic's stages. I propose to make this study.

I have counted at least seventeen separate passages in which Eckhart enumerates the divisions or phases that a mystic might undergo.[16] No two are identical; it is no wonder that there is so much disagreement among scholars.

In terms of the frequency of usage, Eckhart's favorite division is, as in so many things, threefold.[17] For example, he speaks of three developmental "ways into God": seeing God in creatures, finding God through rapture, and "seeing God without means in his own being."[18] Elsewhere he uses Augustine's image of the dawn, mid-morning and midday light.[19] He also employs the related images of morning, midday and evening: as well as night, morning, and midday development. It is striking that in only one reference (which is in the Latin not the German works) does he employ the traditional purgative, illuminative, and unitive division.[20]

He was nearly as fond of a fourfold scheme.[21] He speaks of four "degrees of virtue," in which the first degree is "away from all transient things," and the final one is "right in God and is God himself."[22] He refers to four steps into God: starting with fear of and hope for the religious life and ending in a state in which the soul "enters into God, where she will eternally dwell."[23] This is the division Kieckhefer asserts to be archetypical. There is another division of four, in which Eckhart returns to the light metaphor. One moves from the natural light of the soul, which is like morning, through mid-morning, midday and finally to "the silence of pure repose, and that is evening: then it is hottest in divine love."[24]

Eckhart also employs two different sixfold schema, one based on Augustine[25] and the other on Pseudo-Dionysius, in which the divine light appears to five kinds of people, the fifth of which he subdivides into two.[26] I will discuss the sequentiality of this passage later.

Not only are the numerical divisions multifarious, but the character of the development herein outlined is heterogeneous as well. Some passages enumerate a "moral"-sounding development, a falling-off of fears and attachments to things, as Kieckhefer noted. These express a movement towards an "attachment" to God alone, if you will.[27] Other passages use the dawning day as their metaphor, in which the light rises over creatures and arrives at midday or at evening at God.[28] These passages are more ambiguous in intent. Some are quite mystical, especially those that speak of a progressive development in "ways of seeking."[29]

> The second way is a wayless way, free and yet bound, raised, rapt away well nigh past self and all things, without will and without images, even though not yet in essential being. . . . St. Peter did not see God unveiled, though indeed he was caught up by the heavenly Father's power past all created understanding to the circle of eternity. I say he was grasped by the heavenly Father in a loving embrace, and borne up unknowingly with tempestuous

power, in an aspiring spirit transported beyond all conceiving by the might of the heavenly Father.[30]

Passages that list different "types" of people also suggest a progressive and perhaps mystical development.[31]

I think it is fair to conclude two things from this initial perusal. First, Clark was wrong. Eckhart definitely discusses the phases of progression. The problem is an embarrassment, not a paucity, of riches. From these passages exactly what stages or what type of development Eckhart had in mind is not immediately apparent. Second, Caputo and Barciauskas's account of two phases of progress is never mentioned in these enumerations. That fact alone need not necessarily indicate that Eckhart did not distinguish the two they mention. He did speak frequently of them. Rather, it is surprising that for whatever reason he never focused on this distinction when he spoke specifically of the phases of progress.

Aside from these two observations, there are four points I would like to make from looking at these passages as a group. It is in looking at them *en masse* that we can find them instructive.

First, the very divergences of metaphor, meaning, and number inform us that in Eckhart we are confronted with a lush and supple metaphorical mind. Here we are presented with stages, ways, types, lights, and dawning days. Some passages are reminiscent of traditional stages, others of peculiarly Augustinian ones, and still others of angelology. We have visions. We have silences. Yet we have none of these in any obvious consistency. If "a foolish consistency is the hobgoblin of little minds," as Ralph Waldo Emerson once wrote, then in Eckhart we are dealing with the great.

Second, there is one unquestionable consistency found herein. Each and every passage communicates a progression of some sort, a more or less gradual and lived transformation. That there is a developmental process found in these passages is, of course, a consequence of my selection procedures. That the divisions are more than merely theoretical or abstract, and that they denote existential transformations through which we may pass, is not a consequence of my procedures.

One of the most nuanced accounts of a transformation process comes in the sixfold stage account from *The Nobleman*.[32] There we see a sensitive portrait of a slow and existential development in the life of the religious. In the first stage, the subject "lives according to the example of good and holy people," though he does so haltingly and needs help from others to maintain his zeal. In the second stage, he "runs and hastens to hear the doctrine and counsel of God and of Divine wisdom."[33] Here the truth draws him actively forward. In the third stage, the subject withdraws himself more and more from these sorts of external props and aids, and the development becomes internalized:

> he escapes care, throws off fear so that—even if he were able to do wrong and evil without giving offense to anyone—he would nevertheless have no desire to do so, for he is so zealously bound with love to God until God . . . leads him to joy and sweetness and bliss in a place where all is repugnant to him which is unlike or alien to Him.

In the fourth stage, one becomes "rooted in love and in God, in such a way that he is prepared to face all temptations, trials and distress and to suffer pain willingly and gladly, cheerfully and joyfully." It is clear that these passages are not merely theoretical divisions but represent a development someone may undergo.

The fifth stage is the first stage that can be read as mystical *per se*. There "he lives in peace with himself in all respects, resting quietly in the richness and fullness of the highest ineffable wisdom."

The sixth is an outgrowth of this stage, and again describes a mystical fulfillment:

> The sixth stage is when man is transformed and conformed by God's eternity and has reached full and complete forgetfulness of this transient and temporal life, and is drawn and transformed into the divine image and has become a child of God. There is no stage beyond this or higher, and here there is eternal rest and bliss, for the end of the inward man and of the new man is eternal life.[34]

In summation, in the *Nobleman*, Eckhart describes what might be called a psycho-social development of an increase in religious zeal and a decrease of fear and worldly attachments. This transformative process concludes in two experiences that may be seen as mystical. This general pattern is quite in harmony with the kind of development we will outline in the rest of this book. For now, let me merely note that it is clear that there is undoubtedly a developmental and lived process at hand here.

Though the precise nature of the transformative process is heterogeneous among passages, each and every one of the stage passages does connote, as I have noted, some sort of apparently experienceable or existential process. Some metaphors seem more suited than others to represent such a lived transformation. Those passages employing the light and the daylight metaphors communicate a gradual transformation process eloquently. "When the divine light breaks forth in the soul, more and more until a perfect day comes . . ."[35] So too when Eckhart employs the phrase, "we are wholly transformed . . . and changed," it is clear that he has a lived developmental process in mind.[36] The one traditional stage passage, in which he speaks of purgation leading to an illumination that leads to the unitive life, also is clearly speaking of a process through which someone may or should pass.[37]

On the other hand, those passages that speak of "types of people" or "kinds" of darknesses in a progressive manner seem less suited to describe a transformation process.[38] But their obvious progressivity does imply a transformation, and in fact they describe it with unusual candor. I would like to analyze one of these "types of people" passages in some depth, since in it Eckhart is about as explicit and thoroughgoing as in any stage passage.[39]

Eckhart begins by reminding his audience of Pseudo-Dionysius's assertion, "if the divine light shines in me, it must be shrouded, as my soul is shrouded." This sets up the expectation that he will discuss how an individual's soul might be shrouded and how (or in what stages) it may become unshrouded. And so he does. Here he again hearkens to Dionysius, with the image of the divine light shining in five "kinds" of people.

The first type is "not alive to it. They are like cattle, not capable of receiving it." This is a different *terminus a quo* from the passage we saw from the *Nobleman*. There the subject began by being at least somewhat religious, i.e. "following the example of good and holy people." Here the subject seems utterly unaware of the possibilities, for that this type is "like cattle" implies that its members are as unconscious of the divine light within as are the animals.

"To the second group a little light appears. Like the flash of a sword being forged." Here is the first clue that the types here are progressive and serial, for this second "type" necessarily describes a new phase in someone's life. It is not a fixed or permanent "type." After all, someone who saw a flash of light for an instant was, just before that instant, in darkness. Furthermore, he will necessarily return straightaway back to that darkness. He may be ever after different, since he will perhaps remember the flash, but every member of class two was necessarily once a member of class one. *Ergo* this division clearly describes a class of individuals who are on a transformative journey.

The next several classes are also transformative:

> The third get more of it, like a great flash of lightning, which is bright, and then immediately dark again. They are all those who fall away from the divine light again into sin. The fourth group receive more of it, but sometimes He withdraws Himself for no other purpose but to spur her [the soul] on and increase her desire.

From darkness to the light of a flashing sword to the increasing light of lightning: again we have "types of people" who were previously of another type, and through some sort of transformative process have entered class after class.

In the fifth division this type of analysis gets interesting. It is subdivided into two. Both divisions represent an altogether new level of advancement on this increasing light business:

> The fifth are aware of a great light as bright as day, but still as it were through a chink. As the soul says in the Book of Love: "My beloved looked at me through a chink. His face was comely" (Cant. 2:9, 14). About this St. Augustine says, "Lord, thou givest me sometimes such great sweetness that, if it were perfected in me, if this is not heaven I know not what heaven can be."

While the precise meaning of this metaphor remains perhaps intentionally ambiguous, what is unmistakable is that unlike the preceding phases, it signifies a change that is permanent. Light through a chink does not cease like a flash from a sword or like lightning. Furthermore, this permanent change is characterized as a "sweetness." Finally that he can say, "If it were perfected in me . . ." implies that at this "through-a-chink" stage the religious life is not yet perfected, and that it may yet get even "sweeter."

That perfection, which we might call the sixth stage, is described by means of an exegesis on the Book of Love:

> Is there then no way of seeing God clearly? Yes. In the Book of Love the soul says: My love looked at me through the window"—that is, without hindrances—"and I knew him, he stood by the wall"—that is, by the body, which is perishable—and said: "Open up to me, my beloved"—that is because she is altogether mine in love, for "he is mine and I am his alone"; "my dove"—that is, simple in longing—"my beautiful"—that is, in act. "Arise, make haste and come to me. The cold is past", of which everything dies: all things live in the warmth. . . . Here God bids all perfections to enter the soul.

I will discuss this passage in detail in chapter seven. However, let me note here that this is unmistakably a different level of development from the previous "light-through-a-chink" stage. Like that stage here we see a change that is permanent, for light through a window is not momentary, as is light from a flashing sword. But compared to the previous stages the experience represented by this one is not as narrow in some sense or as limited. This one is fuller, more complete, as vision through a window is more complete than is vision through a chink. Indeed Eckhart emphasizes that this level of development is complete: one sees God "quite clearly," "without hindrances." I am his "alone." Finally it is striking that this final level is said to invigorate what is normally understood as profane: God stands in an intimate connection with "the body" and is somehow found "in act." "All things" are expressly implicated. "All perfections" enter the soul. We will see in chapter seven how *a propos* is this brief evocation to what Eckhart says of the highest experience.

In summation, it is not only reasonable but instructive to construe this passage as describing a dynamic transformative process rather than static "types" of people. Each "type" presupposes the previous type and is an advancement on it. The process Eckhart depicts is progressive, marked by occasional backsliding, and ends in two sequential levels of permanent change. The first is analogous with light through a chink, the second with gazing through a window. The final level seems to involve the full range of life: the body and action, as well as the transcendent.

Continuing my analysis of these stage passages considered *en masse*, there is a third consistent element I see in each of them. The light passage I have been discussing, as well as the other passages, all conclude with a stage that involves the divine. Eckhart consistently depicts a *terminus ad quem*, which is in some sense implicated with the divine. In every progression the adept moves towards and then concludes somehow conjoined with God, the Divine Light, the perfect day of God, etc. "We are wholly transformed *into* God and changed," says St. Paul in Second Corinthians.[40] "My love (God) looked at me through the window."[41] The light that increases over the light of the soul and over the angelic light is the *Divine* light.[42] At the conclusion of the transformation process, the soul "reigns *with* God in eternity. . . . What she then does she does *in* God."[43]

Conversely, the movement is away from "creatures," the natural light of the soul, ordinary fears and desires, etc. The morning light "shines over all creatures."[44] The light moves from "this world."[45] The first phase is "the natural light of the soul."[46] One starts on the journey involved with "transient things."[47] Though an explication of the experiential content of these terms will occupy us for much of this book, for now let us simply observe that this pattern—away from the ordinary, transient, and "creaturely" and towards the divine—is a consistent one.

Finally, when I look at these passages *en masse*, I find a fourth pattern. Many of the passages mention ecstasy, but they do not emphasize this experience. For example, in a discussion of three "ways into God," Eckhart describes the second way as

a wayless way, free and yet bound, rapt away well nigh past self and all things, without will and without images. . .[48]

As his archetype of this way Eckhart appeals to Matthew 16:17, in which Peter was described as "caught up in the higher mind." He was, says Eckhart,

caught up by the heavenly Father's power past all created understanding to the circle of eternity. I say he was grasped by the heavenly Father in a loving embrace, and borne up unknowingly

with tempestuous power, in an aspiring spirit transported beyond
all conceiving by the might of the heavenly Father.[49]

This experience is clearly rapturous.

Such explicit discussions are the exceptions, however, not the
rule. More commonly we find a penultimate stage (e.g., number
three of four, or number five of six, etc.) which, if read literally,
may be taken as a reference to such experiences. For example,
"Forgetfulness of all temporal things"[50] (three of four) or things
becoming "altogether forgotten as if they had never been"[51]
(three of four) can be read in this manner. But such passages may
also be read hyperbolically, as Kieckhefer demonstrates, as steps
in a process of moral development. For example, "forgetfulness
of all temporal things" may be construed as either mystical or as
an advanced grade of a process of detaching oneself from the
emotional attachments to worldly things.[52] At best, from such
ambiguous and obscure passages alone it would be hazardous to
draw any firm conclusions.

In one Latin passage Eckhart discusses four grades of ecstasies.[53]
That he does so may be taken to indicate at least a knowledge of
ecstasy. But that it is so little changed from a parallel passage in
St. Thomas would suggest that, at least at the early stage of his
career when it was probably written, he did not have a great or
abiding interest in the subject. Here are the passages from Eckhart
and St. Thomas:[54]

Eckhart:
The first (kind of ecstasy) is that of
intention, when one spurns all
creatures and is joined to God
alone in love . . . The first is the
ecstasy of love, according to Dionysius.[55]

Thomas:
(In the first kind) this transport
from things outside is taken to
refer to attention only, as when
someone makes use of the external
senses and things about him, but
his whole attention is engaged in
contemplating and loving things
divine. Such is the state of anyone
who contemplates and loves
things divine in transport of the
mind, whether ecstasy or rapture.
For this reason Dionysius says:
"Divine love brings about
ecstasy."

Eckhart:
The second consists in imaginative or spiritual vision, as when one is drawn by some supernatural power to see things supernaturally without the use of the senses or the action of the senses or external sensible objects . . . The second is the spirit in which John (Apocalyspe 1:9–10) and Peter (Acts 9:5–6) found themselves.

Thomas:
(In the second kind) one is also deprived of the use of his senses and sensible things in order to see certain things supernaturally. Now, a thing is seen supernaturally when it is seen beyond sense, understanding, and imagination . . . (Here) the mind is at once transported out of the senses and out of the imagination to an intellectual vision. This is what happened to Peter and to John the Evangelist in the Apocalypse.

Eckhart:
The third is when the mind is withdrawn or rapt from sense and imagination to intellectual vision, whereby it sees God by intelligible infusions . . . The third is the sleep or trance of Adam referred to in Genesis (2:21).

Thomas:
(In this kind) the intellect understands God through certain intelligible communications, and this is proper to angels. Adam's ecstasy was of this sort . . .

Eckhart:
The fourth occurs when the mind itself sees God in himself through His essence . . . The fourth is Paul's ecstasy which we have been discussing. These three terms, *ecstasy, trance*, and *rapture*, are frequently understood in the same sense in the scriptures.

Thomas:
(In this kind:) . . . the understanding sees God through His essence. It was for this that Paul was enraptured . . . (In the beginning of this set of answers, Thomas notes:) In the scriptures, transport of mind, ecstasy, and rapture are all used in the same sense and indicate some raising up of the mind from sensible things outside of us towards which we naturally turn our attention, to things which are above man.

I would like to make two observations about these Eckhartian passages, concerning what they are not and what they are. From their barely concealed paraphrastic character we might deduce that Eckhart put little rhetorical attention on such an analysis of ecstasy. Knowing him, had he cared a great deal about this phenomenon, he would have embellished at great length on Aquinas's suggestions. On the other hand, that it *is* included suggests that Eckhart certainly knew of ecstasy as at least a relatively common phenomenon in the religious life, and one to which scripture relates. Hence we would expect him to discuss it on occasion. And so he does, as I will show in chapter five.

The uninspired character of these passages, and the infrequency of his references to ecstasy elsewhere tend to confirm Kieckhefer's conclusion that Eckhart knew of, but deemphasized, the phenomenon of ecstasy.[56] If ecstasy was a stage in the developing life of the religious, it was not, apparently, *essential*.

The German sermons and tractates were delivered to, and recorded by, listeners in various cloisters and Churches. I would speculate that Eckhart mentioned ecstasy as one of the stages of progress in those places where he knew that among his listeners were those who had undergone such raptures, and he mentioned ecstasy for their benefit. But in other houses he perhaps found it unnecessary or even counterproductive to include such references. If this is correct, it underscores the impression that ecstasy may be an important ingredient in the developing religious life, but not a necessary one, for were it essential he would have mentioned it more consistently.

From this perusal of Eckhart's stage passages, I draw the following conclusions. First, I think it is clear that he does maintain that there is some sort of existential development through which one must pass in the movement towards the Divine, but he leaves its precise nature obscure. He does not typically employ the traditional tripartite division, but there do seem to be various milemarkers. The movement represented here is consistently away from an involvement with creatures and the world and towards a conjunction with God. The precise nature of either pole is left vague. Ecstasy is deemphasized, though not excluded altogether.

CHAPTER FOUR

The Transformation Process

You must give up yourself,
altogether give up self,
and then you have really given up.

In the first section of this chapter I will briefly present Eckhart's doctrinal assertions concerning God and man's relationship to Him—his theology and mystical anthropology. Although I will present his systematic thought in more detail in chapter eight, I will introduce it here for two reasons. First a brief summary will provide a framework for the reader. But even more importantly, Eckhart's mystical anthropology will serve as the most natural springboard into his picture of both the personal transformation and the mystical experiences to which it leads. I will show here where the mystical journey stands as *a* or *the* key element in his thought. At the most intimate level, according to Eckhart, man is in touch with God, but because of the nature of the Creation and the Fall, man is largely inattentive to that contact. This inattention, and the implied possibility of its reversal, set up a soteriological demand: take the mystical journey and rediscover your intimacy with the infinite.

AN OUTLINE OF THE DOCTRINE

Let us start at the beginning.

In the beginning God created heaven and earth.

In his introduction to his commentary on this famous passage, Eckhart notes that he will touch on the essentials of his theories of *bullitio* and *ebullitio*.

> ... these words suggest first the production or emanation of the Son and the Holy Spirit from the Father in eternity, then the production or general creation of the whole universe from the One God in time, and many of the properties of both Creator and creature.[1]

Eckhart's theology combines the Neo-Platonic notions of the one transcendental Godhead with the Christian formula of a trinitarian God. Eckhart is well known for his doctrines of the Godhead as a silent characterless One, beyond all multiplicity. The Godhead is a "solitary One," a "darkness or nescience."[2] It is divine "desert", utterly featureless, a pure untrammeled One without movement or number. Emanating from this desert-like emptiness is the trinitarian God, Father, Son, and Holy Spirit, which are the dynamic, differentiated, creative phase of the Divinity. This "production" or "emanation" of the Three Persons out of the silent Godhead is encapsulated in the term *bullitio*, literally "boiling," which metaphorically expresses the boiling over into itself of the trinitarian God out of the One. Correlatively, *ebullitio* describes the production or general creation of the whole universe from the One God.

The key characteristic of Eckhart's notion of *bullitio* is that while the trinitarian God involves the activity of emanation, distinction, and numerical diversity, the Father, Son, and Holy Spirit never lose their absolute unity with the nondiverse One. There is a "unity of substance and [a] distinction and property of persons in the Godhead."[3] Eckhart's emanationism centers on this fact. Despite the process of boiling and manifesting, the distinct Three persons are ultimately indistinct within the One. They "abide and remain" in the One.[4] In a famous passage from his Latin commentary on the Book of Exodus's "I am who am," (Ex. 3:14), Eckhart says:

> the statement "I am who am" indicates a certain reversion and turning back of his being and into and upon itself, and its abiding or remaining in itself; also a sort of boiling up *(bullitio)* or giving birth to itself: an inward glowing, melting and boiling in itself and into itself, light in light and into light wholly penetrating its

whole self, totally and from every side turned and reflected upon itself. As the wise man says: Monad begets—or begot—monad, and reflected its love or ardor upon itself."[5]. . . This is why John I says: "In him was life." [Jn 1:4] Life means a sort of thrusting out, whereby a thing, inwardly swelling up, wholly bursts forth in itself, every part of itself in every other part, before it pours forth and boils over (ebulliat) outwardly.[6]

This image of the Godhead's boiling "into and upon itself" stresses that the One gives birth to a plurality within itself while yet remaining unchanged and One. I needn't delve here into the technical details of this process, except to note that the plural trinitarian God is not created outside of the Godhead, but remains fused within it.[7] In German this is called *uzbruch* (a breaking out):

The first outburst *(uzbruch)* and the first effusion God runs out into is His fusion into His Son, who flows back into the Father.[8]

The Godhead and the triune God may be distinguished, however. Whereas the Godhead remains simple and unchanging, an unmoving, pure existence, like a "desert wasteland," the triune God has features, differences, and plurality. It, or rather they, actively work to create:

God and Godhead are as different as heaven and earth. . . . Everything that is in the Godhead is one, and of that there is nothing to be said. God works, the Godhead does no work: there is nothing for it to do, there is no activity in it. It never peeped at any work. God and Godhead are distinguished by working and not working,[9]

The Trinity works. Not only does it create the universe and creatures, but it acts in the soteriological process as a magnet drawing man back towards itself. The Godhead, however, remains a "divine desert," a "prior nothing," a simple, unmanifest existence. Though It is rife with possibilities, they remain but potential.

The Three Persons "remain in the One"[10] because the One is their internal principle (Latin *principia*):

The One acts as a principle *(principiat)* through itself and gives existence and is an internal principle. For this reason, properly speaking, it does not produce something like itself, but what is one and the same as itself. For what is "like" entails difference and numerical diversity, but there can be no diversity in the One. This is why the formal emanation in the divine Persons is a type of *bullitio*, and thus the three Persons are simply and absolutely one.[11]

Any differentiating process implies a principle on which it is based, and cannot be fully understood without a knowledge of the operative principle. The triune God, while diverse, can be understood only as the formal emanation of its principle, and is its perfect image, one and the same with it.[12] Again we are driven back to the indistinguishability between the One and the Three Persons.

> In the Godhead, since every production or emanation is not directed to what is outside the producer, and is not from something that is not an existing being or from nothing, and in the third place is not directed to particular existence, what is pro-created does not have the nature of something made or created and is not an effect. It is also clear that the producer does not have the nature of a creator or a cause, and that what is produced is not outside the producer and is not different from it, but is one with it. "I am in the Father, and the Father is in me" (Jn. 14:11); "The Father and I are one" (Jn. 10:30). In the Godhead the Son and the Holy Spirit are not from nothing, but are "God from God, light from light, one light, one God" with the Father. "These three are one" (I Jn 5:7).[13]

There are two factors connected with this doctrine of emanation which I would like to emphasize. First, this doctrine of an emanation of something that remains one with its source serves as the model for the *ebullitio* of the universe and of man. Although the creation process is not one of emanation *per se*, the two processes have parallel structures.[14] Because the material universe is made (*factio*) and is produced (by God) out of nothing (*creatio*), there are differences between the Divine Source and the world. Such disjunctions parallel the difference seen between the Three Persons and the One. On the other hand, the active Trinity, in particular the second Person, serves as the principle, prototype, or Idea of the creation. Hearkening to ancient Platonic notions, Christ serves as the Image, Word, Logos or model of all things, especially man. Because we humans have this divine prototype, and retain Christ as our principle, our spirit was and is, at the depths, conjoined with God. This parallels the notion that the Trinity remained indistinguishable from the Godhead. Speaking in the German sermons of the connection between God and the Soul, Eckhart writes,

> In this Word the Father speaks my spirit and your spirit and every individual human being's spirit equally in the same word. In that

speaking you and I are the natural son of God just like the Word [i.e. Christ] itself.[15]

> *In principio.* Here we are given to understand that we are an only son whom the Father has been eternally begetting out of the hidden darkness of eternal concealment, indwelling in the first beginning of the primal purity which is the plenitude of all purity. There I have been eternally at rest and asleep in the hidden understanding of the eternal Father, immanent and unspoken. Out of that purity He has been ever begetting me, his only-begotten son, in the very image of His eternal Fatherhood . . .[16]

Because God serves as the Logos of man, and man remains thereby conjoined to the Creator, the world and the Soul retain, at the depths, the stamp of God.

Because man is so stamped with the Divine, through the agency of the second Person, all that was said of the emergence of the triune God out of the one Godhead becomes utterly relevant to man.

> All that God the Father gave His only-begotten Son in human nature He has given me: I except nothing, neither union nor holiness, He has given me everything as to Him.[17]

> The Father gives Birth to His Son in the soul in the very same way as He gives Birth to Him in eternity, and no differently.[18]

The second point I would like to make about Eckhart's *bullitio* doctrine is that because man has the Word as his prototype, all that is true of the Son is true of man's Soul (in its ground) as well. Just as the Word has, so the Soul has dwelt in the Godhead for all time and, despite being created, remains in the Divinity even now:

> When the father begot all creatures, He begot me, and I flowed forth with all creatures while remaining within the Father. It is like what I am now saying: it springs up within me, then secondly, I pause in the idea, and thirdly, I speak it out, and all of you receive it, yet really it is in me all the time. Likewise I remain in the Father.[19]

This statement could be taken in a heretical sense, as Eckhart's inquisitors took it, for it seems to apotheosize man. In his Defense he stressed that one is thus pious, noble, just, etc., *insofar* as (*inquantum*) he was just, etc. In such a defense, Eckhart is not speaking of the total man and is not claiming pantheistically that man becomes identical with God in every respect. We will see in later chapters in what sense man does become identified with God.

The connecting link between God and man is existence. "Existence is God" (*Deus est esse*), he argued in the Prologue to the *Opus Tripartitum*.[20] As such God stands as the first principle of everything that exists, which includes virtually all of creation. (It is evil and sin that should not be properly said to exist. See below.) If everything that exists partakes of the existence of God, then nothing can be said to exist "outside of" God. This notion emerges clearly in his commentary on Genesis I:I: "In the beginning (*in principio*) God created Heaven and earth." Punning on *in principio*, Eckhart translates it as both "in the beginning" and "in the principle." He writes:

> Existence is what is first and it is the principle of all intentions and perfections, as I have remarked in detail in my commentary on the first chapter of Wisdom.[21] Second, "He created in the principle," that is, he created in such a way that things do not exist outside him. The case is different with every artificer lower than God. The architect makes the house outside himself. . . . [As] Augustine says, "He did not create and depart, but the things that are from him are in him.[22]

Man, like every other created thing, hence does not exist "outside of" God, but "in him," with him, and through him, just like the second Person. Man retains an inner unity with God at the deepest level, in the "ground." "In the ground of the soul . . . God's ground and the soul's ground are one ground".[23] There God "indwells."[24]

If all creation exists "in such a way that things do not exist outside Him," how, then, does Eckhart explain the facts of sin or of man's lack of awareness of his connectedness with the Divine? First he capitalizes on the notion of the Fall. Originally man's entire system was oriented to the connection with the Divine. Eckhart expressed this notion in the Latin commentary on the *Parables of Genesis* as the ordering of the various "powers" within the Soul, a doctrine which we shall discuss again in the next chapter. Before the Fall, when man was fully attuned to God, the lower three powers of the Soul (lower intellect, anger, and desire) were hierarchically "ordered to" the higher three powers (memory, superior intellect, and will), especially to superior reason. This superior intellect, which some translate as the power of ratiocination, was in turn attentive to God.

> "This was," and is, "man's correct condition,"[25] when the sensitive faculty obeys, looks to and is ordered to the inferior reason, and the inferior reason cleaves and adheres to the superior reason as it in turn does to God. . . . This was and is the state of nature that was set up before sin, "the state of innocence."[26]

Eckhart uses the analogy of a magnet to account for this "ordering" phenomenon. As long as a magnet is present, the first needle points towards and touches the magnet, the second touches and points towards the first, and so on. Remove the magnet, however, and that hierarchy falls apart. Similarly, take away the contact with God, as Adam did when he sinned, and the ordered Soul collapses into entropy.

> When the bond and order of the height of the soul to God was dissolved through the injury of sundering sin ("Your inquities have divided you from your God," Is. 59:2), it followed that all the powers of the soul, inferior reason and the sensitive faculty as well were separated from contact with the rule of the superior reason.[27]

Once immediate contact with the Deity is lost, the powers and the soul become scattered, and mankind loses the simplicity it had in its origins.

Eckhart's second explanation for man's unconsciousness of the indwelling God concerns the status of sin, evil, and the "creaturely." Eckhart follows the Augustinian tradition and asserts that this sin and evil should not properly be said to exist, and hence does not compete with the status of God as the one existence.

> Sin and evil in general are not things that exist, so they are not made through him but without him. This is the meaning of what follows: "Without him was made nothing," that is, sin or evil, as Augustine says. Here it says that all things were made through him, but evil things do not exist and are not made because they are produced as effects, but as defects of some act of existence.[28]

Sin is a nothing, a defect or a privation. And that which does not exist does not threaten the unity of God.

> If [something is] not subject to [God] insofar as he is existence, they are not beings, but are nothing existing at all. All privations, evils, corruptions and defects are of this nature. All of these and things like them are not beings, but lack all existence. They are not effects, but defects, and therefore do not have God as cause.[29]

In the *Opus Tripartitum*, as well as his later German works, not only sin but creatures, too, are said to be nothing in themselves. One of the condemned propositions was:

> All creatures are pure nothing. I do not say that they are a little something, or anything at all, but that they are pure nothing.[30]

That certain things, i.e. evil and sin and creatures, do not exist, preserves the integrity of his notion of God as pure existence and as One by leaving God pure and sacrosanct. But this formulation sets up a dialectical tension. Here we come to the place, a key one, of the mystical journey. Both the notion of man as participating in the existing and the nonexisting, and the notion of the inherently ordered powers having "fallen away" from their innate structure, invite a resolution of that dialectical tension. Man in his fallen state—the *terminus a quo* of every religious journey, I may point out—straddles the two contradictory realms, if I may call them that:[31] the connection with God in the ground and the investment of mental attention in the creaturely world and in sin (both of which "lack all existence," and "do not have God as cause"[32]). I will show in the rest of this chapter and throughout the book exactly what this involvement with the "creaturely" world implies. But for now I merely want to note that an involvement with what "lacks all existence" shrieks out for healing. So, too, does the notion that the powers have "lost" their original orientation. Such a healing would result from coming to recognize the Soul's connection with what properly exists, God. To do so, she first needs to disentangle herself from the nonexisting, making it possible to reorder her powers towards the One true existence.

> The state of man after sin is when through grace he is redirected to God. Then the more that the height of the soul adheres to God himself, the more what is beneath it, even the sensitive faculty, obeys it. In this state the fullness and perfection of grace give perfect men the ability to have the sensitive faculty obey inferior

reason and inferior reason superior reason in such a way that what Isaiah writes is fulfilled: "The lion and the sheep will abide together, and a little child shall lead them" (Is. 11:6). The little child is the superior rational faculty, which cleaves to God and leads together and reconciles the lion (the sensitive faculty) and the sheep (the inferior reason).[33]

This then is the key place which Eckhart gives to the soteriological demands that are his constant preoccupation. Seen in this light, his entire systematic thought—existence as God, God's absolute oneness, the Soul's hierarchical orientation, the Soul's preexistence—above all, point his listeners towards what he knew of as the soteriological teléon. It is not surprising that he should say, as we noted in chapter one, "What does it avail me . . . if it does not happen to me? That it should happen in me is what matters."[34]

What is the nature of the transformation process and teleon so demanded? What is it like, to use the philosopher Thomas Nagel's language, to be entangled with evil or the "nonexistent?" How does Eckhart describe the transformation process of disengagement? And what is the fully transformed man's life like—when it has "happened in me"? That is, what is the experience of rejoining the One like? What are its distinguishing marks? In the rest of this chapter I will discuss the *terminus a quo* and the transformation process as Eckhart depicts it, suggesting at the end an interpretation of that process. The later stages of development, the mystical experiences *per se*, will be the topics of the later chapters.

THE TRANSFORMATION PROCESS

In the last section I concluded that according to Eckhart, in the soul's preexistence, man's powers were oriented like needles to a magnet, towards God. Because of Adam's fall this orientation was lost. It becomes the goal of the religious life to recover that "God intoxication." But rather than attending first to that sublime state, let us analyze the state with which we are each, I am sure, more familiar: the nature of the ordinary life, the *terminus a quo* of the religious life, in which man is yet entangled with sin, evil, and the nonexistent. We will then be in a better position to understand the nature of the recovery process and its goals.

A. *Eigenschaft*

In his fallen state, man finds his attentions taken up with those creaturely worldly things, "this and that," as Eckhart often puts it,[35] and he becomes "attached" (*eigenschaft*) to what does not properly exist. What is it like to be so attached?

The MHG *Eigenschaft*, often translated as "possessiveness" or "attachment," had two interrelated meanings, both of which Eckhart employs.[36] Primarily it signified possession or owner-ship.[37] For example, in his DW Sermon 2 = W Sermon 8, its basic meaning of "ownership" is employed: *mit Eigenschaft* is seen in conjunction with "have" (*begriffen*), "have these things with attachment,"[38] and with "possess" (*besezzen*), "the work to which you are possessively attached."[39] Here he evokes a life in which one considers the fruits of ones labors as owned, attached to oneself. Such phrases connote the sense that "I worked for it and it is mine."

One may be attached to anything. Some are attached to their work,[40] others to their family.[41] Worldly honors attract many.[42] It may be the "failings of other men" that preoccupy some.[43] According to Eckhart, there were many in his day (and how many more would he have found in our own!) who were attached to wealth and goods:[44] many there are who "direct all [their] aims and intelligence towards transient possessions."[45] In his Latin sermon on *Sequere Me*, Eckhart described the wicked in such terms:

> These are the sort of men who never have any thought of God in their actions, who do not care or consider what is good or evil, pleasing God or displeasing. They throw all that behind them as an old woman might throw away bad eggs or rotten apples and *their sole concern is how to gain honors, wealth and pleasure.*[46](italics mine)

More spiritually oriented souls may also be "possessively

attached": not to wealth but to a spiritual technique like prayer, fasting, vigils, etc., such that he or she will care excessively about these.[47]

The key attachment is to the self, Eckhart frequently declares. It is "my" worldly gain, "my" wealth, and "my" pleasures which one seeks. One pursues one's own spiritual flashes.[48] All involvements with the world, all sense of pride or advantage, ultimately come down to the attachment to the self:

> [The Soul's] own honour, her advantage or anything that is hers, she should no more desire or heed than what is a stranger's. Whatever is anyone's property should not be distant or alien to her, be it bad or good. *All the love of the world is based on the love of the self.*[49](italics mine)

We find ourselves attached to the world because we regard its things as intimately connected with the self, and hence as "mine."

This brings me to the second and very important connotation of the MHG term *"Eigenschaft"*: serfdom or bondage. In the same sermon which we analyzed above, Eckhart also employs this second nuance. Attachments, he suggests, make the possessor himself the possessed.[50] People who bind things to themselves are themselves "bound with attachment"[51] and "bound by [those] attachments."[52] Drawing in the term's connotation of "serfdom," people at the commencement of the religious quest "are themselves the slaves, not the masters."[53]

How is one enslaved by one's attachments? Attracted to "this or that"—be it wealth, honor or what have you—the soul draws those things "into herself through the senses,"[54] thereby coming to include such objects in her sense of herself. She comes to feel about objects as if they were intimately bound up with her. The soul thereby becomes "constricted" into them.[55] By focusing on a mere object, one's powers, says Eckhart, are dissipated towards and into them.

> Now there are some men who completely dissipate the powers of the soul in the outward man. These are the people who direct all their aims and intelligence towards transient possessions. . .[56]

Wordsworth meant something similar when he said:

The world is too much with us; late and soon,
Getting and spending, we lay waste our powers.[57]

Because he has brought things into his heart, he works for them and finds his energies and attention "spent" on them. Such a man wastes his energies acquiring, maintaining, and spending in the world. He finds himself "dissipated" in and among his transient possessions. "For as long as you want more and more, God cannot dwell or work in you."[58]

Hence the real crux of the phenomenon of *Eigenschaft* is not mere "possession" or "ownership," but it is the connection one feels between the self and those possessions. Because one associates things with the self "in one's heart," one cares about them excessively. In the following low-ramified passage, the Meister clearly distinguishes between owning things and being attached to them:

> A man once came to me—it was not long ago—and told me he had given up a great deal of property and goods, in order that he might save his soul. Then I thought: Alas! How little and how paltry are the things you have given up. It is blindness and folly, *so long as you care a jot* for what you have given up.[59](italics mine)

Here was a man who was attached, according to Eckhart, to things that he did not actually own. His attachment was a psychological relationship that he had with his things, not merely an economic one. Such an emotional connection is more insidious, since even giving objects away does not cure it.

Here is where the connection with the Latin *proprietas* enters. Things are a property of me not simply by owning them, but inasmuch as I am personally involved with or attached to them. When I regard my wealth, say, as an aspect or extension of myself, it becomes my *proprietas*.

Such a personal investment in things, having them as one's *proprietas*, makes one the possessed in two senses. First, through attachments the soul can be emotionally swayed this way or that by those things. The winds of fortune—good or ill— thereby can take on the power to topple over one's internal sense of self and with it one's emotional stability. One becomes "over"joyed and overly sorrowful. It is in these terms that I read a psychologically insightful passage like the following:

> The summit of the soul is . . . brought so low by . . . joys as to be
> drowned in pleasure. [It does not] rise resolutely above them . . .
> creaturely joys and sorrows [have the power] to drag down the
> topmost summit of the soul.[60]

One is possessed by attachments in the second sense in that if
someone cares a jot for something, he will devote himself to
activities that advance it, be they activities of self-aggrandizement,
spiritual advancement, or whatever. Such activities preoccupy his
soul with the requirements of the work, again distracting him
from the more spontaneous life Eckhart advocates, one of freedom
(W 1:142).

> Your soul will bear no fruit till it has done this work to which you
> are possessively attached, and you too will have no trust in God or
> in yourself before you have done the work you embraced with
> attachment, for otherwise you will have no peace. . . . [Action of
> the attached man] springs from attachment to the task and not from
> freedom. (W 1:73)

The *eigenschaft* soul is bound because it is preoccupied with
accomplishing that to which it is attached.

Attached to things, people and circumstances, the *eigenschaft*
man will be an emotional man, prey to the anger and passions
with which his overinvolvement with others and with things
leave him. For him the "lower powers" of desire and anger
become very real factors with which he must contend. ". . . if any
things anger him, he is not [yet] perfected."[61] Such emotions get
sparked off because he associates things too deeply with himself.

B. *Lâzen, Getâzen*

As the transformation process unfolds, these attachments, which
both bind the world to one and one to the world, are "released,"
lâzen and *gelâzen*.[62] *Lâzen* means "to let" or "to let be." It connotes
a leaving things to themselves, a removal of bindings, a letting go.

What is "released" is that sense of being emotionally attached
to things. Such a deattaching process does not mean that one
withdraws from all contact with the material world. Eckhart was
a Dominican, and that order did not advocate a contemplative
withdrawal, as I noted in chapter two. Even if it had, however,

such a withdrawal would be impossible, for even eating and praying are activities of a sort: "Even if he is given to a life of contemplation, still he cannot refrain from going out and taking an active part in life."[63] No, the withdrawal Eckhart advocates is not from the world but from an attachment to its things.

> Whatever state we find ourselves in, whether in strength or in weakness, in joy or in sorrow, whatever we find ourselves attached to, we must abandon.[64]

This means that one must "let go" of the personal investment one has in one's things and stop "caring a jot" for them. Eckhart describes this process as one of "finding out his weakest points so as to mend them and diligently striving to overcome them."[65] It is not easy. It is long and arduous, accompanied by pain, strife, and unrest.[66]

At the core of this letting go of attachments to transient material goods and honors stands the letting go of the sense of one's own self.

> You must give up (*lâzen*) yourself, altogether give up (*lâzen*) self, and then you have really given up (*gelâzen*).[67]

Self-abandonment comes first; the rest follows inevitably.

> He should renounce himself first, then he has renounced all things.[68]

This does not mean that one somehow gives up being in one's body, or stops being able to live in the world as a distinct being, for of course one must continue to take into account one's social situation, personal qualities, capacities, etc. Eckhart does not advocate stupidity! No, what he advocates is a ceasing to cherish self-aggrandizement over the aggrandizement of others, a ceasing to regard oneself and one's own gain as most important. One stops distinguishing "my" gain from that of others.

> It is necessary that you should make no distinction in the family of men, not being closer to yourself than to another. You must love all men equally, respect and regard them equally, and whatever happens to another, whether good or bad, must be the same as if it happened to you.[69]

One would "as lief be sick as well, well as sick."[70] As a result of not caring about one's own fortunes, the sense of self may be said to die:

That man who is established thus in God's love must be dead to self and all created things, paying as little regard to himself as to one who is a thousand miles away.[71]

He does suggest obliquely two elements of the transformative process. The first is that in the beginning the transformation takes effort on the subject's part: it begins as a lifting oneself up by one's own bootstraps. The process of *lâzen* begins with one's own efforts and determination. One must attempt to abandon those things to which he has been attached.[72] One stops the cycle of accelerating desires, the wanting of "more and more,"[73] by abandoning whatever we find ourselves attached to:

Whatever state we find ourselves in, whether in strength or in weakness, in joy or in sorrow, whatever we find ourselves attached to, we must abandon.[74]

The initial effort always comes from the religious. He must "prepare himself."[75] This self-modification initially demands strife and pain, for it is difficult. "The coming of the fire is accompanied with strife, with pain and unrest. . ."[76] The Soul must be in "labor" to give birth to this new existence.[77]

But with practice and patience, the process of abandoning becomes progressively more natural and easy. The religious does only the initial releasing. The rest comes seemingly from above, automatically, effortlessly.

There is still one work that remains proper and [the adept's] own, and that is the annihilation of self. Yet this annihilation and diminution of the self, however great a work it may be, will remain uncompleted unless it is God who completes it in the self. Humility becomes perfected only when God humbles man with man's cooperation.[78]

What began as hard and as a "labor" ends up "a pleasant burden."[79]

Secondly, Eckhart also speaks occasionally about penitential practices—"fasting, watching, praying, kneeling, being disciplined, wearing hair shirts, lying on hard surfaces or whatever it may be."[80] These can help in the initial self-transformation process, but they are only preparatory. They are often "harsh" and brutal.[81] They can too easily themselves become attachments: one too easily becomes attached to the practice itself, "getting the way and missing God."[82] Following such practices is an error: the "mantle of love" is the best.

> Pay attention. Penitential exercises, among other things, were instituted for a particular purpose: whether it be fasting, watching, praying, kneeling, being disciplined, wearing hair shirts, lying hard or whatever it may be, the reason for all that is because body and flesh are always opposed to spirit. The body is often too strong for the spirit, and there is a real fight between them, an unceasing struggle . . . And so, in order to succour the spirit in this alien realm, and to impede the flesh somewhat in this strife lest it should conquer the spirit, we put on it the bridle of penitential practices, thus curbing it so that the spirit can resist it. All this is done to bring it under control; but if you would capture and curb it in a thousand times better fashion, then put on it the bridle of love! With love you overcome it most surely, with love you load it most heavily . . . He who has taken up this sweet burden fares further and makes more progress than by all the harsh practices any men use.[83]

Thus Eckhart advocates this relatively inexplicit notion of adopting a "bridle of love," a detaching of attachments.

Such a process of *lâzen* will have the correlative result of letting go of attachments to the "required" work and hence will involve the discovery of a new freedom of possible choices.

The process of *lâzen* denotes a process of surrendering. One surrenders both the emotional attachments to things, people, and work, and surrenders the sense of oneself *vis-à-vis* attachments. As a description of the goal, Eckhart uses the derivative term *gelâzenheit*. Clark is right to translate it as "self-abandonment," since one must above all abandon the self.[84] Colledge is also right to translate it as "surrender," since in abandoning the self one surrenders all attachments.[85]

C. Abegescheidenheit

As a result of this *lâzen* process, one comes more and more to a quality of life Eckhart calls *Abegescheidenheit*, detachment. This term is composed of the prefix *ab*, designating a separation, and the verb *scheiden* or *gescheiden*, to isolate, separate, or depart.

Conjoined, *abegescheiden*, means "cut off from" or "away from." The modern German *Abgescheidenheit* denotes "the departed" in the sense of the deceased. Eckhart used his MHG term to translate *abstractus*, that which is removed from matter and its conditions.[86] Thus Eckhart's most common usage of *Abegescheidenheit* is an ambiguous "detached from things"[87] or "pure detachment . . . unable to stoop to anything."[88] Such ambiguous usages, however, are deceptively simple. For being "detached from things" has moral mystical, and theological connotations. As McGinn observes, "at first glance, no concept in his thought seems more simple, though on closer inspection the richness and subtlety of his understanding of detachment becomes gradually evident."[89] In this brief section I will show how Eckhart employs the term to characterize the new relationship with the world. Only later, having seen its other ramifications, will I be able to document the term's fuller—mystical as well as moral or psycho-social—meaning.

In the new "detached" way of relating with the world, one is, of course, unattached to possessions. Most obviously, one is no longer so preoccupied with acquiring and maintaining them. One will be able to "love God as much in poverty as in riches."[90] Even having given "all one hast" to the poor, one no longer "prizes" the goods and possessions one has given up. Eckhart's emphasis is not on the giving away of goods but on the ease one feels in so doing, that is, on one's emotional relationship with one's goods. This was seen clearly in the "care-a-jot" passage and seen, too, in the following:

> For such a man it would be *as easy* to give up everything as a pea or a lentil or as nothing—indeed upon my soul to that man all things would be as nothing.[91]

> A man who loves God could give up the whole world *as easily* as an egg.[92](italics mine)

As a result of such detaching, objects can take on an autonomy. No longer so preoccupied with an object's usefulness for the self, one comes to think of someone or something in terms of its usefulness to itself. Reiner Schurmann describes this transformative journey as:

> the attitude of a human who no longer regards objects and events

according to their usefulness, but who accepts them in their autonomy. This attitude makes him renounce influences, and it produces equanimity.[93]

This equanimity of which Schurmann writes is a symptom of nonattachment. Without a personal attachment to things, one is no longer swayed by one's emotions. Hence one can confront the world calmly. Borne along now by an inner quiet, such a changed Soul will find a "mental satisfaction" under any external circumstances:

> I call that mental satisfaction when the summit of the soul is not brought so low by any joys as to be drowned in pleasure, but rises resolutely above them. Man enjoys mental satisfaction only when creaturely joys and sorrows are powerless to drag down the topmost summit of the soul.[94]

In the following passage we read of an identical sense of equanimity. It concerns the fully transformed man, to whom Eckhart refers in this sermon as a "just" man:

> To the just man nothing gives more pain or distress than when, counter to justice, he loses his equanimity in all things. How so? If one thing can cheer you and another depress, you are not just: if you are happy at one time you should be happy at all times. If you are happier at one moment than another, that is not just.[95]

Losing the sense of emotional equanimity would be a regression to the old attached *modus operandi*. It would again stir up those lower powers of anger and desire. (". . . if any things anger him, he is not [yet] perfected."[96]) Thus when Eckhart defines the word "*Pharisee*" as "one who is detached," the definition includes "being so established in peace that one knows nothing of disquiet."[97]

Finally, or perhaps first, when one is in this state, one is detached from that old attachment to the self. In the detached state one "pays little regard to oneself," as we saw.[98] One feels that I am "detached fully from my own."[99] Being rid of all special attention to oneself and one's wealth and honor, all special emphases on the self are eliminated. As a result, one cares "not a jot" for either things or oneself. "He wants nothing and seeks nothing . . ."[100]

In this new style of living, "detached fully from my own,"[101] a man's own needs, determinations, and even the very sense of being an individual will be forgotten. The man will have "no will at all."[102] Rid of his personal investment in possessions, honors, and the self, he will come to be able to act in the world, doing whatever seems appropriate, while remaining personally uninvolved with the motivations of his own actions. Eckhart encourages his listeners to transform not what they do but their relationship to their actions. The "perfected" man performs no actions because he wills them. Instead he simply does what he does. Desires brought to nil, he stands without will.

> And so, if you were to ask a genuine man . . . "Why do you act," if he were to answer properly he would simply say, "I act because I act."[103]

> . . . nor should one work for any "Why," neither for God nor one's honour nor for anything at all that is outside of oneself, but only for that which is one's own being and one's own life within oneself.

Again speaking of the "just" man:

> The just man does not love "this and that" in God. . . . he wants nothing and seeks nothing: for he has no *why* for which he does anything, just as God acts without why and has no why. In the same way as God acts, so the just man acts without why; and just as life lives for its own sake and asks for no why for which to live, so the just man has no why for which to act.[104]

It is commonly observed that the life Eckhart depicts is without selfish motivations, without ulterior motives and "without why."[105] The growth of such a will-lessness is portrayed vividly in the sermon "The Just Shall Live Forever" (W Sermon 65). The lowest level is that "some people want to have their own way in all things." Here one is attached to certain goals (i.e. gaining honor), and as a result, the outcome of any event matters to him. He retains, in a word, a will. Better than these are the men and women who "truly want what God wants, and don't want anything against his will." While this type would focus on God's will in the main, such a person would still have desires that things should be thus and such for him/herself. It is a little better. . .

> but if they should fall sick they would wish it were God's will that

they should be better. These people, then, would rather that God willed according to their will than that they should will according to His.

Higher than this is a state of true detachment. This is the stage in which one has "no will at all." Whatever befalls such souls, "it is one to them, however great the hardship."[106] Sick or well, rich or poor, it would be all one to them. Here is the passage in its entirety:

> Some people want to have their own way in all things, that is bad, there is a fault in that. Those others are a little better who truly want what God wants and don't want anything against His will, but if they should fall sick they would wish it were God's will that they should be better. These people, then, would rather that God willed according to their will than that they should will according to His. This may be condoned, but it is not right. The just have no will at all: whatever God wills, it is all one to them, however great the hardship.[107]

The lucky man who is attachment-free and therefore content with whatever befalls him—sickness or health, weal or woe—must be very comfortable indeed. For the will that things should be otherwise simply does not arise. *Abegescheidenheit* denotes such an easy restfulness: it represents the affective sense of being uninvested in external and conditioned things. It denotes one's "detachment" from personal aggrandizement and the insidious will to better oneself.

THE PSYCHOLOGY OF ATTACHMENT AND DETACHMENT

Eckhart describes the transformation process as a movement from a life of attachments, through a surrendering and a letting go of them, to a state in which one is unattached and will-less. What are we to make of this portrait? What kind of a transformation is this?

Most scholars, whose primary interests have admittedly not been in Eckhart's transformative process, have contented themselves with a brief mention of the key terms in this process, i.e. *eigenschaft* and *abegescheidenheit*.[108] Some have amplified these in some detail. In the following typical passage, for example, John Caputo describes the process:

> The detached soul is that which does not mix with anything created, which keeps itself pure of created things and even of God as a good for it. To be detached is to be pure and empty:
>
> "It is right that you should know that to be empty of all creatures is to be full of God and to the full of all creatures is to be empty of God."

After introducing the notion of the hidden ground "into which neither thoughts nor desires nor sensible affections can in principle gain entry," Caputo suggests that the way to gain access to it is not through spending one's energies on one's "works." but,

> The only way back to this inner ground is the way of detachment and letting be, the way which lets knowledge go for a silent unknowing, which lets willing go for motionless rest.[109]

Even when I read such passages, however, I still find myself wondering just what it means to be attached or detached from something.

Reiner Schurmann, in *Meister Eckhart: Mystic and Philosopher*, is helpful. He notes that a key feature of being *eigenschaft* is being attached to "images," and through them being attached to "things as a property." He says that, "even from the highest knowledge we must be detached if we want to be as free and as void as we were in our preexistence and as we still are in our intellect."[110] We are avidly attached "to representations."[111] The notion that attachments are principally to images, representations, and things clarifies which are the typical objects to which we become attached. Along with a changed attitude towards works as the mark of the detached soul, Schurmann points to the absence, once again, of images:

> A man disengaged from all attachment (*eigenschaft*) to images and to works necessarily receives Jesus . . . Jesus, both the model and the goal of this union, defines the condition for us to become one with the Word: freed from all possession *of images and works*, following him on the way of detachment . . . His disappropriated mind, *void of images*, likens [one] to the Son of God . . .[112]

According to such passages, the key failing of the attached man is the attachment to works, things, and especially images. The goal is to be free of such. But, like Caputo, he is specifying here the objects of attachments, but leaving the critical question unasked. Eckhart emphasizes "caring a jot," the personal involvement with whatever. What does this mean? Whatever the object, what does it mean to be attached to something?

To bring out the meaning of attachment, I would like to propose a psychological interpretation. I introduce it because this reading has been helpful to me in clarifying the process at which Eckhart hints. I will be drawing upon Herbert Fingarette's very exciting connection between mysticism and modern psychology.[113] Let me say in advance that I am making no claims here that Eckhart was a proto-psychologist. I do not maintain that his thought can be completely accounted for as or by the science of psychology. Rather I merely believe that Fingarette's articulation of the process of mystical or psychological development in general can help flesh out some of the logic, details, and connections in the Eckhartian picture.

I think the key unanswered question is: What does it mean to be attached to something, or, in Schurmann's rephrasing, to "possess an image?" Fingarette draws a parallel between the phenomenon of attachment and neurosis. The typical neurotic patient can very well be described as being "attached" to things and people. In clinical language he or she is said to "cathect" someone or something. "Cathexis" is the concentration of mental energy on an emotion, idea, or line of action, giving such emotion, etc. importance or significance. To be cathected is to be emotionally invested in someone or something, lending to that object an emotional content. For example, Fingarette presents the case of a young woman, Katherine, describing her pretherapeutic state as "cathected" to her friend Alice. Katherine said that she "wanted [Alice] to be shown up in her true colors," "to have people see how wrong she was." Katherine would "dwell on" the wrongs Alice had done, and be "involved" with them. It would "matter" to her. One could appropriately say that she was "attached" to her friend Alice in a neurotic way. That she cared about Alice's failings is undeniably parallel to Eckhart's statement ["heart" of the *eigenschaft* person will be "troubled" by ...ings of other men."[114] Both suggest an excessive and ... concern with another person(s).

Though psychology broadens the number of possible objects of this phenomenon, the notion that someone concentrates mental and emotional energy on a person, thing, or line of action seems to be just the kind of problem Eckhart is describing as the nature *"eigenschaft."* To say that one "cares a jot" for something, or that the "heart" can be "troubled" by someone's failings, is to say something very close to an investment of mental energy in it. As a result of either neurosis or attachment, one is possessed by and emotionally swayed by the very thing in which one has invested oneself.

We saw that, according to Eckhart, at the heart of all attachments stands the attachment to the individual identity, the *self*:

> [The soul's] own honour, her advantage or anything that is hers, she should no more desire or heed than what is a stranger's. Whatever is anyone's property should not be distant or alien to her, be it bad or good. *All the love of the world is based on the love of the self.*'115

Why should attachments to things be said to be based on the love of the self? The connection in Eckhart seems intuitively obvious: one cares about honor, wealth, etc. because they relate to the self and its advantage. But this remains unsatisfying. From where comes the *emotionality* obviously at work here? What is there about caring about the self which makes one "care a jot" for things of the world?

Here again Fingarette may help. According to his analysis, both the psychologist and the mystic speak of the self in two different senses. Normally there is "no more awareness of the ego than of the air one breathes." It is only when there is trouble that we become aware of either. The two senses of "self" correspond to the awareness of the self in the contexts of trouble and no trouble. In technical language, one sense of "self" is used in an anxiety-dominant context and the other is used in an anxiety-free context.116 The first sense can be correlated with the sense in which Eckhart uses the term when he speaks of attachments. In a neurosis, emotional investments arise, according to the psychologist, as an expression of some intrapsychic conflict or anxiety. In technical language one cathects onto something by "displacing" a repressed and emotionally charged memory or memories, thereby making a chronic discharge of emotional energy

Katherine dwelled so negatively on Alice because she was con-
flicted within herself over something—a memory, a self-percep-
tion—the negative side of which Alice represented to her. That
repressed memory, etc., was laden with anxiety. Such anxiety,
brought on by that inner conflict, gives rise not only to a chronic
discharge of energy, but also to what Fingarette calles an "introspected self-conscious I."[117] Such a "self-conscious I" arises when
one thinks of a "particular part, affect, idea or action *as* the self
which is emotionally opposed to the cathected object of one's
emotions."[118] In Katherine's case she introspected her "self" as
that which is "right" as opposed to Alice's being "wrong."
Another form of the "introspected, self-conscious I" might
perhaps involve the sense that "I am worthless," which may be
opposed to "so and so is worth a great deal"; or one may think of
the self as "I am hated by it or him or her," which will be
opposed to "so and so is loved." Whatever the exact details, the
emotional context within which one defines the self will in part
give rise to and condition that self-definition.

> The matter may be put briefly and suggestively, if not too preci-
> sely, as follows: the introspected, self-conscious "I" is not in fact a
> perception of one's own total person; it is some particular part,
> affect, idea or action of the person as perceived by the person in a
> context where the dynamically dominant affect is some form of
> anxiety. These experiences are often expressed in the language of
> self: "I feel," "I am so worthless," "I desire," "I believe," "I love,"
> "I am hated by," "I must have," and so on. "Consciousness of
> self" is not an awareness of some self-identical entity; it is, rather
> *any consciousness colored by intrapsychic conflict and anxiety.* (italics
> his).[119]

Because one is emotionally "caught up" in external things,
"attached" to them, one identifies the self in the terms that are
specified by that emotional context. Katherine's sense of her self
as "right" will be laced with the anxiety about her own "wrongness." Her sense of herself is thereby colored by this intrapsychic
conflict and anxiety. In sum, interior psychic conflict brings
about neurotic cathexis, and in its terms we define the self.
   Here is how I see Fingarette elucidating Eckhart. When Eckhart says "all the love of the world is based on the love of the
self," he is suggesting a process similar to the one Fingarette here
outlines as the mechanism of the "introspected self conscious I."

One neurotically cares about the world—invests things and lines of action with emotional energy—in a way that is determined by the anxiety-laden definition of the self. Just to flesh this out with one plausible rendering: The "rich man" of Eckhart's example may define himself as rich, but he may have repressed how he regards himself inside as "really worthless." His "caring a jot" about his wealth may then be a screen that represses and conceals that displaced self-definition. Such a caring about his wealth will, of course, be emotionally loaded, for it grows out of his interior conflict between the sense of himself as worthless and as worthy.

This is how I understand Eckhart's assertions that the love of the world is "based on" the love of the self. Emotional attachments to the world grow out of an anxiety-laden self-definition. We displace inner conflicts and express them as caring excessively about "this and that." In this view, the problem which stands as the source of our attachments to the world is not the love of the self but the love of certain emotionally loaded conceptions (images) of the self.

Just as Eckhart speaks of the process of *lâzen*, letting go, of such attachments, Fingarette, too, speaks of a "letting go," by which he means "the cessation of defensive striving."[120] If the neurotic attachment expresses a repressed emotionally charged memory or self-conception, to bring that memory to conscious awareness or by some other means to rid oneself of it would result in the elimination of the whole syndrome, both self-conception and neurotic attachments.

Eckhart is frustratingly unclear about exactly how one is to bring about a transformation. "Finding out his weakest points so as to mend them and diligently striving to overcome them"[121] is at best vague. He does obliquely suggest two ingredients of the transformation process as we saw—starting the process by one's own efforts and perhaps using some penitential practices—but both are unclear enough to leave the key question unanswered: how is one to actually bring about the goal?

Fingarette, however, with the years of psychotherapeutic history behind him, can be more explicit. He writes that the successful patient will gradually build up insights into the character of his/her defensive striving: the psychoanalytic insight "proceeds (ideally) by limited and partial insights."[122] Gradually gaining insight into the character of his/her neurotic attachments the patient learns to function without them. This process entails nothing short of a major and possibly stormy reorganization of the character, for such conflicts are utterly seminal. But if those conflicts are somehow resolved, and the personality is so transformed, the individual comes to be able to conduct his or her affairs in a more anxiety-free atmosphere, no longer conditioned by the conflict-generated neuroses and obsessions.

Such a form of life requires an extremely well-developed and mature personality:

> The central task of the mystic is that of achieving an unusually strong ego within an unusually well-integrated personality. This implies maximal ego-autonomy and neutralization of drives, and it implies minimal conflict, anxiety and defense.[123]

There is no doubt that the endeavor is a long, arduous, and difficult one. It is not hard to see a parallel here with Eckhart's assertion that the path at times involves "strife, pain, and unrest."

The psychotherapeutic tradition maintains that the transformative process results from bringing repressed memories to consciousness and thereby eliminating them as unconscious sources of defensiveness. Eckhart, of course, had no such psychotherapeutic techniques at his disposal. But I think that psychologists would be the first to admit that much progress has been made by individuals naturally, that is, neuroses have been resolved without bringing repressed memories to clear, conscious awareness. It is my guess that this is the kind of thing Eckhart had in mind. Though more vaguely understood, the process Eckhart evokes and the one of which Fingarette writes are strikingly similar in outline. Both advocate a letting go of the self and of attachments—however that may be accomplished.

If, indeed, intrapsychic conflicts are the source of neurotic drives, attachments, and the introspected sense of the self, then we should expect that the elimination of such conflicts would eliminate these symptoms as well. That is just what occurs according to Fingarette. Each aspect of the personality touched upon before is affected. To begin with, it means that those attachments to which one had clung drop off. One ceases defensive striving towards "this or that", and the old bugbears simply cease mattering so much. Without such, one comes to live with an "absence of pretense, absence of anxious dependence or 'clinging,' 'openness' to life."[124] After Katherine had undergone a successful psychotherapy, she said of her old nemesis, Alice: "Well, I don't have any desires now. I used to want Alice to be shown up in her true colors, to have people see how wrong she was. Now I just don't think about it. I just act. I get along. ..."[125] Having resolved her intrapsychic conflict, her behavior and feelings cease being neurotically centered on Alice, and it ceases mattering to her excessively. When Alice did something she considered wrong, "I wouldn't *dwell* on its being wrong. I'm just not involved. It doesn't matter in the same way." This is strikingly similar to Eckhart's assertion that the detached soul would no longer be "troubled" by the "failings of other men,"[126] or a "mental satisfaction" would be found in which "creaturely joys and sorrows are powerless to drag down the topmost summit of the soul."[127] When neurotic drives are neutralized, one simply is no longer so preoccupied with the objects of attachments.

The resolution of intrapsychic conflicts would also have its effects on the sense of the self. As we have noted, Fingarette distinguished between the two uses of the term "self"—anxiety-laden and anxiety-free. The non-anxious sense of "self" does not signify an inability to identify and distinguish oneself from others. It marks instead the attitude towards the self of someone who, no longer emotionally opposing a notion of the self to a cathected object, ceases thinking of a particular image or part of the self *as* the self. Instead, one simply conducts one's affairs without paying undue attention to (the neurotic notion of) the self. Katherine no longer cared about showing herself "right" in opposition to Alice's "wrong." "Where . . . the ego functions are anxiety-free, we have that 'self-forgetfulness' so characteristic of autonomous ego functions using neutralized instinctual energy."[128]

It is in this sense of ceasing to be so preoccupied with a self-definition that grows out of neurotic drives that I read such Eckhart passages as, "you must give up yourself, altogether give up self, and then you have really given up,"[129] and "he should renounce himself first, then he has renounced all things."[130] I understand Eckhart here to be advocating a process similar to ceasing to care about the "self-conscious I" *vis-à-vis* the world, and a coming to determine one's action with greater autonomy and context sensitivity.

This brings me to the final aspect of this new form of life, what Eckhart has called "acting without a why," or will-lessness. Fingarette clarifies the obscurity of such expressions by adding that it is the aims of repression or obsession which one comes to function without. Devoid of such drives, the transformed soul comes to be "aimless" and "open to experience,"[131] which are expressions Eckhart himself could have uttered. This transformed man is open to an unlimited variety of behavioral choices; he may "pursue and enjoy whatever concrete aims seem appropriate."[132] Eckhart's expression "to be will-less" is hence misleading: one is not devoid of all autonomously chosen behavior, but is devoid of those lines of action generated out of one's attachments.

As I said, I find Fingarette helpful in understanding the transformative process at work in Eckhart. He is at his best when he is describing the nature of neurotic drives and their neutralization, and these help in understanding what it is to "care a jot" for, or be attached to, something.

I do not find him especially helpful, however, in understanding the experiences associated with the *terminus ad quem*. There is more to the experiences of *gezucket*, the Birth of the Son in the Soul, and the Breakthrough of the Soul to the Godhead than merely the *absence* of drives and the *absence* of an introspected self-conscious I. These states have certain more positive and novel aspects than such formulae would indicate. It is now time to turn to them. Let the reader not forget, though, that the process leading to these intriguing states involve a transformation in the character of the individual regarding how he feels within himself, towards his possessions, and towards the world. We will see that this transformation in the inner workings of the soul may be carried to a very high degree. It may carry one to mysticism.

I have one final somewhat personal observation. I have asserted that Eckhart describes the process in modest detail but provides precious few specific directions about how to accomplish it. Perhaps meditative instructions or something like them were forthcoming in a more intimate manner. The *orison secrae* might have been just such a teaching. Perhaps in the day-to-day life of the Dominican friar or nun the patterns or habits of living we noted briefly in chapter two helped the adept to release his or her attachments. Perhaps Eckhart thought that merely understanding his sermons would transform the listener. Perhaps he taught in private some such theory of the mechanics of transformation. But such a theory is not to be found in the material we have from him.

Eckhart would presumably argue that he gives no instructions about physiological or mental manipulations because they themselves can too quickly become attachments (see chapter five). But in this thought, it seems to me that Eckhart may be throwing out the baby with the bathwater.

I suspect that Eckhart was one of those lucky few who underwent the transformation he describes spontaneously and without using any systematic transformative techniques. Possibly it was like a "becoming pregnant with nothing," as Walshe suggests, and later a kind of giving birth to God within himself. Yet having spontaneously undergone such a transformation, or having developed a theoretical system admirably suited to communicate the results of such a transformation, is no guarantor of being able to lead others to it.

In mystical literature one often sees the image of a path and a goal.[133] This image communicates one thing in this context. The knowledge of, say, San Francisco, is no guarantor of knowledge of the roadways leading there, or of the mechanics of the vehicle in which one may ride on those roads. Because Eckhart was aware of the characteristics of San Francisco (e.g., the advanced mystical states), he needn't necessarily have understood the roads (e.g., the techniques of attaining those states). The two ranges of knowledge are by no means identical.

If the techniques of psycho-physiological transformation he inherited from his tradition had been more highly developed and reliable,[134] he might have held them in higher regard. As they were, however, they were less than reliable. Indeed, Eckhart found them to be counterproductive. The Beguines' self-flagellations produced little more than visions, hallucinations, and sore backs. Their results were at best ephemeral and passing. Eckhart advocated something more lasting and significant, and given the knowledge available to him, this may have been the only appropriate attitude.

That Eckhart's philosophical poesy helped to produce what he taught in his followers is at best doubtful. The writings of Suso and Tauler suggest transformed men.[135] We have little record of Eckhart's immediate female disciples, though the evidence of a half-century later retains a visionary tone rather than the mystical tone Eckhart advocated. What we know about his followers as a whole would suggest a lack of success on Eckhart's part, though obviously this is partly conjecture and a matter that involves phenomena far more complex than merely Eckhart's influence.

From the vantage point of today, it is unfortunate that Eckhart saw fit to discourage his listeners or readers from taking up some effective technique. It is naive to think that people can transform themselves in the deep and fundamental way he/she seeks without effective tools. Throughout the centuries many such tools have been developed and are available to us now. Some are presumably more effective than others. Which are most effective is a judgment each individual must make for him or herself. But there is no doubt that an advocacy of a more efficacious path would have made Eckhart a more productive spiritual advisor in his own time, and certainly more useful to us.

The Rudimentary Mystical Experience, *Gezucket*, and the Dynamization of Silence

Now you might say
"But Sir
What of the silence
you told us so much about?"[1]

When Eckhart speaks of the *terminus ad quem*, he employs three key terms. Two of them he emphasizes consistently: the Birth of the Son in the Soul, and the Breakthrough of the Soul to the Godhead. Both of these are "habitual." However, before discussing them, I must begin with the third term, the only one which marks a brief episode: *gezucket* (rapture). This mystical event plays a significant but smaller role in this thought than either of the other two. I will investigate it first for two reasons. First, as I will show, though not a requirement of the more advanced experiences, rapture may be an unmixed experience of them; in the Birth and the Breakthrough one may be understood to retain a key element of the enraptured mind. The second reason, not unrelated to the first, is pedagogical. A presentation of this temporary form of mystical experience will make it easier for me to introduce the nature of those two more advanced and, indeed, interesting experiences.

Gezucken, and the related terms *verzücken* and *entzücken*, terms with which Eckhart names this temporary mystical experience, has never to my knowledge been explicated in the secondary literature. Eckhart translates the Latin *raptus* with *gezucke*, and hence the latter is usually translated as "rapture," "enraptured" or sometimes "borne up." Paul was *gezucket* to the third heaven, says Eckhart's version of Second Corinthians 12:2[2]. Peter was *entzucket . . . unwizzende*, (transported . . . unknowingly).[3] I have found nine passages in the German works in which this experience is discussed using the term *gezucket*, and two discussions in the Latin works.[4] Other passages do not use *gezucket* but are unquestionably discussing rapture.[5] *Zücken*, the infinitive, means to draw quickly and forcefully, to seize or tear away from. It indicates a force beyond the individual which grabs one, as when a sword is drawn from its sheath. As used by Eckhart in its mystical sense, especially in the passive voice, it indicates that the mystic is, as it were, pulled up or out of himself or herself by something (or some One) beyond his or her control. *Gezücket werden*, the passive voice, becomes the participial adjective *gezucket* on occasion.[6] Since this form is closest to English phraseology, I will generally use it.[7]

One of the clearest (and relatively low-ramified) characterizations of *gezucket* is found in the sermon *Dum Medium Silentium* (QT 57 = W 1), a sermon to which we return frequently in this chapter. Eckhart there introduces the medieval notion of the powers of the soul.

> Whatever the soul effect, she effects with her powers. What she understands, she understands with the intellect. What she remembers, she does with the memory; if she would love, she does that with the will, and thus she works with her powers and not with her essence. Every external act is linked with some means. The power of sight works only through the eyes; otherwise it can neither employ nor bestow vision, and so it is with all the other senses. The soul's every external act is effected by some means.[8]

In addition to the five senses there are six powers: three lower (lower intellect, desire, and anger) and three higher (memory, higher intellect, and will). It is by their activity that the soul enters into and interacts with the external world.[9] We look at objects with our eyes, hear sounds with our ears, etc.[10] The activity of the six higher powers generates thought and desire, that is, willing and cognitive, or mental, activity. So far, pretty standard scholastic psychology.

The powers in our fallen state, that is, in the state with which all of us are most familiar, are not hierarchically oriented to God as they were in man's preexistence. What this means is that, in a word, our hearts and minds *wander*. Here is why. No longer focused on the "One," the powers attend to their respective roles within the external world. Because the soul is "so firmly attached to the powers," she "has to flow with them wherever they flow, because in every task they perform the soul must be present and attentive, or they could not work at all."[11] As a result of being thus drawn into the world, the mind attends now to this and now to that. The attention turns, in short, "from one thing to another."[12] Elsewhere Eckhart calls this phenomenon the "storm of inward thoughts."[13]

Despite Eckhart's implicit interpretation of this phenomenon by means of the doctrine of the Fall, in such expressions I think we can detect a phenomenological portrait of a very common-place pattern of mental activity. It is one with which each and every one of my readers is, no doubt, all too familiar. One sees, hears, touches, and thinks about the world, the self, images, or whatever. Such activities, and especially thoughts themselves, are in constant flux, a "storm." In a word, the mind wanders.

Perhaps because Eckhart's listeners, like my readers, were no doubt familiar with this prosaic fact of life, Eckhart needn't have dwelt on it in great detail. This is very much his style, for he focuses almost exclusively on the "goal" to be attained rather than the starting point.[14] To draw out its nature, let me quote one of the clearest descriptions of this, the ordinary pattern of mental activity, in Christian mystical literature. It is found in the immensely popular and the seminal fifth-century volume, *The Conferences of Cassian*, a book which, by the way, Eckhart knew.[15] Cassian's Abba Moses describes the ordinary mind as "fluttering." It "flutters hither and thither," he says, "accordingly to the whim of the passing moment and follows whatever immediate and external impression is presented to it."[16] Abba Isaac describes thoughts similarly as "career[ing] about the soul," and like bubbling, effervescent "boiling water."[17] In a more extended description of these mental "flutterings," Abba Isaac states:

When the mind has begun to take the meaning of a psalm, it passes on unaware and unintentionally to some other text of Scripture. When it has just begun to meditate upon that text and has half considered it, its attention is caught by another passage and it forgets all about the earlier matter for meditation. And so it goes on, hopping from text to text, from psalm to psalm, from Gospel to Epistle and thence to a prophetic book and thence to a narrative in the historical books of the Old Testament, meandering vaguely . . . At the time of the office it totters about like a drunkard, its worship very inadequate. During the prayers it is thinking about a psalm or lesson. During the singing of the psalter, it is thinking about something quite outside the text of the psalm. During the lesson, it is thinking about something that has to be done, or remembering something that has been done. So it receives or rejects nothing in a disciplined and orderly manner, but seems to be knocked about by haphazard assaults, powerless to keep or to linger over the text which pleases it.[18]

Cassian's Isaac calls this state, as I did, the "wandering mind."[19] It is obvious that Cassian and Eckhart are pointing to the same fact of life. It is that the mind wanders, weaving from hither to thither, and flitting about from fantasy to thought to sensation to concern to. . .This pattern of mental activity may be roughly characterized in terms of two primary characteristics: first there is some *intentional content* to the mind, be it thought, sensation, emotion, etc.[20] In Eckhart's similar (though not identical) notion, the Soul, through the agency of the powers, attends to some "outward" content.[21] Second, that content is in a *constant state of flux or mutability*. It "wanders," "flutters," or "meanders," as Cassian put it. We constantly, as Eckhart puts it, "turn from one thing to another."[22]

After having introduced the powers in *Dum Medium Silentium*, and alluding thereby to this phenomenon of the wandering mind, Eckhart writes of the *gezucket* of St. Paul, the archetypical "man."

. . .the more completely you are able to draw in your powers to a unity and forget all those things and their images which you have absorbed, and the further you can get from creatures and their images, the nearer you are to this and the readier to receive it. If only you could suddenly be unaware of all things, then you could pass into an oblivion of your own body as St. Paul did,. . .[In this experience] memory no longer functioned, nor understanding, nor the senses, nor the powers that should function so as to govern and grace the body. . . In this way a man should flee his senses, turn his powers inward and sink into an oblivion of all things and himself.[23]

He says that in this phenomenon St. Paul, or any "man," is "unaware of all things." Here Eckhart specifically asserts the absence of sensory content ("nor the senses"), as well as mental objects (devoid of memory, understanding, senses, etc.).

In another passage Eckhart specifically notes that the contemplative "withdrawal" from cognitive activity includes both "internal" and "external" powers.

> If a person wanted to withdraw into himself with all his powers internal and external. . .

The "external" powers are, as I mentioned, the senses, the lower intellect (common sense), anger, and desire, the powers by which we notice and respond in rudimentary ways to the external world. The "internal" powers are intellect, will, and desire, the "higher" powers with which we generate thought and desire. Hence withdrawal of both implies that neither the powers of thought nor of sensation "flow out" into their usual activities. In other words, both the sensing and the thinking aspects of the mind are inactive. Responding to his conditional, Eckhart continues,

> . . .then he will find himself in a state in which there are no images and no desires in him and he will therefore stand without any activity, internal or external.[24]

With both internal and external powers withdrawn, one experiences neither thought, affective feeling, sensation, nor vision.

In *gezucket* one is therefore unaware, according to Eckhart, of thought, word, speech, and even vague daydreams. Oblivious even to "himself," such a man becomes completely silent and at rest, without cognitive content: one is blank, yet open and alert. Restated, according to this passage, in *gezucket* one is merely awake, simply present. No manifold for awareness, either sensory or mental, is encountered.

According to Eckhart, then, the two primary characteristics of the ordinary waking pattern of mental activity stated above, intentionality and mutability, are absent, then, in *gezucket*. First, he denies any sensory or mental *content* of the mind, since without the operation of the mental or sensory powers no particular thought or sensation is encountered. Second, he denies flutter or *mutability*. Quoting Anselm a few lines later, Eckhart exhorts:

> Withdraw from the unrest of external activities, then flee away and hide from the turmoil of inward thoughts. . .[25]

While the "turmoil of inward thoughts" (*gesturme inwendiger gedanken*) connotes an emotionality, it also denotes a constant change within the thinking mind.[26] To withdraw from a "storm" implies that one will go to a calmness. Such a calmness is inevitable, given the lack of mental content in *gezucket*, since without any particular thought no change from one thought to another thought or sensation is possible. In short, both intentionality and changeability are absent in this quiet state. These two features make *gezucket* profoundly unlike ordinary waking experience.

As I noted, there are nine or more passages in which Eckhart speaks of such an experience. It would be boringly redundant to do an exhaustive study of them all, since they all bear similar phenomenological nuances. Let me give, then, just one or two more examples to confirm and amplify the characteristics of Eckhart's *gezucket*.

In the oft-quoted *intravit Jesus* (DW 86 = W9) Eckhart characterizes the three ways into "the circle of eternity." The first is seeking God "in all creatures with manifold activity and ardent longing." The second way involves rapture, *gezucket*. Peter is the example here. Eckhart says:

> The second way is a wayless way, free and yet bound, raised, rapt away (*gezucket*) well-nigh past self and all things, without will and without images, even though not yet in essential being. . . .St. Peter did not see God unveiled, though indeed he was caught up by the heavenly Father's power past all created understanding to the circle of eternity. I say he was grasped by the heavenly Father in a loving embrace, and borne up unknowingly (*unwizzende*) with tempestuous power, in an aspiring spirit transported (*entzücket*) beyond all conceiving by the might of the heavenly Father.[27]

Note here that Peter was borne up "beyond all conceiving." His rapture was beyond the use of the rational powers; he was borne up "unknowingly" (*unwizzende*).

This term, *unwizzen*, (sometimes "Nihtwizzen") literally "to unknow," expressly opposes the activity of the powers which cause the mind to "turn from one thing to another." When the passage discussing the mutability of the mind continues, it juxtaposes an unknowing "silence and stillness" with the chattering, dissipated mind. One must collect all of one's powers away from such outward activity and thought, he wrote, and bring them to quietude:

> Accordingly a master says: "To achieve an interior act, a man must collect all his powers as if into a corner of his soul where, hiding away from all images and forms, he can get to work." Here he must come to a forgetting and an unknowing (*unwizzen*). There must be a stillness and a silence. . .[28]

Hence when Eckhart speaks of the "unknowing" that Peter underwent in his rapture in the circle of eternity, he alludes to such a stillness and silence. (Indeed, he associates heavenly eternity with unchanging stillness. Letters traced there in the sand will remain unchanged forever.[29]) The silence gained in this experience results from a "forgetting" of the ordinary sensory and ratiocinative powers. Obviously Eckhart means that one forgets in the sense of ceasing to employ and use those powers, but not in the sense that one forgets things permanently, or ceases being able to use one's powers forever. No, the point is that in his *gezucket* St. Peter ceased thinking.

A similar portrait comes into the treatise *On Detachment*. The truly detached man is sometimes

> . . .*gezücket* into eternity in such a way that no transient thing can move him and he experiences nothing at all that is physical. He is said to be dead to the world, for he savors nothing worldly.[30]

Sometimes such a thoughtless moment is depicted without use of the term *gezucket*. For example, the following passage, in which Eckhart quotes Pseudo-Dionysius, may be read in this light. It says that one must have an "untroubled mind," by which I understand that the worries and anxious mental storm have been "stilled." One must "soar above" the powers of thought and activity, arriving at a place of "stillness" and "darkness."

> Dear son Timothy, do you with untroubled mind soar above

> yourself *and all your powers, above ratiocination and reasoning*, above
> works, *above all modes and existence,* into the secret still darkness.[31]
> (italics mine)

By such a "soaring into a darkness" I understand the comtempla-
tive quiet of *gezucket.* It is beyond the powers, above ratiocination
and reason, and leads to a dark (without content) and still state.

In sum, I characterize the pattern of mental functioning denoted
by Eckhart's term *gezucket as a mind which is simultaneously wakeful
and objectless.*[32] I assume that the mind is awake, i.e., not unconscious or asleep, primarily because it would be absurd to suppose
that Eckhart would spill such ink over a mere state of sleep or a
blackout. If confirmation is needed, in one discussion of St. Paul's
rapture, Eckhart specifically asserts that the senses remain alert,
which implies that the subject is not asleep.[33] Had anyone touched
St. Paul with a needle during his rapture, would he have felt it? I
say, "Yes.". . . if anyone had then touched him with the point of a
needle, he would have been aware of it. . .he would have known
it.[34] Paul's powers were alert and awake; they could have responded had a need arisen, only there was no such need. Had he
been utterly blacked out, he could not have felt anything. This
capacity to respond to sensory input implies that the mind was not
unconscious.[35]

As for the second characteristic, if the powers cease active functioning, if all images are utterly "forgotten," one can indeed be
"unaware of all things."[36] It is fair to say that one who is thus is
without mental or intentional content.

Before I continue, let me note that however paradoxical and
strange this contentless but alert mind may sound, it is not idiosyncratic to Eckhart. Not only is such a silent wakefulness described
by other Christian writers such as St. Paul, St. Augustine and St.
Thomas, all of whom Eckhart glosses over in various discussions of
gezucket, but structurally similar events are also described by
writers from a wide array of traditions. W. T. Stace devotes about
forty pages to documenting the cross-cultural evidence for such
events. He calls it an "introvertive mystical experience."

> Suppose that, after having got rid of all sensations, one should go on
> to exlude from consciousness all sensuous images, and then all
> abstract thoughts, reasoning processes, volitions, and other particu-
> lar mental contents; what would there then be left of consciousness?
> There would be no mental content whatever but rather a com-

plete emptiness, vacuum, void. One would suppose *a priori* that consciousness would then entirely lapse and one would fall asleep or become unconscious. But the introvertive mystics—thousands of them all over the world—unanimously assert that they have attained to this complete vacuum of particular mental contents, but that what then happens is quite different from a lapse into unconsciousness. On the contrary, what emerges is a state of *pure* consciousness—"pure" in the sense that it is not the consciousness of any empirical content. It has no content except itself.[37]

If Stace's research is correct, such an experience does exist. I have argued elsewhere that there is virtually incontrovertible evidence that it is reliably reported.[38]

GOD AND *GEZUCKET*

Returning to the Meister, by now his theological direction should be growing clear. He speaks of the "powers" as those "agents" within the soul that lead one into the external world. They are the machinery, as it were, of the outward "dissipation" experienced by "fallen" humanity. But they are not man's essence. Notice this distinction in a passage we have seen before:

> Whatever the soul effects, she effects with her powers. What she understands, she understands with the intellect. What she remembers, she does with the memory; if she would love, she does that with the will, and thus she works with her powers and not with her essence.[39]

If she works with her powers and not with her essence, when she eliminates the activities of her powers she must arrive at her "essence," also called her "ground" (*grunt*).

We said before that man has two levels within: his internal and external "powers." However, Eckhart sometimes describes not two "men" within the soul but three: external, internal, and "innermost." Through the external "man" the soul perceives sensory data and performs the bodily functions.[40] By means of the "inner man," the soul generates cognitive data and desires. Everything the soul does it does by these powers. The powers, however, are only the external aspect of the soul. Like spokes around a hub, they emanate from the "innermost" within man, the "ground," but they do not enter it. In fact, they cannot even have any knowledge of the ground. The ground is thus like an inner sanctum, a holy of holies,[41] "akin to the nature of the deity."

> There is something that transcends the created being of the soul, not in contact with created things, which are nothing; not even an angel has it, though he has a clear being that is pure and extensive: even that does not touch it. It is akin to the nature of the deity, it is one in itself, and has naught in common with anything. It is a stumbling-block to many a learned cleric.[43]

To this "innermost" man Eckhart devotes much of his most enthralling language, speaking of "the ground of the soul or the spark of the soul." [44] Within the soul there is a nameless place,[45] an "inmost man,"[46] a "silent middle." It is one's "being" or one's "essence." Eckhart creates nearly as many names for it as he wrote passages! It is *in dem höchsten der sele*, what is highest in the Soul; *der sele geist*, the spirit of the Soul; *das innigeist*, the inward spirit; *der grunt*, the ground; *das burgelin*, the little castle; etc. Most often, however, it is the *scintilla animae*, or *das funkelin der sele*, the spark of the Soul.[47]

It is here, to this "place" within, that man retires when he drops all external and internal works. When Eckhart continues the passage about the place "akin to the nature of the deity," he describes this transcendent "place":

> . . . It is a strange and desert *place*, and is rather nameless than possessed of a name, and is more unknown than it is known. If you could naught yourself for an instant, indeed I say less than an instant, you would possess all that this is in itself. But as long as you mind yourself or anything at all, you know no more of God than my mouth knows of colour or my eye of taste. . .[48]

The key fact to be remembered about this "place" within the soul is its utterly apophatic status. No activity enters there, no images can be made of it. It is no-thing, utterly silent and restful.

> . . . in the soul's ground and innermost recess, into which no image ever shone or (soul) power peeped.[49]

> In the summit of the soul. . .where time never entered, where no image ever shone in. . .[50]

> In the soul's essence there is no activity, for the powers she works
> with emanate from the ground of being. Yet in that ground is the
> silent "middle": here [in the ground is] nothing but rest and
> celebration.[51]

Isn't it strange that a location within the Soul should be characterized by terms like *rest* and *celebration*? Elsewhere Eckhart calls this
place "silent":

> There is the silent 'middle', for no creature ever entered there and
> no image, nor has the soul there either activity, or understanding,
> therefore she is not aware there of any image, whether of herself
> or of any other creature.[52]

This place, in other words, is the place to which one retires when
one has dropped all of the activity of the powers of the Soul, i.e.
all cognitive activity. It is the place of rest.

> When the soul comes to the nameless place, she takes her rest.
> There . . . she rests.[53]

"There" no soul power "peeps" and no thing enters. In short, the
ground is consistently portrayed as devoid of motion, content, or
even cognition. Nothing "gazes into it." Without attributes it is a
"nowhere" and a "nothing" which encounters nothing. It is "that
place which is nameless," which is remarkable, since the term *ineffabi-
lity* is generally reserved not for a place but for an experience.[54]

When I read Eckhart I am often struck by how consistently his
philosophical terminology seems almost phenomenological in
intent: his highly ramified language is defined in significant ways in
terms of experiential characteristics. Philosophy and theology are
shot through with experience. Here the "ground" or "spark" within
the soul is *defined* with precisely the same features as those characterizing the experience Eckhart calls *gezucket*. The terms become
virtually interchangeable.[55] Both are "without work."[56] Both are
"silent."[57] Both transcend names, forms and ideas.[58] Both are
"exalted" or "uplifted" above this and that.[59] Both are "ineffable."[60] Both are "bare" in the sense of being without ephemeral
connectedness.[61] In neither can one have activity[62] or knowledge.[62]

Let me try a brief language experiment. I will write two
passages below, as if either "ground" or *gezucket* were their
subject. One was originally a description of the ground, and the

other of the experience of *gezucket*. See whether you can tell which was originally which.

> no creature ever entered [there/then] and no image, nor has the soul [there/then] either activity or understanding, therefore she is not aware [there/then] of any image, whether of herself or of any other creature.[64]

Here is the other passage.

> [Where/when] the powers have been completely withdrawn from all their works and images. . .[there/then] memory no longer function[s/ed], nor understanding, nor the senses, nor the powers that should function so as to govern and grace the body. . .[65]

Aside from the fact that I have quoted the second passage before, could you tell any difference? Perhaps the context suggests one or the other to you. But is it not striking how easily one passage can be read as if it were characterizing the other subject? What this little experiment demonstrates is how significantly parallel are the implications of the "ground" and *gezucket*. The primary difference between them is that one is a verb (the act of experiencing this silence when the powers are still) and the other is a noun ("where" in the soul one "goes" when the powers are still). These two grammatical classes provide Eckhart with different implications and usages, yet they have virtually identical experiential nuances.

Now here is where it gets interesting. This ground or essence is not only defined with parallel phenomenological implications, as is *gezucket* (and perhaps was so defined in part *because* of the nature of this experience), it is also presented as the locale in which God is within man: "Christ within me."

> Here [in the ground] God's ground is my ground and my ground is God's ground.[66]

> There is something in the soul [namely, the ground] in which God is bare and the masters say this is nameless, and has no name of its own. . .God is always present and within it. I say that God has always been in it, eternally and uninterruptedly. . . .[67]

> . . .God is nowhere so truly as in the soul, and. . .in the inmost soul, in the summit of the soul.[68]

As we have seen, for Eckhart God shares a ground with the

soul's ground, and He has so shared it since man's preexistence. But in "ordinary" experience, in which man is attached to various cognitive objects, the soul attends to the powers and through them to the external world. As a result, his thoughts bubble incessantly, and what he perceives as "his" needs enthrall his attention. Activities cover over this place "like a mist over the sun."[69] By looking in the wrong direction, outward instead of within, the religious "overlooks" this "place" within himself, and hence attends not to God but to the creaturely. Yet the possibility of encountering this "locale" always remains, at least in theory.

> The soul has something in her, a spark of intellect, that never dies. . .But there is also in our souls a knowing directed towards externals, the sensible and rational perception which operates in images and words to obscure this from us.[70]

If God is at the summit of the soul and the ground is that which is realized during the moments in which the powers are brought to stillness, then, we might predict, Eckhart will assert that God is encountered during these moments of emptiness and is experienced as that emptiness. Describing Paul, the archetype of all *gezucket* experiencers, Eckhart wrote:

> "Paul rose from the ground and with open eyes saw nothing." I cannot see what is one. He saw *nothing, that is: God.* . . . When the soul is unified and there enters into total self-abnegation, *then she finds God* as in Nothing. It appeared to a man as in a dream—it was a waking dream—that he became pregnant with Nothing like a woman with child, and *in* that nothing God was born. He was the fruit of nothing. God was born *in* the Nothing. Therefore he says: "he arose from the ground with open eyes, seeing nothing."[71] (italics mine)

God is the nothing, is in the nothing, and it is God who is "born" when one is "pregnant" with nothing. The act of silencing the cognitive mechanism and the senses is identified as—is equated with—the encounter with God. As far as *gezucket* is concerned, theological doctrine is shot through with experiential characteristics.

A similar passage in which God is presented in part in terms of experience appears when Eckhart describes what happens when the religious becomes aware of God and "tastes" him. From that moment onwards his or her soul takes on certain properties. We have seen them before:

> The first is that it becomes detached from here and now. . .everything that touches or smacks of time must go. Again, it is detached from here. . .The place where I am standing is small, but however small, it must still go before I can see God.
>   The second point; it is like nothing. . .by virtue of being like nothing, this power is like God. Just as God is like nothing, so too this power is like nothing.[72]

Thus the experience of *gezucket*, the achievement of the oneness within one's soul, becomes archetypical also for the encounter with the Divine.

Eckhart's message fairly jumps out at us: it is *God* who is met in the silence, and he has been "there" all along. We have been so busy, we never noticed. Simply remove the busyness, and *voila!*, there he will be. *Gezucket* is man's first access to the Divine, though not its final perfection. That will come later.

IS *GEZUCKET* NONINTENTIONAL?

The reader may ask: although such experiences may be reported in some mystical literature, is Eckhart himself speaking of an *objectless* experience? After all, as I have pointed out, Eckhart uses the terms *God* or *Godhead* to describe "what" is encountered during rapture. St. Paul encountered the "Godhead."[73] These terms certainly sound like object-talk! However, I do not think that Eckhart is referring to an encounter with God that is intentional. Let us look closely at the relationship between God and the Soul into which one enters in *gezucket*. Eckhart is very careful. Paul did not see something; he was "locked in the embrace of the Godhead."[74] Peter did not stare wondrously at a God "over there", as it were, he was "caught up by the heavenly Father's power" and was "grasped by the heavenly Father in loving embrace."[75] Such expressions, reminiscent of the mystical marriage motif of many Rhineland mystics, the so-called "Braut-mystik" (bride mysticism), may be understood to be construc-tions designed to avoid asserting the presence of an object—God—which is phenomenologically distinguished from the soul. When Eckhart says that Timothy soared above himself "into the secret still darkness," he connotes again the absence of any object for the mind. It is striking that he typically avoids more natural phraseologies like "one sees God there" or "one thinks of God."

The nonintentionality of the purported "object" of *gezucket* is also inevitable given the nature of that "object." As we have said, Paul was locked in the embrace of the *Godhead*. While this term grammatically sounds like an object, what kind of an object might it be? The Godhead, you will recall, was God beyond God, utterly without numeration or distinguishing marks. If one were to encounter something without distinctions, then there would be nothing by means of which one might distinguish the subject from the object. This concept needn't imply pantheism. There can be analytical distinctions without phenomenological ones, as we shall see. But phenomenologically, without distinguishing marks there would be no "borders" between self and "other." Nothing could be sensed as "over there against me" if there were no boundaries. The same lack of distinguishing marks hold true of the "Father," for in this context, as is generally the case when the trinitarian God is spoken of without mention of the Godhead, the "Father" is equivalent to the distinctionless aspect of God. Hence to be "grasped by the heavenly Father in loving embrace" asserts both by syntax and also by theological implication that Peter experienced no intentional object.

That he is speaking of no object distinct from the self itself also emerges from a consideration of his doctrine of the hierarchy of the soul. In the previous chapter, I mentioned that in Eckhart's doctrine of the soul the lower powers are hierarchically inferior to the higher powers, and they in turn are below the highest in the soul. That "highest place," called variously the ground, little castle, spark, or summit, it will be recalled, shares a ground with, or is part of, the Divine. "In the ground of the soul . . . God's ground and the soul's ground are one ground."[76] Some imma-nent contact with God therefore persists within the soul's own ground, despite fallen man's unawareness of that contact.

> God is nowhere so truly as in the soul, and. . .in the inmost soul, in the summit of the soul.[77]

> There is something in the soul in which God is bare and the masters say this is nameless, and has no name of its own. . .God is always present and within it. I say that God has always been in it, eternally and uninterruptedly. . .[78]

Now if one is able to drop off all the preoccupying activities of the powers, one will come not to some object which is experientially distinguished from the self. Any such object will be encountered via the powers, and here the powers are silent. No, one will arrive at none other than one's own ground within oneself. It is this "ground" that is analytically understood to share a ground with God. But that does not imply that one comes to something like an intentional object. It is none other than the subject itself to which one comes, for it is the summit of "my" soul to which I retire when I drop all mental content. It is the self itself, not an object "over against" the subject, to which I retire. Stace says:

> Suppose then that we obliterate from consciousness all objects physical or mental. When the self is not engaged in apprehending objects it becomes aware of itself. The self itself emerges. The self, however, when stripped of all psychological contents or objects, is not another thing, or substance, distinct from its contents. It is the bare unity of the manifold of consciousness from which the manifold itself has been obliterated.[79]

Hence when Eckhart says that in *gezucket* one comes to the highest within the self, and that God is "there," he does not mean that the self goes anywhere or sees anything external. Rather it simply rests in itself, "becomes aware of itself." This self within is what is analytically understood to "share a ground" with God. To retire away from the activities of the powers is to retire to the summit of the soul, and here God is asserted to continually persist.

It is more in harmony with Eckhart's thought to say that with reference to *gezucket*, the objective character of his God-talk is analytical, not phenomenological. The phenomenology of the experience is that one simply ceases to pay attention to or use the powers. One ceases to think or feel anything. This self—or rather the summit—Eckhart *analyzes* to be associated with God or the Godhead. Hence to be without intentional content (phenomenological description) is just the same thing as being "locked in the embrace of the Godhead" (analysis) or soaring "into the secret still darkness."

May someone plausibly speak of a nonintentional experience with intentional language?[80] W. T. Stace implies that one can:

> Since the experience has no content, it is often spoken of by the mystics as the Void or as nothingness; but also as the One [viz. the "Godhead"], and as the Infinite. That there are in it no particular existences is the same as saying that there are no distinctions in it, or that it is an undifferentiated unity. Since there is no multiplicity in it, it is the One. And that there are no distinctions in it or outside it means that there are no boundary lines in it between anything and anything. It is therefore the boundless or the infinite.
>
> The paradox is that there should be a positive experience which has no positive content—an experience which is both something and nothing.[81]

Hence when Eckhart asserts that one is "locked in the embrace of the Godhead" in *gezucket*, he is offering a term, *the Godhead*, for the "something" encountered in this "nothing" experience. He may be understood to be providing an analytical, theological "content" for a phenomenological contentlessness.

Rather than a new object or a new way of perceiving an intentional object, Eckhart's *gezucket* would be better conceived as naming a new phenomenological pattern of mental functioning. Instead of an intentional and ever-changing manifold, the pattern of one's mind comes to be nonintentional and quiescent.

If that is the case, then I can suggest a technical term here: Eckhart is describing a new State of Consciousness.[82] A State of Consciousness has been defined for any given individual as a state

> in which [the subject] clearly feels a *qualitative* shift in his pattern of mental functioning, that is, he feels not just a quantitative shift (more or less alert, more or less visual imagery, sharper or duller, etc.) but also that some quality or qualities of his mental processes are *different*.[83] (italics his)

According to this definition, the key feature of a State of Consciousness involves subjectively recognizable changes in mental functioning. Such changes are not in a particular aspect of mental functioning such as feeling especially happy, or focused on any particular image, but rather are changes in the overarching character of the mind's functioning. Let us take a relatively common example of a new State of Consciousness: inebriation. Think of the difference between ordinary waking consciousness and inebriation. The perception that one is now drunk is not made on the basis of simply being particularly happy, sad, or clumsy, although such may be part of it. Nor is it recognized on the basis of some different subject matter to the mind, though again such may be the case.[87] Rather, we might say that the *overall pattern of functioning* of the mind and of awareness subjectively appears different from normal. As the psychologist Charles Tart puts it, the immediate experiential basis of the recognition of a new State of Consciousness

> is usually gestalt pattern recognition, the feeling that "this condition of my mind feels *radically different* from some other condition, rather than just an extension of it." (italics his)[85]

The sense or recognition that this overall condition of my mind is radically different from some other condition may be thought of as the distinguishing mark of a new State of Consciousness.

While I find this definition of State of Consciousness adequate on the whole, I would like to refine this notion of "gestalt pattern recognition" by noting that what is radically different about the mind's condition in the *gezucket* event is a novel "cognitive structure," the way in which the mind handles its content. This notion will become more important in the next chapter. Here, however, the cognitive structure is such that no sensory or mental content is allowed to come to conscious awareness. It does not matter what the usual content of the mind may be, whether one may be generally happy or sad, or whether one usually thinks in English, Latin, or Medieval German. No content is entertained.

Now, is it appropriate to think about someone like Eckhart in terms of a State of Consciousness if he, himself, didn't use such a term? Such a question concerns the old problem of translating belief systems: that it is impossible to translate one culture's or age's set of terms and concepts into another's. In this case I am translating Eckhart's set into those of modern psychology. I think here however, with reference to the structure of cognition, we can and should legitimately apply our set. This is because two people from any culture—no matter how different may be those cultures' systems of belief—may both be said, without danger of error, to be in the same, i.e. waking, State of Consciousness.

Being awake does not involve using any particular term, thinking of any one thing, working within any particular belief system, or what have you. Rather, the notion of the waking state describes a manner of handling content—a mind which encounters any content intentionally and with a constant mutability, if you will. Nor do you need to use any special term, language, or belief system to be drunk, or to be in any different State of Consciousness. Conflicts of belief systems do not enter into evaluations of States of Consciousness. An American Indian may think of his new fire-water state as a gift from the spirits. No matter, we could still rightly describe him as "intoxicated."

"States of Consciousness" may form a kind of trans-cultural or meta-language. Terms and concepts differ from age to age and across cultures, while patterns of mental activity appear to remain largely the same. Psychological research on State of Consciousness over the last several decades has intentionally included subjects from a range of ages and cultures, and has found no sharp differences in the psycho-physiological structures between them—despite the enormous differences in their linguistic and conceptual systems.[86] It would make sense that States of Consciousness would remain constant across cultures if any particular term or belief counts as part of the content that is entertained within a State, for according to our definition it is not the content that defines a new State but the overarching manner or pattern of handling that content.

In conclusion, I think it is appropriate—and indeed revealing—to think that when Eckhart (or Stace) describes a state in which one is "unaware of all things," devoid of "the turmoil of inward thoughts," he is describing quite clearly a new State of Consciousness, one which is nonintentional and nonfluctuating.

THE PLACE OF *GEZUCKET* IN THE MYSTICAL LIFE

Eckhart scholars may object that whether or not Eckhart was describing a new State of Consciousness, he certainly did not emphasize or advocate rapture. Rather he advocated something closer to what Professor Kieckhefer called *habitual* mysticism— i.e., a permanent or semi-permanent lived experience of union with God. Kieckhefer writes:

> Eckhart did not view ecstatic or abstractive union with God as integral to the life of the soul, or even as a goal to be sought or particularly treasured. The state to which he invites his reader is that of habitual and nonabstractive union; he nowhere says that other forms are necesary or even helpful in the attainment of that goal.[87]

I agree. Rapture is no *summum bonum* for Eckhart. I will show in the next two chapters that he advocates a more permanent trans-formation.

However, it would be false to claim, as some scholars have done, that Eckhart denigrates rapture in itself.[88] Authors who believe that Eckhart denigrates rapture have appealed to passages like the following:[89]

> But now some complain that they have no inwardness nor devotion nor rapture nor any special consolation from God. Such people are still not on the right way: one can bear with them but it is second-best . . . [These] people want to see God with their own eyes as they see a cow, and they want to love God as they love a cow. You love a cow for her milk and her cheese and your own profit. That is what all those men do who love God for outward wealth or inward consolation—and they do not truly love God, they love their own profit. I truly assert that *anything* you put in the forefront of your mind, if it is not God in Himself, is— however good it may be—a hindrance to your gaining the highest truth.[90]

One can hardly be blamed for reading an antagonism towards rapture in this. The desire for rapture is the "wrong way." People desirous of rapture want to "see God with the eyes one sees a cow." This passages certainly sounds antimystical!

Yet, on closer scrutiny, it is not antiecstatic at all. In fact it is just the opposite! Eckhart does not inveigh against *rapture*. What he preaches against here is the *desire* for it. People who crave it are on the wrong track not because they seek something evil in itself but because they have a craving at all. The desire for inwardness or rapture functions as nothing more than a placeholder for some other desire: such people still seek their own profit. Now instead of something material, the profit is the ecstatic "flash," as it were.[91] It is profit and desire against which he rails.

Not only does he not devalue these rapturous moments, but he twice herein affirms them: "good as [inwardness, devotion, or rapture] may be:" and "however good it may be." He does not deny their value. He knows that rapture is a momentary taste of something worthwhile, indeed a taste of the *summum bonum*. Addressing himself to those (the Beguines perhaps?) who sought the ecstatic flash, what he disparages is either seeking or being attached to such moments. This is a theme in virtually every passage discussing rapture.

Here is another popular passage among those who claim that Eckhart was antiecstatic:

> I say truly, as long as you do works for the sake of heaven or God or eternal bliss, from without, you are at fault. It may pass muster, but it is not the best. Indeed, if a man thinks he will get more of God by meditation, by devotion, by ecstasies or by special infusion of grace than by the fireside or in the stable—that is nothing but taking God, wrapping a cloak round His head and shoving Him under a bench. For whoever seeks God in a special way gets the way and misses God, who lies hidden in it.[93]

Note again the overt debunking and the covert affirmation. Seeking God by some special way represents an attachment to the process rather than to the goal. Yet experiences in meditation, devotion, or ecstasy are indeed experiences of God: it is *his* head around which the cloak gets wrapped. Eckhart's point is that to desire Him via these special ways and consolations is to have a desire at all. Desire implies a self-will, perhaps the self-definition founded in a context of anxiety, and the whole syndrome of *eigenschaft*, attachments. In this case the attachment is to the way, the contemplative routine: "all those who are bound with attachment [*eigenschaft*] to prayer, fasting, vigils, and all kinds of outward discipline and mortification."[94] And for Eckhart, attachment remains attachment.

Rather than debunking it utterly, Eckhart presents *gezucket* as one form of real contact with God, but in itself not worth pursuing. One key factor marring it is that Eckhart seeks habitual changes and *gezucket* is but temporary. Eckhart mentions its transiency frequently. Paul's archetypical rapture into the third heaven lasted but a short while.[95] Even the residual effects lasted but three days.[96] Peter, tempestuously borne aloft, soon returned.[97] No one in the world can be withdrawn for very long: perhaps an instant,[98] perhaps an hour, perhaps even as long as Moses, forty days.[99] But even Moses's forty days were but a brief interlude in his long years. Temporary experiences, no matter how wonderful, are wonderful only as long as they last. One is left with but a memory.

What Eckhart advocates is no ephemeral flash, but a permanent and more far-reaching change in the entire constitution of the religious. He is not interested in a life of light, as it were, which is prey to intervening "spells of darkness."[100] He seeks neither "gifts of the Holy Spirit" (visions, auditions, or other consolations) nor his "likeness" in transient transcendental moments, for these do not abide with one. Rather he seeks to establish a relationship with God that is constant.

> It is true that you may receive the gifts of the Holy Ghost, or the likeness of the Holy Ghost, but it does not abide with you—it is impermanent. In the same way a man may blush for shame or blench, but that is accidental and it passes. But a man who is by nature ruddy and fair, remains so always. So it is with a man who is the only begotten Son, the Holy Ghost *remains* in his being.[101]

Eckhart advocates an habitual union with God, in which the Holy Ghost "remains" in his being.[102]

However, though he does not advocate pursuing such experiences, the relationship between *gezucket* and the more habitual forms of mysticism may illuminate something of the character of the latter. In fact *gezucket* may be understood as an unmixed experience of the novel aspect of a life in habitual union. This is why I chose to present it first, for by understanding it and the development out of it, we can better fathom the peculiarities of the Birth and of the Breakthrough experiences.

Let us look at a passage in which Eckhart discusses the relationship between contemplative silence and the rest of life. It follows a passage we have seen before:

> If a person wanted to withdraw into himself with all his powers internal and external, then he will find himself in a state in which there are no images and no desires in him and he will therefore stand without any activity, internal or external.[103]

Here Eckhart describes the rapturous encounter in which one "withdraws" all of the powers from their objects, and hence attends to neither sensation, image, thought, nor anything else. One becomes herein one with the "inward man." How, according to Eckhart, is one to respond to this encounter with inward silence? Is one to merely escape from the silence, forget "it" or "him" altogether, and jump headlong into activity? Definitely not. Eckhart continues:

> Not that one should escape from the inward man, or flee from him or deny him, but in him with him and through him, one should learn to act in such a way that one breaks up the inwardness (*innicheit*) into reality and leads reality into inwardness, and that one should thus become accustomed to work without compulsion.[104]

What does "breaks up (*breche*) the inwardness (*innicheit*) into reality (*würklicheit*)" mean? "Inwardness" or the "inward man" is what is discovered in that moment when one is "without any activity, internal or external." Eckhart instructs his listener to drag the inwardness outwards, as it were, bringing it into activity. One is to learn to act in such a way that reality (*würklicheit*)—activity, thought, perception, etc.—is perceived and undergone *while not losing* the interior silence encountered in contemplation. Simultaneously one is to lead "reality into the inwardness," i.e. make the silent inwardness, if you will, dynamic. In other words, the advanced adept is to learn to think, speak, walk, and work without losing the profoundest quietness inside. However active, the interior silence is not lost. The silence becomes, to coin a term, "dynamized."

A phenomenologically clear portrait of the first step in this dynamization of silence may be found in *The Nobleman*. This treatise portrays the God-illumined man as analogous with a lord or a nobleman. The passage begins with a description of the contemplative moment with which we have grown familiar, in which one is unaware of knowledge, or of love, or of anything at all.[110] The soul knows nothing in an intentional sense, but rather persists "in" one's being or "in" God.

> For the first thing on which blessedness depends is that the soul should contemplate God unveiled. In this experience the soul receives all her being and her life, and draws all that she is from the

> ground of God, and knows nothing of knowledge, or of love, or of anything at all. She becomes entirely and absolutely passive in the being of God. There she knows nothing but being and God.[105]

But this passive resting in God, this contemplation of God without image, thought, or hence "intermediary," is short-lived. Without even knowing how or when, the soul begins *thinking* about this contemplative union, and in so doing (Catch 22) destroys the pure (thoughtless) connectedness.

> But when she knows and recognizes that she contemplates, knows and loves God, that is a breaking out and a reversion to the previous stage, according to the natural order. . .[106]

To commence thinking *about* God or one's relationship with God is to lose the very relationship one had enjoyed. Hence at this point the silence is incompatible with thought: to think is to lose the silence.

However, the passage then suggests an advancement. Using an analogy with whiteness (appropriately enough for such a contentless experience), Eckhart suggests that one may be white and also *know that* he/she is white. This is a development on merely being white.

> . . .If anyone knows himself to be white, he is building and making a foundation on whiteness, and he does not receive his knowledge without medium, nor unknowing direct from colour, but he receives the knowledge of colour and about colour from that which is now white [i.e. himself]. He does not draw knowledge from the colour alone in itself, but he draws knowledge and cognition from that which is coloured, or that which is white and knows itself to be white.[107]

In this new and more mature integration, on the one hand one persists as white and on the other hand one is aware *that* one is white. If one can maintain both capacities simultaneously, i.e., be white yet also know that one is white, or, more to the point, maintain a silence yet also be aware of being silent—draw one's ground from the ground of God and also know that one is so doing—this indeed would be an advancement.

> Hence I say that beatitude cannot exist unless man knows *and* is aware *that* he contemplates and knows God. . .Hence our Lord

says very rightly: "A nobleman went out into a far country to obtain for himself a kingdom and returned." For a man must be one in himself and must seek this in himself, and in One and receive it in One: that is to *contemplate God alone*. [This is like the first capacity, that of being white.] *And then* he must return, that is to know *and* to be aware that one knows and is aware of God. [This is like the second capacity, that of knowing that one is white.][108] (italics mine.)

To be immediately aware of sharing a ground with God (i.e. to persist in silence), and also to know that one so persists without losing that "sense" of silence, must be an early step towards dynamizing the interior silence. To carry such a sense throughout all activities, Eckhart's ultimate goal, first requires, according to this passage, that one be able to think a thought without losing the sense of silence within.

There is a movement of meaning here. The ability to maintain and also be aware of a silence means that that silence must be more palpable or more like what William James called "a quasi-material something" than the mere being without content of *gezucket*. The silence must be like "something" of which someone may be aware along with or through other mental content. This concept is not unrelated to W. T. Stace's assertions that the lack of multiplicity may be experienced as the One, or that an experience without positive content may be, paradoxically, a positive one. But the capacity to think, along with maintaining an inner quietness, seems to be a development upon the capacity to merely maintain silence, for Eckhart states that to do so, like being white and knowing it, is an *advancement* (like "building and making a foundation on whiteness"). Perhaps we could say that the more "positive" character of *gezucket* seems to come to the fore here. What is this positive character of *gezucket* and of the more advanced experience? This is a big question, and it will take the better part of a chapter to answer it. Thus in the next chapter I will document what Eckhart presents of the character of this quasi-material "content" and suggest why Eckhart might plausibly call it "God."

However it is to be conceived, for now let me just emphasize that Eckhart repeatedly says that the silence encountered without thought in contemplation must come to be experienced along with activities. Furthermore, as we saw before, all of reality (*würklicheit*)—activity and perception as well as thought—must be undergone while not losing the *innicheit* (inwardness, interior silence) usually thought to be encountered only in contemplation. That the interior silence should be dragged into activity, or experienced along with activity, may be seen in Eckhart's somewhat novel use of terms prefixed by *inne* (inner): e.g., *innwendicheit, innicheit, innen,* etc. Medieval German mystics generally used in *innwendicheit* in the special sense of devotion or contemplation.[109] Sometimes Eckhart used it to indicate full attention to the *innwendicheit* within man, the innermost within man, becoming senseless and enraptured (*verzücke*), gaining a state transcending reason and image.[110] Similarly, the related term *innerkeit* (inwardness) is found in conjunction with contemplative devotions (*andâht*) and ecstasies of contemplation.[111]

But Eckhart redirects the contemplative nuances of these *inne*-terms into something entirely more dynamic. We have already seen him say that one must "break up the inwardness [*innicheit*]" into reality and lead reality back into the *innicheit*, thereby becoming habituated to working within it.[112]

So, too, one must learn, says Eckhart, to live in this silence, using silence as a preliminary "school." "At the beginning there must be attentiveness and a careful formation within himself, like a schoolboy setting himself to learn."[113] Only based on this elementary sort of "learning" can one hope to "cultivate an inward (*innerlich*) solitude, wherever or with whomever one may be."[114] To gain the *innen* man, one "accustoms the ground and the heart" to function in the new way. One learns to work "in the light of the soul," thereby learning to "abide in the *inwendic* and not come out."[115] One learns to "bring the self to the point" whereby he acts, though "locked up internally":

> One should learn to be free and unimpeded in one's activities. . . [so that] God can be present to us continually and can shine unveiled at all times and in all surroundings. . .[for this] a man should be *locked up internally*, that his heart should be protected against the images that stand outside, to see that they remain outside him and that they do not in any unbefitting manner wander and associate with him. He must see that they find no place in him. . .A man should not allow himself to be distracted or disturbed or exhausted by multiplicity, either in the shape of internal images, such as fancies or pride of the heart or external images or whatever it may be that is present in a man. He should

devote all his energies to fighting them and should have his
inwardness present [*gegenwartig haben sine inwendicheit*][116]

To "have the inwardness present" is to have present what one
may encounter in its purity in *gezucket*. This is not to say that one
must experience *gezucket per se*. Rather, Eckhart is saying that the
inwardness which one may gain in *gezucket* must be brought into
reality.

Not only does he communicate this new, active mysticism of a
dynamized silence in his restructuring of the German language,
but he amplifies it at some length in the more well-known of the
two sermons entitled *Intravit Jesus in Quoddam Castellum*.[117] This
sermon concerns the Luke 10:38–42 story of Mary and Martha, in
which Mary sits meditatively at the Lord's feet, while Martha
bustles about serving the guests. Eckhart's monastic predecessors
had a fairly free interpretation of this passage. Martha signified
the ordinary active life, the *vita activa*. This, monastics held, was a
lesser life than was Mary's more perfect *vita contemplativa*.[118]
Monks held that this story demonstrated that Jesus advocated
their contemplative life, noting that Jesus called Mary's way the
"better part," while chiding active Martha with, "Martha,
Martha, you are anxious and troubled about many things, one
thing is needful." (Luke 10:42).

By straining this exegesis one further step, Eckhart reverses its
conclusions. To Eckhart Mary represents a *less* advanced adept
who sits in mere inward contemplation.[119] Because hers is but the
rudimentary encounter with the ground, it remains frail. Like
Paul's, hers is a life of light, but exposed to darkness, he says.[120] It
is good but not yet the best.

Martha, on the other hand, represents the dynamized silence,
which Christ acknowledged by calling her twice, "Martha,
Martha," claims the Meister. The first "Martha" signifies that she
had located the ground through a contemplative life; the second
implies that she *lived* with it. Although she worked, she preserved
her inwardness. "Martha was so well grounded in her essence that
her activity was no hindrance to her."[121] She was thus not Mary's
opposite, as the monastic authors implied, but her fulfillment.
Mary, having lived awhile with the contemplative joy, as Martha
had, will find it leading her into good works.

And so, when Mary sat at the feet of our Lord she was learning,

> for she had just gone to school to learn how to live. But later on, when Christ had gone to heaven and she received the Holy Ghost, she began to serve . . . Only when the saints become saints do they do good works. . .[122]

In contemplation Mary was as if in school. She was growing acquainted with the silence, as it were. Once familiar with it, she could "maintain" it and also act; acting without losing her interiority. Note also that this is archetypical for every saint. Gaining the inward quietness and *also* working out of it is the saintly formula.

Hence Paul, too, Eckhart notes in this sermon, made his first discovery of the ground in his rapture. Only by living with and through it, could he bring the silent, detached core of the virtues into dynamism.[123]

Eckhart's attitude towards such contemplative ecstasy discourages any potential attachments to this or any other transient experiences. By making ecstasy the goal, one overlooks more valuable, permanent transformations. Mary's problem, in the sermon on Mary and Martha, was not that she had found something other than the true God in her *contemplatio*. It was *Christ's* feet at which she reposed. Her problem was that she had become attached to the transient bliss she discovered therein.[124] Any longing for it makes it into an attachment and it can thereby become counterproductive.

> We suspect that she, dear Mary, sat there a little more for her own happiness than for spiritual profit. That is why Martha said, "Bid her rise, Lord," fearing that by dallying in this joy she might progress no further.[125]

One may "profit" from ecstasy, Eckhart suggests, by being drawn on by it, or by becoming withdrawn enough to develop one's detachment in the world, etc.

> It is given by our LORD to such people as a bait or stimulus, and also in order that one may be effectively kept away from others thereby.[126]

But the potentially worthwhile, short-lived, "perfectly simply, wholly unoccupied" experience is not a necessary roadmarker on the journey towards permanent perfection. Instead, Eckhart maintains that every religious, indeed every person—is given according to "what is best and most fitting" for him or her. Only to those who are "ready" or most "capable" of profiting from it is this experience given.

> He gives to each one according to what is best and what is suitable for him. If one has to cut a coat for someone, one must make it to his measure, and a coat which would fit one person would not fit another. One takes everyone's measure according to what fits him. In the same way God gives each one the very best in accordance with the fact that He best knows his needs urgent.[127]

And, apparently, it is best for only a few adepts. "This [*gezucket*] happens rarely and to few people."[128] In short, though a possible and preliminary experience, *gezucket* is not requisite. Desires for it or attachments to it, unless one is one of those "few people" (and even then attachment won't do), will only lead one astray.

In his downplaying of the experience of rapture, Eckhart compensates for what he must have perceived as an overemphasis on it in the ecstatic mysticism of his day. The teachings of the Beguines and the Beghards, Mechthilde de Magdeburg's *The Flowing Light of the Godhead, The Mirror of Simple Souls,* etc., all communicate his century's emphasis on ecstasy. In his shifting of emphasis, Eckhart downplays the short bursts of the life of ecstatic "light" and encourages a more permanent advance upon it.[129]

Despite Eckhart's deemphasis of it, I think it should be growing clear by now why I have emphasized *gezucket* to the extent I have. Let me repeat: Eckhart does not advocate the pursuit of such transcendental moments, nor it is apparently essential on the path he envisions. The space I have devoted to it, in this sense, distorts him. I have chosen to emphasize it both because he does talk about it and because in a pure and uncompounded way one seems to gain in this State of Consciousness something novel, and that something becomes an important aspect of the experiences called the Birth and the Breakthrough. The silence found by Mary, Paul, or anyone else in *gezucket* is an aspect of the fuller, integrated life he seeks. The Dominican motto, "to contemplate and to share with others the fruits of contemplation," Eckhart takes seriously. He advocates learning to contemplate, sharing in a pure way (without intervening thought, sensation, etc.) the ground of God, *and then also* acting without losing this quiet interior sense. But one may also, he implies, dispense with this intervening step and enjoy the mixed life of a dynamized silence even without ever experiencing its pure, enraptured form. In other words, as an experience, *gezucket* may form part of the mystical journey, but it is *not* essential. As an element of the complete life, the silence gained in *gezucket* is indispensable.

It may, in fact, be one of the very last steps on the path towards the complete life. Eckhart is inconsistent here, but in several passages he seems to suggest that this is so. It may be that the process of sloughing off attachments and moving thereby towards *abegescheidenheit* (detachment) will lead to *gezucket* if and only if one is able to eliminate at least for some time the effects of attachments entirely. In a passage from *On Detachment* (part of which we have already seen) Eckhart suggests this:

> And the man who thus stands in complete detachment (*ganzer abegescheidenheit*) is rapt (*gezücket*) into eternity in such a way that no transient thing can move him and he experiences nothing at all that is physical. He is said to be dead to the world, for he savors nothing worldly.[130]

Hence Eckhart may believe that only those who come to a state of complete detachment can achieve the absolutely thoughtless moment. A similar sense of thoughtlessness coming as a result of complete detachment may be seen in the following:

> What is the prayer of the detached heart? I answer that detachment and purity cannot pray. For if anyone prays he asks God that something may be given to him, or asks that God may take something away from him. But the detached heart does not ask for anything at all, nor has it anything at all that it would like to be rid of. Therefore it is free from all prayer . . .[131]

To contemplate while being "free from all prayer" may be understood as being free from any cognitive activity. And this is the result of the completely detached heart.

Hence it may be that only those who are enabled to gain or temporarily maintain a state utterly devoid of attachments can maintain such a pure and untrammeled State of Consciousness as *gezucket*. This would, of course, rule it out for most people. Most of us can rid ourselves of attachments only to a partial extent. Perhaps this is why Eckhart deemphasized it so.

Whether *gezucket* is a milepost at the middle or end of the journey, what is clear is that Eckhart advocates a process of the releasing (*gelâzen*) of attachments, which leads towards a progressively greater level of detachment (*abegescheidenheit*). The detachment so achieved may result sometimes in a state of pure detachment, and one may find oneself enraptured. While this experience is not necessary, it does mark an aspect of the habitual experience Eckhart advocates. In some way the Birth and the Breakthrough will involve an inner, non-"creaturely", non-thinking, silent side of the Soul. And they result from, as it were, bringing an inner silence into reality and bringing reality within.

I believe the Birth and the Breakthrough mark two different experiential relationships between the silent, unmoving One and the "creaturely" many. The positive character of the interior silence, and how that silence and the active come to coexist with each other will be the subjects of my next two chapters.

CHAPTER SIX

The *Geburt:*
The Intermediate
Mystical Experience

> . . .the soul's life was with the body
> but above the body immediately in God
> without any obstructions.[1]

It is now time to turn towards the experiences of the Birth of the
Son (or Word) of God in the Soul and, in the next chapter, the
Breakthrough of the Soul to the Godhead.[2] These terms, unlike
gezucket, are Eckhart's primary focus: the problem here is an
embarrassment, rather than a paucity, of riches.

The key feature of the Birth and the Breakthrough is that
unlike *gezucken*, they are permanent or semi-permanent.

> And so I say, if this child is born in you, then you have such great
> joy in every good deed that is done in the world that this joy
> *becomes permanent and never changes.*[3] (italics mine)

> . . .cast out all *grief* so that perpetual joy reigns in your heart.[4]

(I say "semi-permanent" because there is a development from the
Birth to the Breakthrough, as I will show in the next chapter.
While the characteristics we see in the Birth themselves remain
permanent, the Breakthrough brings new attributes or functions
to it: hence the Birth is not the final development.)

Again and again Eckhart emphasizes that the Birth he advocates is continual and permanent:

... God gives birth to Himself fully in me that I may *never* lose Him, for whatever is born to me [spiritually] I *cannot lose*.[5]

...the soul that gives birth spiritually...gives birth *every moment*. The soul that has God is fruitful *all the time*.[6]

Sometimes he speaks of an inwardness (*innwendicheit*) which lasts for a considerable time, "a week, a month, or a year."[7] More commonly he discusses a state that is unending. For example, after having discussed a man to whom "God gave him to contemplate for one fleeting moment how he is in this power [in the soul]. . ."[8] Eckhart extolls the state in which "a man's spirit were *always* united to God in this power."[9] In short, the experience of the Birth, unlike *gezucket*, is permanent.

The Birth and Breakthrough experiences crown the process of releasing attachments I discussed in chapter four. Indeed, they may result only from releasing those attachments entirely. Speaking of the Birth, Eckhart writes:

If you grieve in your heart for *anything*, even on account of sin, your child is not yet born. If your heart is sore you are not yet a mother—but you are in labour and your time is near. . .But the child is fully born when a man's heart grieves for *nothing*.[10] (italics mine)

Even attachments to one's closest relatives and dearest friends must, apparently, be abolished before the Birth can be experienced. Continuing the above passage:

. . .cast out *all grief* so that perpetual joy reigns in your heart. Thus the child is born. And then if the child is born in me, the sight of my father and all my friends slain before my eyes would leave my heart untouched. For if my heart were moved thereby, the child would not have been born in me, though its Birth might be near.[11]

If this is not hyperbole, and I have no reason to believe that it is, then Eckhart envisions something virtually unheard of in modern psychology. As Fingarette put it, the completely analyzed patient is but a myth.[12] Eckhart tells us that he is speaking of a virtually complete abolition of attachments: not even the attachment to one's father or mother, all of one's friends or whatever "touches the heart."[13] One's heart remains untouched by *any* grief. Such an unusual psyche should lead, we might expect, to some rather surprising results.

BIRTH THEORY AND BIRTH EXPERIENCE

How does Eckhart use this expression, "The Birth (*geburt*) of the Son in the Soul?"[14] Occasionally he uses the term *geburt* as we commonly do, i.e. as physiological gestation: someone has a ". . . birth . . . into the world."[15] Hence *geburt's* fundamental meaning connotes the emergence of a new individual from the body of another. In a Birth one brings out something that had not previously existed, or gives rise to something through the agency of one's own person. This basic meaning of bringing out a second is never far from the surface.

While he does occasionally use the term in this sense, primarily he uses *geburt* in a more spiritual sense, the Birth of the Son *of God*. As you might expect, this expression bears both theoretical and experiential overtones. In what follows I will outline both and show how the theory serves to describe, to point one towards, and indeed to evoke the experience it marks.

In its theoretical sense, *geburt* describes a metaphysical or theological fact about the human soul: when he gives existence, God "gives Birth" to an aspect of himself, the Son, within the soul. It derives from the emanationist's Christological portrait we have seen before. Christ as model and as historical person is little emphasized by the Meister.[16] But for their role as background symbols, nor do the sacraments or the Eucharist play a large role in his thought. Some attention is given them in the Counsels[17] and in several sermons,[18] but these are not large roles. Instead, Christ is primarily an element in the Godhead-Trinity schema, and for man He is critical.

This schema is based on the famous prologue of St. John's Gospel, "In the beginning was the Word" (*In principio erat verbum*). Eckhart took this to mean that God's being gives life to itself as the Trinity. The first person of the Trinity is the *principium*, hence it is the "Father." The Father's principle role is to give rise to Himself as the Word (*Logos, verbum, wort*) in which he expresses Himself. Hence, according to Eckhart's reading of John, in the Father the Son is born. Into this Son the Father pours his entirety, his whole essence. The Son "was the Same as God and of the same nature."[19] In the *Opus Tripartitum* the essence of God is identified with Being. Since there is no time in God, this giving Birth to Himself occurs continuously.[20]

This process of God's giving Birth to Himself as the Son has enormous relevance for man. For as I have stressed, God's ground is one ground with man's ground. Hence the Birth occurs within man's Soul in just the same way as it occurs in eternity. Assertions to this effect were common in Eckhart:

> He [God] has borne him in my soul. Not only is she [the soul] with Him and He equally with her, but He is in her: the Father gives birth to His Son in the soul in the very same way as He gives birth to him in eternity, and no differently. He must do it whether He likes it or not. The Father begets His son unceasingly, and furthermore, I say, He begets me as His son and the same son. I say even more: not only does He beget me as His son, but He begets me as Himself and Himself as me, and me as His being and His nature. . . . All that God works is one: therefore He begets me as His son without any difference.[21]

This passage was condemned as article twenty-two of the Bull. The Bull also condemned the following:

> All that God the Father gave His only-begotten Son in human nature He has given me: I accept nothing, neither union nor holiness, He has given me everything as to him.

> Everything that Holy Scripture says of Christ is entirely true of every good and holy man.[22]

Fundamentally we have at this point an assertion of a theory of a relationship between God and man in his ground. To exist means that one draws existence from or shares in the Divine existence. "Even though one does not know it,"[23] it is a fact in which one may believe. One may or may not be aware of the Divine Light firsthand. "There the Divine Light is without interruption, working within, even though one does not know it."[24] The true Light shines in the darkness although one does not know it."[25]

For someone who is only beginning the path, this theory of a Birth within the Soul would be all that is known of the connection.[26] He or she would be unaware, except through belief and/or Eckhart's teaching, of being an "image" of God. For such a tyro the notion that "a creature without Birth would not exist," is a fine doctrine, but only that.

However, Eckhart does imply that for the person more advanced along the path, the Birth can be more than another theory. When Eckhart describes his teachings, he tells his listener that the birth can be "consummated" and confirmed in the advanced adept:

> What does it avail me that this birth is always happening, if it does not happen in me? That it should happen in me is what matters. We shall therefore speak of this birth, of how it may take place in us and be consummated in the virtuous soul, whenever God the Father speaks His eternal Word in the perfect soul. For what I say here is to be understood of the good and perfected man who has walked and is still walking in the ways of God.[27]

That the birth can be so consummated leads him to use the term with an experiential meaning. In a passage like the following, *geburt* suggests principally an experience. That experience is a Birth of emptiness within:

> The soul should *give* Birth *to nothing inside herself*, if she wishes to be the child of God in whom God's Son shall be born—in her nothing else should be born. (italics mine)[28]

Similarly, in the following passage the related image of pregnancy denotes a similar experience of "Nothing":

> It appeared to a man as in a dream—it was a waking dream—that he became pregnant with Nothing like a woman with child, and in that Nothing God was born, He was the fruit of nothing. God was born in the Nothing. Therefore he says: "He arose from the ground with open eyes, seeing nothing."[29]

Frequently both experiential and theoretical nuances are used side by side. In the following passage God is said to be "ever begetting the Son" within the soul; there He is "verdant and flowering." Such assert a constant theoretical relationship between God and creature. Yet this theory is then colored by assertions that "here" (i.e. where God bears the Son) one will find "heartfelt delight" and "inconceivably deep joy." Such adjectives suggest a possible experience. One may *undergo* this Birth and it would feel "inconceivably" lovely. *Grammatica*, to use Jean Leclercq's formulation of the monastic dichotomy, is here overlaid with *experientia*.[30]

> . . .[T]here is a power in the soul which touches neither time nor flesh, flowing from the spirit, remaining in the spirit, altogether spiritual. In this power, God is ever verdant and flowering in all the joy and all the glory that He is in Himself. There is such heartfelt delight, such inconceivably deep joy as none can fully tell of, for in this power the eternal Father is ever begetting His eternal Son without pause.[31]

The outlines of the relationship between the theory of the Birth and its experiential consummation should, by now, be obvious. Through the Fall man loses cognizance of his inherent relationship with God, that is, of the Birth within himself. As a result, he grows attached to "this and that" and becomes thereby preoccupied with things. By releasing those attachments, he can become aware of the light that has been glowing within all along, i.e. aware of the Birth of the Son within himself. The capacity to experience the Birth is, therefore, *innate*. If one simply releases obfuscating concerns, God's presence becomes obvious. In the following passage, for example, taken from QT 58 = W 2, Eckhart asserts that "the freer you keep yourself," i.e. the less attached you are, the nearer you come to the ground where the Birth is constantly occurring. So if you want to experientially verify the truth of this Birth doctrine, you do not have to make something happen within yourself. Simply remove your attachments, and thereby get to your own ground. Then just watch.

> . . .the freer you keep yourself, the more light, truth, and discernment you will find. Thus no man ever went astray for any other reason than that he first departed from this [i.e. the union with God], and then sought too much to cling to outward things. . . . [such people] go out so far that they never get back home or find their way in again. Thus they have not found the truth, for truth is within, in the ground and not without. So he who would see light to discern all truth, let him watch and become aware of this birth within, in the ground. Then all his powers will be illuminated, and the outer man as well.[32]

In short, by removing the attachments that preoccupy and cloud the attention, the theory of the Birth can be verified firsthand.

DICHOTOMY OF THE *GEBURT*

If the theory of the Birth can be personally consummated and confirmed, what is it like for it to occur? What is it like to have the Son of God born within the Soul?

The first fact that strikes me in the phraseology of the above "Birth" passages—and in most of Eckhart's Birth passages in general—is a suggestion of two distinct characteristics that continue simultaneously. A dichotomy between the inner and outer man, the spiritual and material dimensions, was a common Pauline and Augustinian division that Eckhart adapts to his focus on mystical experience. He uses this image to express the notion that there is something that occurs *inside* the soul and is more or less clouded by the preoccupation with the external world.

When Eckhart speaks of the Birth which one may undergo, he consistently formulates it in dichotomous language. The Birth of "Nothing" takes place "inside." The Son is born "within" the Soul, "inside" of the Soul.[33] It occurs within the power "in" the Soul, "in the inmost part of the Soul,"[34] "in the inmost recesses of the spirit."[35] This is "that which is one's own being and one's own life within oneself."[36] The soul must be "outdrawn" from the world and "indwelling."[37] One is born "there" where all is timeless, not "in the world." One is "pregnant with Nothing" within oneself.

Even the very Birth analogy itself as Eckhart uses it also connotes a dualistic process, i.e., mother and infant become irreversibly separate. In the spiritual Birth, however, rather than a baby's being delivered away from its mother's body, the Son is born "within" the self. The separation is not between one person and another, but between interior and exterior aspects of a single person. The dichotomy is between what occurs in the ground and the powers.

> [Grace] flows out of God's essence and flows into the essence of the soul and not into her powers.[38]

As Eckhart employs it, the Augustinian dichotomy between inward and outward ultimately comes down to the dichotomy between the experiences of a silent interior aspect and an active exterior:

The soul has two eyes, one inward and one outward. The soul's inner eye is that which sees *into* being, and derives its being without any mediation from God. The soul's outer eye is that which is turned towards all creatures, observing them as images and through the "powers."[39] (italics mine)

When he describes the reborn man, this experiential dichotomy dominates. In the following passage Eckhart uses Jesus as the paradigm of the union of human and divine. Since "everything that Holy Scripture says of Christ is entirely true of every good and holy man," it is appropriate to take Jesus here as the model for mystical experiences of good and holy men.[40] The image Eckhart uses is that Jesus's soul is like a grain of wheat that perishes on the hearth of His humanity. When Jesus said "My soul is grieved unto death" (Matt. 26:38)

He did not mean his noble soul according as this is intellectually contemplating the highest good, with which he is united in person and which he *is* according to union and person: that, even in his greatest suffering, he was continually regarding in his highest power, just as closely and entirely the same as he does now: no sorrow or pain or death could penetrate there. So it is in truth, for when his body died in agony on the cross, his noble spirit lived in this presence. . . . the soul's life was with the body but above the body, immediately in God without any obstructions.[41]

Now, why might Eckhart go to such lengths to communicate such a dualism between two aspects of man, silent ground and active powers? Perhaps what we have here is little more than a *façon de parler*. After all, Eckhart inherited the notion of a power or a "spark" within the Soul, and he added to it his doctrine that the Son is Born there.[42] Perhaps Eckhart is doing no more than writing in dichotomous terms based on such an old doctrine. On the other hand, perhaps he used this image because the experience to which he appealed or evoked in his listeners was in some way dualistic.[43]

While I would not know how to prove this issue with finality one way or the other, I believe that it was the latter. For confirmation I suggest that we look at some of Eckhart's less highly ramified descriptions of the Birth experience. We will find that there is an enormous number of passages that describe a two-sided life in considerable detail. In part because there is such remarkable detail, and considering that he stressed the personal verification of the Birth theory, it is most in keeping with the texts to think that Eckhart had in mind an experience which was itself dichotomous.[44]

One of the clearest low-ramified characterizations of this form of life is from the treatise *On Detachment*. It analogizes the two aspects of man with a door and its hinge pin. Like the outward boards of a door, the outward man moves, changes, and acts. The inward man, like the hinge pin, does not move. He—or it—remains uninvolved with activity and does not change at all. This Eckhart concludes is the way one should really conduct a life: one should act yet remain inwardly uninvolved. Here is the passage:

> And however much our Lady lamented and whatever other things she said, she was always in her inmost heart in immovable detachment. Let us take an analogy of this. A door opens and shuts on a hinge. Now if I compare the outer boards of the door with the outward man, I can compare the hinge with the inward man. When the door opens or closes the outer boards move to and fro, but the hinge remains immovable in one place and it is not changed at all as a result. So it is also here. . .[45]

To act and yet remain "in her inmost heart in immovable detachment" depicts precisely the two sides of the new life. Our Lady acts. Yet at a deep level within herself there remains a sense of something that does not. She lives a dichotomous existence. Like a door swinging around a hinge pin, she both moves and does not.

Such a dichotomy of experience is seen elsewhere in *On Detachment*. The detached spirit is said to stand "as immovable in all the assaults of joy or sorrow, honor, disgrace or shame, as a mountain of lead stands immovable against a small wind."[46] Again we have two sides of life. As a wind rippling across the surface makes leaves flutter and grass bend, there is activity and motion, joy, honor and sorrow. Underneath the flutter however, within at one's heart, one feels like a "mountain of lead." Again an interior stability is juxtaposed with an active side of life.

This inner unchangingness *vis-à-vis* an active outer life is seen in the Sermons as well. Though one is rocked by water, one is not "carried away by it."[47] In one passage Eckhart speaks of remaining "equally distant" from all earthly things—i.e. hope, joy, sorrow—and remaining aloof as it were from them.

[T]he soul that is to know God must be fortified and established, so that nothing can penetrate into her, neither hope nor fear nor joy nor grief nor suffering or anything that could disturb her. Heaven is at all points equidistant from earth. Likewise the soul should be equally distant from all earthly things, no nearer to the one than to the other. Where the noble soul is, she must maintain an equal distance from all earthly things, from hope, from joy and from sorrow: whatever it is she must rise superior to it.[48]

To rise superior to what is earthly is to enter into the peace of heaven, which is unmixed with any creatureliness. Eckhart continues: "Heaven is also pure and clear, free from all impurity but for the moon."[49] Despite living, breathing, and working, in that aspect which "rises superior" to externality, one feels as pure, as clear, and as stable as a clear nighttime sky.

The two sides of life are graphically illustrated elsewhere. In the sermon *Fluminus Impetus Lateificat Civitatem Dei* (DW 81 = W 64), the soul is said to be "collected into the single power which knows God." When this occurs, God's grace is "impressed without cooperation in the soul with the Holy Ghost, and forms the soul like God."[50] For this to occur the soul "must exalt herself and shut herself *away* from all that is creaturely." When it does so, the world comes to taste "bitter" and "nauseous."

To the soul that has received the infusion of divine grace and tasted divine perfection, all that is not God has a bitter, nauseous savour.[51]

Within, one enjoys the divine essence. It is pure, clear, and silent: "a desert place."[52] Outside, however, the world is unconnected with it and so retains a bitterness or a nauseous quality.

In part because I find such surprisingly down–to–earth descriptive passages, I believe that Eckhart was describing a dichotomous form of existence, and not simply speaking in terms of a dichotomous theory.

Such a dualistic state is described by others.[53] One such description was made famous by Sigmund Freud, and was penned in a letter to him by the French critic and erstwhile mystic, Romain Rolland.[54] Rolland describes a "spontaneous religious feeling or more exactly a religious sensation" which he distinguishes from all doctrines and religions. He calls it a "peculiar oceanic feeling," a term to which we shall refer again, and a "sensation of the eternal," which is not far from Eckhart's own notions of the eternity of the Son within and of heaven. He says that he was himself aware of such a religious sensation, and says:

> This constant state (like a sheet of water that I can feel under the bark) does no harm to my critical faculties and my freedom to exercise them, even against the immediacy of this interior experience. Thus I lead at the same time, without discomfort or pain, a "religious" life (in the sense of this prolonged sensation) and a life of critical reason (which is without illusion)[55]

I could give other illustrations, but this shows that to have an unchanging sense within while being outwardly active is at least not utterly idiosyncratic to Eckhart.

THE BIRTH WITHIN AND WILL-LESSNESS

Some of my readers are probably asking, "Aren't you making too much of this two-tiered structure of the mind? Isn't Eckhart really just describing a life of detachment, in which one is removed from things in something like a psychological sense? Isn't he really describing not something akin to Rolland's "sensation of the religious" but rather just a new—detached—way of acting? As he says in *On Detachment*, he pursues "how to act rightly."

Many Eckhart scholars have asserted this to be so. That is, many have suggested that the mystical transformation is primarily a transformation of the *will*. "It is a union of wills, not of essences," states Clark boldly.[56] Schurmann, and Caputo both emphasize working "without a why."[57] McGinn here agrees.[58] Kieckhefer and Tobin regard the final goal as "a state of moral perfection."[59]

Certainly there is much in Eckhart to suggest this. For example, the above passage concerning a boat anchored amidst a rocking sea is preceded by "Our Lord Jesus Christ was often 'moved,' and so were his saints, but they were not flung from the path *of virtue*".[60] In the early treatise, "The Councils on Discernment," Eckhart spoke of a "true and perfect will."

> A true and perfect will means to tread absolutely in the will of God and to be without self-will. The more one has of this, the more and more truly one is placed in God. Indeed, it is more profitable to say one Ave Maria if one has forsaken oneself than to read a thousand Psalters without this.[61]

Clearly the Birth does involve actions and a change in the will.[62] I argued in chapter four that a change in the will is a key element in the transformation.

However, the change in the will is neither the only novel element nor primary. Eckhart's principal emphasis is not on the modification of will and action. Rather his consistent emphasis is on the new discovery of the "ground" within, which is experienced in the Birth. This ground is altogether transcendental to will as well as intellect, Eckhart states repeatedly. It has nothing to do with either.

> Grace enters neither into intellect nor into will. For grace to enter into intellect, intellect and will must transcend themselves [*uber sich selben komen*]. . . . Accordingly, a master said there is something very secret above these [intellect and will], which is the head of the soul.[63] It is here that true union takes place between God and the soul. Grace never did any virtuous work: It has never done any work at all, though it flows forth in the doing of good works.[64]

Primary here is where grace enters. The discovery of this transformed "secret head of the soul" comes first; the "flowing forth" of its grace into activity follows. Similarly, for blessedness:

> Some masters look for blessedness in the intellect. I say blessedness lies neither in intellect nor in will: blessedness lies above them, where blessedness lies *as* blessedness not as intellect, and God is there as God and the soul as God's image. Blessedness is there, where the soul takes God as God. There soul is soul and grace is grace, blessedness is blessedness and God is God.[65]

The true revolution takes place when one becomes aware of the ground—and of that ground's connection with God. This spark has absolutely no truck with action, will, or any *thing*.

While the change in will (as well as intellect) is clearly involved, Eckhart's emphasis is consistently on the personal encounter with the new ground. Only having "received" the Son, does one become "perfect" in deeds—i.e., only then does one's will effortlessly coalesce with God's.

> You should traverse and transcend all the virtues, drawing virtue solely from its source in that ground where it is one with the divine nature.[66]

One "transcends" the virtues, drawing them from something beyond them and the powers which affect them.

Let me be clear. Detachment is unquestionably involved here. "Our Lady" was detached from her outward aspect. But to say only that she is detached is insufficient to describe her experience completely, for *de*tachment is a negative characteristic. It marks a removal *from* things, be they possessions, power, or whatever. To describe her new life fully, a more *via positiva* description is required.

Can anything more positive be said of that aspect of the reborn man that is unattached? What is it like—on the inside? Eckhart says there is a "Birth of Nothing" inside. This suggests an experience of some unchanging aspect within. Sometimes he suggests that this new Birth is like being amidst an ocean, which might imply a new spatial and/or temporal sense.[67] However, it should be noted that this new aspect of life is the really primary aspect. It is not a change in action or will, but is a discovery of a novel aspect of the subject. If and only if one discovers the "true union" between God and the soul does the Birth occur. Only then does one's relationship with one's action really and permanently change.

The steps in the development may be drawn out as follows: One detaches oneself from all worldly attachments. Having done so, something (as it were) comes: the establishment of a "nothing" inside. When this "nothing" is encountered in a brief but overwhelming way, one may become temporarily enraptured: *gezucket*. But when it is permanently established, the changeover will become more complete. One experiences then the Birth of the Son of God in the Soul. Then and only then will one's actions be in accord with God's will effortlessly. Notice that detachment is only complete when it brings about a complete nothing inside:

> When the detached heart has the highest aim, it must be towards the Nothing, because in this there is the greatest receptivity. Take a parable from nature: if I want to write on a wax tablet, then no matter how noble the thing is that is written on the tablet, I am none the less vexed because I cannot write on it. If I really want to write I must delete everything that is written on the tablet, and the tablet is never so suitable for writing as when absolutely nothing is written on it.

The emphasis in this passage is on the achievement of emptiness within. One has "deleted" everything inside; one comes to a "Nothing" inside; the tablet is "blank." When one is truly empty within (experiencing "the Nothing"), then what goes on outside is of little significance. Only once this interior "nothing" is established does one truly begin "acting rightly." Eckhart continues,

> In the same way, when God wishes to write on my heart in the most sublime manner, everything must come out of my heart that can be called "this" or "that;" thus it is with the detached heart. *Then* God can work in the sublimest manner and according to His highest will.[68] (italics mine)

Eckhart's principal focus remains on the emptiness within. This is experienced as separate from action. When and only when this is "owned," God brings about the true change in actions.

Such a dichotomy in experience is precisely what we might expect from the last chapter. There I noted that sometimes one can, for some time, retain an inner silence so profound that it excludes all other input. But such an utter quietude, says Eckhart, should be brought into active life. Were one to do so, he or she would live with precisely this structure. One would maintain the very inwardness which one may discover in *gezucket* alongside of activity. Two distinct characteristics—working and not working—would be enjoyed side by side.

How can we understand such a phenomenon? In chapter five I suggested that *gezucket* marks a new State of Consciousness. The key feature of such a State of Consciousness I called "cognitive structure," the way in which the mind handles content. I think that in the Birth we have another State of Consciousness, and it, too, is characterized by a new cognitive structure. It is one in which a silent, unchanging aspect of the mind is maintained alongside of a changing manifold of awareness. This is suggested by the fact that the inner Birth is permanent. It is even more permanent and abiding than a lasting intention, for it abides through all thoughts and intentions.[69] This implies that no matter what the content may be—whether one is thinking about the unchanging aspect or not, whether one is happy or sad, or whatever—an unchanging silence within coexists with that content. Hence this aspect of the new cognitive structure necessarily has nothing to do with the particulars of mental content.[70] What remains consistent is: (1) The persistence of a two-sided cognitive structure; this is a structural consistency; (2) A silent aspect within the self; this constancy is in a particular side of the cognitive structure.

My argument from the last chapter, that the term *State of Consciousness* may be plausibly applied to Eckhart, who did not use the term, may be applied here as well.

We are all familiar with the changing manifold of awareness. What is unfamiliar is this new silent aspect within the self, one's "own being and life within oneself," which one comes to know and experience.[71] Hence to it I must now turn. What is it like to experience this?

THE NATURE OF ONE'S OWN LIFE
WITHIN ONESELF

What is it like to experience one's own life within oneself? As I have stated, this life within is one with the Son of God; indeed, one ground with God. Eckhart often expresses this as the *imago Dei*, the image of God. The implications of this doctrine should alert us to the character of the experience at hand here.

In the *imago Dei* doctrine Christ is the "image" of the Father or the Godhead. Through Him man's soul itself is, in its ground, the *imago dei* as well. Many mystical theologies of the patristic and early medieval periods centered on this doctrine that man is made in God's image and likeness, that he loses it in the Fall, and that he needs to be restored to it through salvation.

For Eckhart there are two requirements for images. First there must be a likeness between the archetype and its image. Two eggs are similar, yet they are not images of each other.[72] What is also necessary is that the image must "take its being immediately and solely from that of which it is an image."[73] For example, a face in a mirror is the "image" of the real face. It persists if and only if the real face is present: the existence of the image is dependent on the existence of the archetype.

Christ, who is the image of the Father (and hence of the Godhead), receives His entire existence from the Father. This reception is due to the nature of images in general. In his Latin commentary on John, Eckhart writes:

> An image insofar as it is an image receives nothing of its own from the subject in which it exists, but receives its whole existence from the object it images. Second, it receives its existence only from the object, and third, it receives the whole existence of the object according to everything by which it is an exemplar. For if the image were to receive anything from another source or did not receive something that was in its exemplar, it would not be an image of that thing but of something else. . . . the image has the whole existence of the exemplar in itself. "I am in the Father, and the Father is in me" (Jn. 14:11).[74]

The relationship between the Father and the Son is also described as the Father's speaking the eternal word. In medieval theology the second Person was said to be the "thought" in which the Father knows himself. He is that which is "conceived" by the Father in the sense of a silent inner word (*verbum cordis*) as opposed to a vocal word (*verbum vocis*), which is its outer sign. Hence the Father knows himself through the Son as a Silent Inner Word."[75]

Here is where this doctrine alerts us to the key feature of the novel aspect of the Birth. Christ as the *imago dei* is the image of the Father and hence of the Godhead itself. But the Godhead, for Eckhart as well as other writers in the Dionysian tradition, was a solitary one, utterly featureless, distinctionless, and still. It is the One, pure existing, the merest "I am" as it were. Its only characteristic is that it boils up within itself, creating the dynamo of

Father, Son, and Holy Spirit, and through their agency of the world, as we saw in chapter four. To be in union with the Godhead is, therefore, to be a perfect image of just this solitary desert-like distinctionless One. That is, the image of God is itself the Word of pure Being. If one discovers the presence of this image within oneself, he or she will discover the presence of the image of the solitary One, a pure Being, within oneself.

This is not to assert that man would become God, or identical with God. Man becomes at best a Son by adoption, as Eckhart stressed in his own defense (and as Eckhart's modern defenders repeat). But the distinction between Son by nature and by adoption does not change the experiential character of what it is like to be such a Son. To discover this is to discover that one is within oneself, like the Son by nature, an image of the distinctionless One.

In Eckhart's less highly ramified writings something quite near to this is portrayed. The discovery of one's own being and life within oneself is a discovery of a silent One within. This novel element of the Birth is at its most vivid in the following benchmark passage. It is taken from the sermon "Intravit Jesus" (DW 86 = W 9), which discusses Mary and Martha. Eckhart here speaks of Martha, who is, according to him, in a higher union than the contemplative Mary. This union he expresses as:

> When I and you are once embraced by the eternal light, that is one. Two-in-one is a fiery spirit, standing over all things, yet under God, on the circle of eternity. This is two, for it sees God but not immediately. Its knowing and being, or its knowing and the object of knowledge, will never be one. God is not seen except where He is seen spiritually, free of all images. Then one becomes two, two is one: light and spirit, these two are one in the embrace of the eternal light.[76]

Eckhart here states that he advocates something more intimate than a seeing of God. Any (intentional) seeing could result in a knowing that could be distinguished from the knower. He pursues a deeper union: an "embrace" of the eternal light in the circle of eternity in which knower and known and process of knowing are one.

There are three ways into this circle of eternity, he continues. The first is through creatures. The second, which we studied in the last chapter, is the way of *gezucket*. While this was good, it is not enough, for one who is enraptured is "not in unity beholding God in His own Being."

Such a unity comes through the third way, "seeing God without means in His own Being." This is the way in which one becomes conjoined with Christ, i.e., enjoys the Birth of the Son within the soul. To be thus, says Eckhart, is to truly be at home in God.

> The third way is called a way, but is really being at home, that is: seeing God without means in His own being. Now Christ says, "I am the way, the truth and the life" (John 14:16): one Christ as Person, one Christ the Father, one Christ the Spirit, three-in-one: three as way, truth and life, one as the beloved Christ, in which he is all. Outside of this way all creatures circle, and are means. But let into God on this way by the light of His Word and embraced by them both in the Holy Spirit—that passes all words. Now listen to a marvel! How marvelous, to be without and within, to embrace and be embraced, to see and be the seen, to hold and be held—that is the goal, where the spirit is ever at rest, united in joyous eternity![77]

It is in these last few sentences, where Eckhart explicates what it is like for Christ to be the member of the Trinity, that Eckhart communicates the nature of this Birth. Since every man has all that Christ has, to describe Christ is to simultaneously declare what it would be like for Martha, or for any soul who experiences this rebirth. We may draw out its principle features as follows:

A. The Self Itself

The first thing that strikes me about this passage is that its peculiarities concern the *subject*. Something odd happens to the person in whom this takes place. We are used to events in which we see things—in which our knowing and our objects of knowledge remain forever separate, in which we remain separate from what we see, touch, or think. Eckhart has characterized this kind of phenomenon as that in which "its knowing and the object of knowledge will never be one." In this "marvel," however, the subject itself is not separate from its object, but rather has expanded as it were to embrace what it had formerly just looked at. The subject is not separate from its object, but encompasses it. It is best viewed not as a new object but as a new characteristic of the subject itself.

I said in the last chapter that in *gezucket*, when all other contents for the mind are dropped, one becomes nothing other than one's own self without any additions. That is, one remains awake and oneself but is not conscious of anything.[78] Thus, if *gezucket* is similar to or the forerunner of the Birth experience, it is plausible that we should look to the self itself for the locus of the changes that occur during the Birth.

And, indeed, it is towards the nature of the perceiving agent him/herself that Eckhart consistently directs his listener. In the Birth one has one "awareness" with God's awareness (*ein bekennen mit gotes bekennenne*).[79] The new modification is to the "eye with which I see;"[80] it occurs to that in the soul that "knows" and "sees,"[81] or to the agent that "hears,"[82] etc. Eckhart is speaking not of the physical eye or ear, of course;[83] rather he is pointing to that agent of the Soul, the "spark," which is *aware* of knowledge, sounds, and sights. *I* know such and such, or hear such and such. The tranformation is not in some content or sensation but in the "I" itself.

B. An Expanse

What happens to the self? The second unusual phenomenon suggested by this passage is that one is said to be "without and within." That is, one senses oneself as not limited to one's ordinary physical (bodily) boundaries. To be thus is to perceive oneself as being or participating in something like an expanse. Elsewhere Eckhart describes this expansion as a "breadth without breadth, expanseless expanse."[84] It may be characterized as a quasi-physical sense of expansion.

He refers to this frequently. He uses images of the sea and the ocean to communicate it.

> . . . God places the soul in the highest and purest place that she can attain to, into space, into the sea, into a bottomless ocean, and there God works mercy.[85]

It is like a "drop of water in a butt of wine."[86] In a Latin sermon Eckhart states:

> ... the inward man is not at all in time or place but is purely and simply in eternity. It is there that God arises, there He is heard, there He is; there God, and God alone speaks. "Blessed are they that hear the word of God."[87] There the inward man attains his full amplitude because he is great without magnitude.[88]

And in a German sermon:

> If you were to cast a drop into the ocean, the drop would become the ocean and not the ocean the drop. Thus it is with the soul: when she imbibes God she is turned into God.[89]

This oceanic image is reminiscent of the driving metaphor of the contemporaneous *The Cloud of Unknowing*. Eckhart, too, uses the cloud metaphor, calling the expanse at one point, a "divine mist."[90]

What does such an image communicate about an experience? Think of yourself as a drop being cast into an ocean. While still a discrete drop, you would regard yourself as limited—perhaps a centimeter in diameter. This is akin to the limited soul before she gains the Birth. Then you splash into the ocean. Instantly your borders dissolve. When you now attend to yourself, what are you? You are now the endless ocean.

This is not something which you look at which is in any way separate from you. That is, this is no mystical marriage between a self and something other and separate from it. Eckhart emphasizes that there is no separation between the self and what is encountered frequently. The drop in the above passage does not look at the ocean, float on the ocean, or what have you. It "becomes" it. There is not even a hair's breadth of difference: "where I am, there God is; and then I am in God, and where God is, there I am."[91] The one is changed into the other like wood is into fire.[92] This expanse, this endless breadth, is none other than the subject him/herself. To be within and without is to be expanded beyond all traces of boundaries. It is, in a word, to be endless.

Such a quasi-physical expanse, "being within or without" or being an "expanseless expanse" is not idiosyncratic to Eckhart. Rolland calls what he encountered a "peculiar oceanic feeling."

This expression is quite *à propos* to what we have seen in Eckhart. It is "peculiar" because it is not exactly a physical expanse, nor exactly a sensation, but is similar to each. It is "oceanic" because it carries a sense of being expanded like an ocean. "Feeling" is strictly a misnomer, since it is unlike any other sensation or emotion inasmuch as it is permanent and unchanging. But it is like a feeling in that it is no thought or perception of the external.[93]

I also think here of several passages from James's *Varieties* that describe a similar quasi-material sense of being expanded. He speaks of a mystical feeling of enlargement and union, which he says are direct perceptions of fact parallel with ordinary sensations.[94] The conscious person feels himself continuous with a wider self.[95] In one of his most famous passages he wrote that the individual:

> becomes conscious that [his real being] is coterminous and continuous with a *more* of the same quality, which is operative in the universe outside of him, and which he can keep in working touch with, and in a fashion get on board of and save himself. . .[96]

Hence both James and Rolland depict an experience in which the everyday sense of being physically limited or bound by the physical body are transcended, and an expanse comes to be felt.

Imagine what this is like. One maintains the constant sense of being amidst an oceanic expanse, merged with the vastness of God. It does not require thinking in any special way to maintain it. It is even more constant than a steady intention. Hence it must be more like a sensation than a thought, a steady "sensation of the eternal," as Rolland put it. Simultaneously one conducts one's affairs, lives, works, and thinks. It must be like *living and working from within an expanse*.

C. Reflexivity

While this third feature is implicit in the above two, I want to draw it out. In my benchmark passage, not only is one said to be "without and within" but that which "sees" is also "the seen." In other words, the same "seer" which sees is also its own object, as it were, the "seen." One is reflexively aware of one's own self!

This is no mere peculiar turn of phrase, but appears several times: "The eye with which I see God is the eye with which God sees me."[97] Similarly, for knowing:

> You must know that this is in reality one and the same thing—to know God and to be known by God, to see God and to be seen by God.[98]

> Then *God is known by God* in the soul; with this Wisdom *she knows herself* and all things, and this same Wisdom knows her with itself.[99] (*italics mine*)

The reflexivity of such statements indicates to me a reflexivity of awareness.[100] The knowing *of God by God* takes place within the Soul. Hence it occurs within the awareness of the agent who experiences the Birth. Drawing this passage out, it means that within the Soul God is known by the same agent of knowing which is being known by God. There are no two separate agents of knowing that turn and "face" one another, for to know God and to be known by God, or to see and to be seen by God are "one and the same thing." Knower and known are one in one act of cognition. "God is known by God in the soul" means that the subject and the object are one and the same unit, as it were, here. We have seen that any dualism between subject and object has been expressly ruled out, for they would be two, and here, at the ground of the soul, the self-conscious awareness is a pure One.

Such a reflexivity of awareness seems nearly inconceivable, does it not? But viewed in terms of the drop in the ocean image, it may perhaps be a little more intelligible. Again imagine yourself to be that drop. When you attend to the ocean into which you have merged, you are aware of its expansiveness, let us say. But there are no borders between you and that ocean, I noted. You *are* it. Hence to be aware of the oceanic breadth is to be aware of that expanse with which you have merged. It is to be reflexively aware of yourself.

Perhaps a diagram will help. When I (or the drop) ordinarily try to perceive myself, the act is something like this:

In ordinary introspection, when we try to perceive ourself, consciousness can only turn back on itself. It can never catch itself.

Turning back on itself, an introspecting consciousness might seem like this as it tries to perceive itself. Consciousness is no narrow straight line, of course, but is more amorphous, multifaceted, and abstract. But the diagram does suggest that if I try to attend to myself it is like trying to turn in and catch myself "in the act." By the time I turn my attention back on myself, I am already at the new position, now looking *for* myself. This is, of course, precisely the well-known philosophical problem that Hume described. When we look within, Hume asserted, we only see individual perceptions, but never the self itself.[101] If I can perceive myself at all, I can only perceive myself as an object, and thus as separate.

The case of the drop in an ocean that is greater than its (former) boundaries is different, however. It might be diagrammed like this:

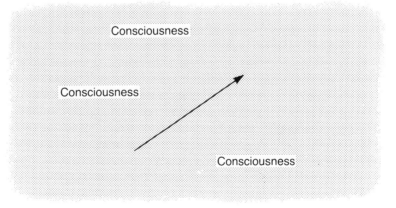

In a transformed state, as described by Eckhart, in which the "drop" which is us has "merged" with a larger "ocean". Reflexive self awareness is possible in a new way.

When the awareness that is within an expanse looks "out," what will it perceive? The expanse. Furthermore, it will recognize that there are no perceptible borders separating itself from the expanded quasi-material "stuff." There are no fissures between its awareness and this expanded "stuff." The problem of consciousness's curving back on itself is avoided by the fact that it has "something" to look "towards," and that "something" is continuous with itself. What is "without" is also "within," the "seer" is also the "seen."

The only technical term I can give to this aspect of the dichotomous cognitive structure in this State of Conciousness is "expanded reflexive awareness." This side of the mind knows itself as "quasi-spatially" nonlimited, an "expanseless expanse, breadth without breadth."[102]

Now, how is such reflexive consciousness possible? It is so unusual! Certainly in all "ordinary" experience all consciousness is, as phenomenology rightly says, "consciousness of something," i.e., something other than consciousness itself.[103] Here we have a consciousness aware of itself only. By way of explanation let us remind ourselves that Eckhart was himself an example of, and was speaking to, people who devoted their lives to not a philosophical but a religious quest: a quest for self-purification. They were able, hopefully, to release all their attachments, and be without any distinctions whatsoever. Thus no "this or that" would lead them away from being simply their own "true" nature. No thing would "peep in" or "peep out" of their souls. Thus no thing would place "limits" on their consciousness.

> As long as the soul perceives any distinction, that is not right. As long as anything peeps out or peeps in, there is no oneness. . . . As long as any distinction of any created things can look into the soul, she is disconsolate. . . . All that is created or creaturely is alien. It is a single one in itself, and takes in nothing from outside.[104]

Because it takes in nothing from outside, such a perfected soul will be led to this unlimited "one," Eckhart tells us, at the depths. Of the mechanics involved, the etiology of this peculiar reflexivity, this is really all we can say. It happens when all distinctions are dropped. When they are, an innate capacity to encounter this is turned on, as it were, and one sees the self itself which has perhaps been there all along. Of this process we can say *that* but not *how* it happens.

Unless you are like Rolland, this is probably no part of your experience. But there is a certain plausibility to this phenomena. Having sloughed off all that leads us outwards, what would we be? Nothing! What would the experience of nothing be? No limits, no borders, no boundaries—though in a body, one would be unlimited. It is to such a nonbounded situation that one retires in *gezucket*. So too, were one to act without even the slightest attachment, one would be acting but remain equally nonbounded within. Whatever the circumstances, one would be at rest and peace within oneself. Such must be the Birth of the infinite, immortal Son of God within the Soul: the Birth of a boundless emptiness within.

THE BIRTH AS A STATE OF CONSCIOUSNESS

There remain two major questions that the astute reader is probably wanting to ask. One is the question of reductionism: have I reduced Eckhart's theology to psychology, especially the psychology of States of Consciousness? I shall argue at the end of this chapter and in the next that I have not *reduced* Eckhart at all, but *explained* him appropriately. Before doing so, however, I want to be somewhat clearer about the characteristics of an altered State of Consciousness and further substantiate my belief that Eckhart is here describing one.

One of the most complete summaries of recent findings on States of Conciousness is Arnold Ludwig's "States of Consciousness."[105] In his section "General Characteristics of ASCs," he enumerates the "common denominators or features" that are typically found in altered States of Consciousness (ASC). Ludwig was attempting to characterize states that were both drug and hypnogogically induced as well as those brought on by more traditional mystical procedures, and he illustrates his points with examples drawn from all of these. But since the characteristics more typical of hypnosis and LSD-induced ASCs are largely irrelevant to my present concerns, I have simplified his list to include only those aspects of a State of Conciousness which, according to him, a traditional mystic might encounter. Here then, largely in Ludwig's own language, are the characteristics of a new State of Consciousness.[106] Following each characteristic I have noted the Eckhartian parallels.

1.   Change in Subjective Boundaries[107]

A wide array of distortions in body image may occur. There is also a common propensity for individuals to experience a sense of depersonalization, a schism between body and mind, or a dissolution of boundaries between self and "others," i.e. an individual, people in general, the world, or the universe. These may be interpreted by the mystic as transcendental or mystical experiences of "oneness," "expansion of consciousness," "oceanic feelings," or "oblivion."

We have already seen that the Birth carries a sense that is analogous to a spatial expansion. Paradoxically this sense seems both infinitesimal and huge, a "breadth without breadth, expanseless expanse."[108] One is "translated into the expanse and breadth."[109] There is an intuited sense of being "wider than the whole world," yet the greatness feels somehow located in the smallness inside oneself.

> . . . God places the soul in the highest and purest place that she can attain to, into space, into the sea, into a bottomless ocean, and there God works mercy.[110]

Analogous to Romain Rolland's "oceanic feeling," one is "filled to capacity."[111] The soul feels itself "capacious [*muge*].[112] Of the prophets who walked in the light and knew and discovered the secret truth, Eckhart says everything they had seen in God was alike, so vast and so sublime that they could find no image or form in which to express it.[113] Associated with such changes in subjective boundaries are the well-known Eckhartian remarks concerning the sense of being "equally near" to everything, being everywhere, etc.[114]

> Where I sat yesterday I said something that sounds quite incredible: I said Jerusalem is as near my soul as the ground I stand on now. Yes, in holy truth! whatever is a thousand miles further off than Jerusalem is as close to my soul as my own body is. I am as sure of this as that I am a man, and learned priests can easily understand this![115]

2.   Disturbed Time Sense

The sense of time and chronology may become altered. Subjective feelings of timelessness, time coming to a standstill, acceleration or slowing of time and so on may be encountered. Time may also seem infinite or infinitesimal.

In *gezucket*, when one is aware of nothing but the unchanging, all sense of change collapses. Inevitably all sense of time will go with it. In the dichotomous cognitive structure of the Birth, one will participate in change but also know oneself at some level to be separate from it. The sense of being outside of time, eternal, or "in eternity, no more no less," is frequently noted by Eckhart:[116]

> All time must be gone when the Birth begins, for there is nothing that hinders this Birth so much as time and creatures. . . . For God to be born in the soul, all time must have dropped away from her, or she must have dropped away from time with will or desire.[117]

> As long as a man has time and place . . . he is in the wrong way, and God is remote and strange to him.[118]

> There time is one present now.[119]

The sentiment of these passages parallels Rolland's "direct feeling of the eternal."

Sometimes Eckhart speaks of time not as empty but as full.

> When is the fullness of time? When time is no more. If anyone has, in time, set his heart on eternity so that in him all temporal things are dead, that is the "fullness of time."[120]

Parallel to the paradoxicality of the "expanseless expanse," time seems like an eternal now, in which all time collapses into a single "now." Six thousand years seem like six days; things seem eternally "new."[121]

It may be objected that here Eckhart is speaking only of the theoretical character of the Divine. This objection would be wrong since, the reader will recall, one shares in that character within the soul. Hence by retiring to that ground, and by gaining habitual access to it in the Birth, one will find that very timelessness within the soul. The Birth experience, therefore, carries a timeless aspect.

3.   Alterations in Thinking

Subjective alterations in concentration, memory, and judgment may be found. Archaic, more "primitive" and less rational, modes of thought may come to predominate.[122] The distinctions between cause and effect may become blurred and an ambivalence may be pronounced whereby incongruities or opposites may coexist without any logical or psychological conflict.

Eckhart's notions of acting "without a why" denote just such primitive modes of thought and behavior. One simply acts, relying less on rational justifications. However, if Ludwig has in mind the distortions in thinking we associate with drug-related experiences, they should not be applied to Eckhart. In the more permanent transformation he advocated, thinking must be relatively clear and productive, not the reverse. One must have access to normal justification procedures. I would say, then, that this characteristic is less readily applied to Eckhart than the others. The same thing is true of the following characteristic:

4. Perceptual Distortions

Perceptual aberrations may occur, including hallucinations, increased visual imagery, subjectively felt hyperacuteness of perception, and illusions. The content of these perceptual aberrations may be determined by cultural, group, individual, or neurophysiological factors. Hallucinations of light, color, geometrical patterns, etc. are common.[123]

Here again Ludwig's characteristic is more typical of transient and/or ecstatic experiences, not the permanent transformation Eckhart advocates. Perceptual aberrations are precisely what Eckhart depreciated as counterproductive and leading toward attachment.

5. Loss Of Control

As a person enters a new State of Consciousness, he may experience a fear of losing his grip on reality and losing his self-control.[124] He may actively resist the onset of the state, or he may actively relinquish his volition and give in to the experience. The experience of this loss of conscious control is a complicated phenomenon. It may arouse feelings of impotence or, paradoxically, may represent the gaining of greater control and power through the loss of control. One may relinquish conscious control in the hope of experiencing divine truths, clairvoyance, "cosmic consciousness," etc.

Eckhart speaks frequently of the sense of will-lessness and passivity. This represents a sense of losing conscious control, which emerges not out of an impotence but rather out of a sense of participating in a greater whole.

> A rational God-conformed will submits to the insight and bids the will stand back from it, and the will answers, "I will, gladly."[125]

> If our will is God's will, that is good, but if God's will is our will, that is far better. . . . when God's will is your will, then if you are sick: "In God's name!" if your friend dies: "In God's name!"[126]

So too we should read the *lâzen* passage, "if you have given up self, then you have really given up," as a movement towards such a loss control.[127]

6.   Change in Emotional Expression

With the loss of conscious control, there is often a marked change in emotional expression. Sudden and unexpected displays of more primitive and intense emotion than shown during normal, waking consciousness may appear.[128] Emotional extremes, from ecstasy and orgiastic equivalents to profound fear and depression may occur.[129] Another pattern of emotional expression may occur: the individual may become detached, uninvolved, or relate intense feelings without any emotional display.

While Eckhart does not advocate pursuit of experiences marked by emotional extremes, he does emphasize the emotional detachment and uninvolvement which Ludwig notes. When Eckhart says, "You should be firm and steadfast, that is, you should be the same in weal and woe, in fortune and misfortune," he is depicting just such an emotional detachment.[130] The detaching process discussed in chapter four may be viewed as leading towards such a characteristic of this State of Consciousness.

7.   Feelings of Rejuvenation

On emerging from some alterations of consciousness, many persons claim to experience a new sense of hope, rejuvenation, renaissance, or rebirth.[131]

Ludwig is characterizing ASCs which are generally transient, again unlike Eckhart's Birth. Hence, we would not expect one to emerge from it with any particular feelings, since there is no emerging. However the Birth, as the very name suggests, is shot through with a sense of a transformation and rejuvenation, a new ease to and sweetness in life.

> Jesus reveals himself, too, in infinite sweetness and richness, well-
> ing up and overflowing and pouring in from the power of the
> Holy Ghost, with superabundant richness and sweetness into all
> receptive hearts. When Jesus reveals himself with this richness and
> this sweetness, and is united with the soul, the soul flows with this
> richness and this sweetness into herself and beyond all things. . .[132]

Elsewhere it is called "a feeling of inner riches."[133] The "merging" into "something" larger than oneself is associated with a
merging into "sweetness."

> One of the saints has said: "I sometimes experience such sweetness
> in me that I forget myself and all creatures and wish to dissolve
> right into thee."[134]

It must be marvelous!

By the way, the factors enumerated here and especially this
one, may be the key reason why Eckhart should view this union
at the ground as primary and the changeover in will as its result.
The interior quietness must be so satisfying, grand, and enormous
that in comparison everything else must seem trivial and puny.[135]

> God's presence in the soul by grace brings in more light than any
> intellect can give: and all the light that intellect can give is but a
> drop in the ocean beside this light, indeed a thousandfold less.
> Thus it is with the soul that is in God's grace: to hear all things,
> and whatever the intellect can grasp, appear small and mean. . . . it
> would be strange indeed if the soul that had once tasted and tried
> God could stomach anything else. One saint says that the soul that
> has tasted God finds all things that are not God repugnant and
> stinking.[136]

A will-lessness would come inexorably if all worldly things
seemed worthless. Someone would have no motivation towards
worldly gain if such a *summum bonum* were maintained constantly. Hence one would have no self to strive for, for it would
seem small and mean.

8.   Sense of the Ineffable

Because of the uniqueness of the subjective experience, persons
frequently claim a certain inability to communicate the nature or

essence of the experience to someone who has not undergone a similar experience. A degree of amnesia about the state may also contribute to the sense of the ineffable.[137]

Eckhart did not use the term "ineffable." But he frequently insists that the ground is beyond all thought, naming, and image. In the tradition of negative theology he asserts, "Whatever we say God is, He is not; what we do not say of Him, He is more truly than what we say He is."[138] If you think of anything, then you are not there, he says.[139] The model-lessness within is beyond speech.[140] All such expressions mark an inability to communicate the nature of the new level within and are therefore ways of asserting that the new aspect of the dichotomous cognitive structure is ineffable.

9.   Change in Meaning or Significance

Ludwig remarks that persons in these states are predisposed to attach an increased meaning or significance to their subjective experiences, ideas, or perceptions. (This may be correlated with James's suggestion that the mystical experience is "absolutely authoritative" for the individual who has it.)[141] Ludwig suggests that the person seems to be undergoing an attenuated "eureka" experience during which feelings of profound insight, illumination, and truth frequently occur.[142]

That Eckhart should speak so frequently and with such eloquence about the Birth within the Soul is proof enough that he finds it significant. The entirety of his sermons and tractates may be viewed as an explanation of the significance he attaches to it. That it is "God" or the "Son of God" who is encountered there demonstrates that to Him this experience is of utmost significance.

In conclusion, most of the relevant features of Ludwig's ASCs are found in Eckhart's descriptions of the Birth experience. The first major difference is that Eckhart's was permanent, whereas Ludwig characterizes experiences that were by and large transient. Furthermore, Eckhart deemphasized ecstatic and hallucinatory experiences. The emotional and perceptual distortions often seen there are missing in him. The new State of Consciousness that Eckhart sought was a more practical and truly significant state because it was permanent. In it the participant becomes emotionally settled and perceptually normal (i.e. without bizarre hallucinations). With these caveats I think it is fair to say that Eckhart's portrait is near enough to Ludwig's to believe that he was describing a state that has nearly all of the common features of a State of Consciousness.

THEOLOGY AND THE BIRTH

The key question yet to be asked is the question of reductionism. Have I *reduced* Eckhart's theological assertions to psychological assertions? Do I maintain that Eckhart's God-talk is nothing but psychological or States of Consciousness talk?

Of course not. "God" is more than a term describing an aspect of a State of Consciousness. Behind Eckhart's use of this highly ramified term stand such assertions as God created the Universe, Jesus Christ lived in the time of Pilate, Christ was the Son of God, etc. The experience of the Birth of the Son of God in the soul does not replace any such notions. Rather, it capitalizes on the history of such terms and adds the nuances of the new experience *to* them. One can become like Jesus (who lived at Pilate's time) in having the Son born within him.

Nor do I claim that Eckhart asserts that man becomes God, or even becomes Christ. God and Christ remain in wholly different categories, *sui generis*, because they are God and Son by nature, born thus in the emanation of the Trinity *ab origine*. As is emphasized in Eckhart's commentary on John, man only becomes the Son by adoption.[143] Humans were not created with this experience as a common feature of our experience, but by God's grace we can be brought into a union with God. Thus I do not maintain that he was asserting that the Son is nothing but a psychological factor, if you will. Christ as Son was specifiably different from the experienceable union between man and God.

However, in a way similar to what I said in the previous chapter, the differences I have just stated among God, Son, and man are *analytic* but not *phenomenological*. Eckhart can specify numerous analytic differences which carry little or no phenomenological weight. That God created the Universe, that Jesus lived in such and such a time, that at the temporal beginning of creation Christ was made, that man fell from his original union with God, etc.—such assertions specify beliefs about God which need not necessarily be part of this particular experience.[144] In our benchmark passage the soul is said to "see God without means," i.e., without thought, idea, word, image, or what have you. If it is true that one transcends all these—and this is one of Eckhart's most heavily emphasized facts—then that inner side of the soul is devoid of the very media by means of which analytic truths are communicated: words and thoughts. If this aspect of the Soul is truly without thoughts, memories, ideas, or images, then no analytic truths *can* be part of that side of the Soul. The difference between "son by adoption" and "son by nature" is therefore no part of the mystical experience. Theology should not be reduced to psychology, but nor should the experience be reduced to theology.

The phenomenology of the experience can be discovered, however, emerging through the theology. For what Eckhart repeats tirelessly is that God is born in the soul and that there is no perceptible difference.[145] There is "no distinction between God and the soul."[146]

> I am converted into Him in such a way that He makes me *one* with His Being, not *similar*. By the living God it is true that there is no distinction.[147]

The coalescence between God and the soul is even more intimate than is the relationship between water and its surrounding barrel:

> Now he says: "I and the Father are One (John 10:30): the soul in God and God in her. If anyone put water in a barrel, the barrel would surround the water, but the water would not be in the barrel, nor would the barrel be in the water: but the soul is so *wholly one with God* that the one cannot be understood without the other. We can understand heat without fire, and the shine without the sun: but God cannot understand Himself without the soul nor the soul without God—so completely are they one.[148]

Experientially, though again not analytically, God and the soul become absolutely indistinguishable. The subject of the soul and the knowing God are one indistinguishable knowing.

> . . . he has one knowing with God's knowing, and one action with God's action, and one awareness with God's awareness.[149]

One becomes "consubstantial with the Father."[150]

Now, what does it mean for Eckhart to say that the Soul becomes "wholly one with God" if God is utterly beyond all thoughts and images? Well, what is God if he transcends all thoughts and images? He cannot be understood as the temporal originator of the universe: that would require a thought about Him. He is not Christ as model or historical figure; again these would call up memory. The same could be said for any of his acts or of analytical truths about him (like Anselm's, than which no greater can be thought).

Stripped of all analytical attributes perhaps we could say that we are left with only certain quasi-sensory attributes: a mere presence (or Being) which is not limited by any boundaries or borders and which does not change through time: an eternal boundless presence, if you will.[151] This is precisely what I have observed is encountered in the silent side of the Birth. Seen in this light, *the phenomenology of the experience emerges out of the theology*.

Not only does the phenomenology emerge out of the theology; the experience is its goal. It will be recalled that I stated on the first page of this book that the experience of the new relationship with God is Eckhart's principal emphasis. I quoted:

> What does it avail me that this Birth is always happening, if it does not happen in me? That it should happen in me is what matters. We shall therefore speak of this Birth, of how it may take place in us and be consummated in the virtuous Soul . . .[152]

It is now growing clear how this may be so. The *theory* that God is constantly giving Birth to the Son within the Soul points towards the Birth experience in three interconnected ways. First, the theory announces and describes the experience, as we have seen. Secondly, his theory passages are one and all hortative in intent. By means of the Birth theory Eckhart's listener is exhorted to discover this truth for him or herself. "Look within, consummate it within your own soul," it fairly shouts.

This hortative function of the Birth theory can be seen in a passage from *The Nobleman*. Both uses—theoretical and experiential—of *geburt* are present. In its theoretical sense, God is said to give Birth to his Son in that part of the Soul which "moves upward." Such a theoretical Birth, however, is like a light which shines in darkness which no one sees: true perhaps, but not perceived.[153] It is "covered over."

> . . . that part of the soul which ascends is a bare image of God, the Birth of God, uncovered and bare in the bare soul. Of the nobleman, as an image of God, God's Son, the seed of the divine nature that is never destroyed in us, but only covered over, King David says in the Psalms: "Though a man may be afflicted by all kinds of vanity, sorrow and distress, still he remains in the image of God, and the image in him." The true light shines in the darkness, but we are not aware of it.

Having stated the theory—that the light of God persists and that man is an image even if he is unconscious of it—Eckhart then begins exhorting his listeners. Remove your attachments, "take away the rust from the silver," and you yourself may perceive this. You may discover within your own Soul that the Son has indeed been there, even though hidden. You may consciously receive the Son, and know yourself to be the Son in the "buxom and heart of the Father." He continues:

> . . . "Take away," Solomon says, "the rust from the silver, and there will gleam and shine out the most pure vessel" (Pr 25:4), the image, God's Son, in the soul.[154] And that is what our Lord means by these words when he says, that "A nobleman went out," because man must go out of every image and out of himself and out of everything, he must go far off indeed, and become quite unlike all this, truly, if he wishes to and shall receive the Son, and become Son in the buxom and heart of the Father.[155]

In this passage, as in most of this preacher's utterances, the theoretical use of the term *geburt* ultimately serves to exhort. The theory serves to call for and perhaps evoke an experience. Slough off your attachments, it declares, and know yourself to be the Son of God![156]

In nearly all of this preacher's utterances the seemingly strictly theoretical passages similarly serve to exhort his listeners. One more passage should suffice to demonstrate this. In this one the theory is that "truth" is what is covered over with some falsehood:

> That which is truth in itself, we are not; rather, we are true, but something of falsehood is mixed in us too.

But it is not enough to know that this is so in a theoretical way only. One must discover this truth firsthand: the Soul should stand and "declare it" for herself:

> . . . But in the primal eruption where truth breaks forth and originates, there, in the doorway of God's house, *the soul should stand* and pronounce and declare the Word . . . [T]here God speaks in the soul and utters Himself completely in the soul.[157] (italics mine)

As before, the point of this passage is hortative: because the Soul is imperfect, man is generally only intellectually cognizant, if cognizant at all, of the spiritual Birth within. Thus far theory. But then Eckhart swings his hortative punch: "In the primal eruption . . . there . . . the soul should stand." The soul, exhorts Eckhart, should discover for herself this locale of truth. Theory here is again employed to bring on salvation.

The Birth theory has a third relationship to its soteriological function as well. This one is not explicit. As I noted, implicit in the Birth theory is a doctrine of an "innate capacity." This doctrine may be correlated with the nature of the transformation process advocated by Eckhart.

A process described as a releasing of attachments is fundamentally negative. To say "rid yourself of X" says nothing about what more positive attribute or experience Y may result.[158] And indeed Eckhart never provides any new notion or line of action which might serve as a substitute to which one may become attached. We have seen that he refuses to advocate ecstatic experiences, penitential procedures, etc. to which one may become attached. He also refuses to provide any concrete *ideas* of self or of God as possible substitute attachments. He provides no crutches. His listener should simply "slough off" things, not add them.

But this approach presents a theoretical problem. If anything valuable results from this process of deattaching—and he, like so many other mystics, declares that something eminently valuable results—then he must intelligibly account for it. A doctrine of an innate capacity (that a relationship with the *summum bonum* has been present to man at the ground of the Soul all along and that man was incapable of gaining access to it) serves just this function. Were he to say almost anything else, that is, were he to say that the soul should draw in *anything* from outside of itself, then that doctrine would be in danger of reopening the Pandora's box of attachments. When Eckhart claims that by merely dropping off all other concerns, what was innately "there" will come inevitably to the surface, he allows one to remove attachments and substitute nothing. Hence this doctrine preserves the notion that a valuable "something" can be achieved through his *lâzen* process while protecting it from any new attachment-substitutes.

In these three ways the theory of the Birth hence lends plausibility to the deattaching process while leaving it free to take place.

In sum, Eckhart's God-talk concerning the Birth is not completely reducible to psychology. But it should be understood as a way of describing and evoking the novel experience that Eckhart advocated, while leaving it free to occur. The Birth doctrine expresses and evokes mystical experience by means of theology: the Mystic as Theologian.

Read in this light, some of his more opaque statements regarding the Birth begin to make good sense. For example, one of the seemingly strangest of the Birth's nuances is that when the Son is born within the Soul, the Soul is immediately born "back" into God. That is, the reborn Son leads one back to God: the Birth is reflexive.

> If a soul stands in this present now[159] the Father bears in her His only-begotten Son, and in that same Birth the soul is *born back* into God. It is one Birth: as often as she is born *back* into God, the Father begets His only-begotten Son in her.[160]

> But the child is fully born when a man's heart grieves for nothing: then a man has the essence and the nature and the substance and the wisdom and the joy and all that God has. Then the very being of the Son of God is *ours and in us* and we attain to the very essence *of God*.[161] (italics mine)

One takes on the essence of God "within," and that essence is "God's." God, I have suggested, is encountered as an "expanseless expanse." In the Birth I am "in Him" and He is "in me," i.e., the expanse is me and I am it. As Eckhart states elsewhere, "Where I am there God is and then I am in God and where God is there I am."[162]

When Eckhart states that the Birth is reflexive, he communicates both of its critical elements. First, it is to say that one is aware of being within an expanse, or in his language, the very Being of the Son of God is ours and in us and we attain to God's essence. Secondly, the Son is "within" me, at the head of the Soul. That is, when I attain to this sublime state, the Son is none other than me myself. I *am* this. By saying that in my Birth I am "born back into God," Eckhart neatly ties together the sense of an expansion with its reflexivity of awareness. I am aware of myself *as* the expanse, and in the self-same knowing, the expanse is aware, as it were, of being me.

In the following passage Eckhart emphasizes this reflexivity of awareness. God's awareness is said to be a "bright pure light." We come to know in it; that is, it is the light amidst which we are conscious. Furthermore, it knows itself. Ergo, the soul "knows herself." "God is known by God" thus is logically equivalent with the Soul is known by the Soul, for they are both a single "light."

> When this Wisdom is united with the soul, all doubt, all error and all darkness are entirely removed, she is set in a bright pure light which is God Himself, as the prophet says: "Lord, in Thy light shall we know the light" (Ps. 36:9). Then *God is known by God in the soul;* with this Wisdom *she knows herself* and all things, and this same Wisdom *knows her with itself.*[163] (italics mine)

There is one knowing: my knowing God and God knowing me. Elsewhere the reborn Soul is said to know itself "with God's knowing."[164] That is, the Soul is self-aware from within the expanded "oceanic feeling." Eckhart's expression concerning being "born back into God" may be viewed as a way of expressing an expanded reflexive consciousness, of a single knowing subject that is both "without and within," "embraced and embracer," "seer and seen," "holder and held."

CONCLUSION

The key fact to be understood about the Birth—and about each of the three modalities of mystical experience that Eckhart portrays—is that the change is not in any object, but rather in the subject. The perceiver undergoes a change in vantage point, as it were. In *gezucket* the vantage point is inside of the divine "expanseless expanse," but cognizant of nothing else. In the Birth one comes to live amidst this expanse. All activity is then conducted while maintaining the sense of a presence. That is, in the Birth *one perceives and acts from within this oceanic expanse*. One sees, hears, thinks, etc. in the old way, but the seer is now different. One's awareness is now as if broader or larger.

To repeat: the novel element in the Birth is not a change in any object, but rather one in the subject, who now comes to experience from within a sense of the expanded presence. It is in this sense, and only this sense, that one becomes divine. This new vantage point—perceiving from within the expanse—is the novel element in the dichotomous cognitive structure. Ordinary activity is continued. One encounters in the ordinary way objects for consciousness. But simultaneously and continually one also maintains an awareness of oneself as infinitely expanded. It is as if one lives two lives simultaneously. It is just as Rolland said:

> Thus I lead at the same time, without discomfort or pain, a "religious" life (in the sense of this prolonged sensation) and a life of critical reason.

Such a dichotomous cognitive structure—as if living two lives—is not a thought, or a trying to keep this new, "religious" awareness. Rather it is a change in the very structure of the aware subject. Without trying, one knows oneself as expanded, yet is also aware of the finite, transient, and bound "ordinary world." One lives, indeed, between time and eternity.[165]

In the following passage Eckhart employs Augustine's image of the Janus-like two faces of the Soul, one turned towards God and the other towards the world. It is a nice review of many of the points we have touched on in this chapter: the theory of the Birth, although one is not aware of it; the discovery of God within the Soul in the Birth, etc. The two-faced image in it is especially pertinent here, for it suggests that the restructuring of the mind into a dichotomous cognitive structure is, as I have noted, permanent. Although in the Birth one is "facing" God, the worldly face does not cease gazing outwards. It continues to work "virtue, knowledge and holy living." The two-faced structure goes on "all the time."

> St. Augustine speaks—and with him another, pagan master [Avicenna]—of the two faces of the soul. The one is turned towards this world and the body; in this he works virtue, knowledge and holy living. The other face is turned directly to God. There the divine light is without interruption, working within, even though she [the soul] does not know it, because she is not at home. [*That is, God is present in the soul in theory, though one may not be conscious of this fact. Now Eckhart turns to the Birth:*] When the spark of intellect is taken barely in God, then . . . the Birth takes place, then the Son is born. [*One becomes aware of this presence. Furthermore, it is permanent.*] This Birth does not take place once a year or once a month or once a day, but all the time, that is, above time in the expanse where there is no here or now, nor nature nor thought.[166]

CHAPTER SEVEN

Der Durchbruch:
The Advanced
Mystical Experience

"My love looked at me through the window"—
that is, without hindrances—
"and I knew him, he stood by the wall"
—that is, by the body, which is perishable
. . ."Come wind from the south, blow through my garden
and make my spices to flow"—
here God bids all perfections to enter the soul.[1]

In chapter five I noted that Eckhart regards the contact with God as a contact with a silent, unmoving One, and that he advocates bringing that silence into activity through a process I called the dynamization of silence. In chapter six I observed that as a result of that dynamization process, a sense of internal silence is established alongside of activity in the State of Consciousness called the Birth of the Son of God in the Soul. Once established, that silence within is never lost. There is a further stage in the dynamization process though. Something yet remains to be added: a silence with even more wide-ranging implications. This broadening of horizons takes place in the state Eckhart calls the breakthrough (*Durchbruch*) of the Soul to the Godhead.

Let me warn the reader about two things. Although I have probably stretched my credibility beyond all reasonable limits, it is about to get worse! In this chapter I will describe an experience which may sound pretty strange. My only defense is that Eckhart himself says of this next milepost in the mystic's journey that it "sounds even stranger."[2] If I (or anyone else) am to represent this state as Eckhart himself does, inevitably I will sound equally strange. I am sure I will not disappoint the reader!

I have a second *caveat*. Eckhart is not very clear about the nature of the Breakthrough of the Soul to the Godhead. Probably his listeners could have made little of what he was talking about; perhaps that is the reason he did not dwell on it. Whatever, what we have is very sketchy. I have tried to draw out its nature, but I, like everyone who ponders it, am making an educated guess at best. Perhaps I have drawn the borders between this state and the Birth too sharply; perhaps we do not have a form of experience but a theory only; perhaps I have simply misunderstood him: many such questions have plagued me throughout my labors on this subject. I hope that the reader takes what follows in the proper light—and all of this book, for that matter—as the record of my halting attempts to understand what it might be like for a Soul to experience a Breakthrough to the Godhead.

DURCHBRUCH: LINGUISTIC USAGE

Although *Durchbruch* has been frequently analyzed as a key to Eckhart's doctrine,[3] the term appears in the Eckhart corpus a scant twenty-three times. This infrequency is hardly surprising, considering what I noted above, that the majority of his audience had had, in all likelihood, few encounters with the Birth, much less its refinement. Yet, though the term appears infrequently, it does play a critical role in characterizing the lattermost development of the religious life.

Durchbruch literally means a breakthrough. Eckhart used this neo logism to translate the Dominican term *motus*, the movement beyond the distinctions in the drive towards the One.[4]

Eckhart uses the term in several related senses. As a verb, it meant breaking through boundaries, a bursting of limits like physical borders. Things once impenetrable become penetrated, as when one bursts through a shell: "the shell must be broken [*zerbrechen*] and what is inside must come out."[5] A similar meaning is seen in the quotation "one must learn to break through things (*durchbrechen*) and to grasp one's God in them . . ."[6] In another analogy with a material bursting through, Eckhart suggests a breaking through topsoil to reveal what lies hidden beneath: the intellect is said to "burst through" the ground and "break through" (*durchbrechen*) to the roots from where the Son "wells up" and the Holy Ghost "blossoms forth."[7] Elsewhere, the term appears not in a quasi-physical context but in a moral one. One "breaks through" (*durchbrechen*) what seem to be the limits of virtue established by the saints.

> Now attend closely: Neither John nor anyone else among all the saints has been put before us as a limit, or as a compulsory goal beyond which we may not go. . . . In very truth, if there were a single man who could go beyond the measure of the highest saint whose virtuous life has brought him to blessedness—if there were a single man who could in any way at all transcend (*durchbrechen*) that measure of virtue . . . there is no saint in heaven who is so perfect but that you could transcend (*durchbrechen*) his holiness by the holiness of your life, and come to stand above him in heaven and eternally remain so.[8]

Thus in its first sense the term signifies the act of overstepping ordinary boundaries, whether physical, spiritual, or moral.

In one passage, this breaking through boundaries is associated with an ephemeral "something" that emerges ghostlike out of a physical body. In Christ's grave Mary had hoped that something of God had "broken forth (*durchbrechen*) out of man," i.e., out of his physical body, while something had remained within it.[9] Eckhart's use suggests that a quasi-physical substance or residue may exist in and then break through a body.[10]

This quasi-physical character leads us to Eckhart's second sense of *durchbruch*: a penetrating and being penetrated by. Speaking of physical heat, the midday heat is said to "*durchbrichet* the air and [make] it hot."[11] According to such a medieval scientific image, heat is presented as penetrating the air and filling it with its substance. Where air is, there is the stuff of heat; where heat is, is air. Drawing out the analogy, Eckhart says that a man must be "thoroughly penetrated (*durchbrechen*) and made incandescent with divine love."[12] Here it is man, not air, which is penetrated and filled with something. Elsewhere the Meister uses related terms to communicate such an interpenetration: "a man should

be so penetated (*durchgangen*) with the Divine presence and transformed into (*durchformet*) the form of his beloved God and he
essential in Him . . . "[13] Finally, mutual interpenetration is sometimes depicted in terms of a reflexive activity: "Just as He breaks
through into me, so I break through in turn into Him."[14]

Thus Eckhart's term *"durchbruch"* carries two characteristics:
First, an activity of breaking through boundaries which hitherto
were impenetrable, like a bursting through a shell; second, a
"bursting through" that results in a becoming penetrated by that
very "thing" into which one penetrates. Eckhart capitalizes on
both nuances of this term.

FROM THE BIRTH TO THE
BREAKTHROUGH

One of the clearest passages describing the relationship between
the Birth and the Breakthrough comes in the latter part of the
sermon *Surge Illuminare Iherusalem* (DW 14 = W 50). It begins
with the suggestion that God must become internalized, and that
this process will take on the character of a reflexivity of awareness.

> . . . God should be brought down, not absolutely but inwardly.
> . . . This means God is brought down, not absolutely but
> inwardly, that we may be raised up. What was above has become
> inward. You must be internalized, from yourself and within
> yourself, so that He is in you. It is not that we should take
> anything from what is above us, but we should take it into
> ourselves, and take it from ourselves, and take it from ourselves
> into ourselves.[15]

This internalization of God, the being "within yourself," etc., I
hardly need to say, is typical of Eckhart's Birth-talk.

But, Eckhart now continues, to discover that one has the Son
of God within is not enough: "And yet the Noble and humble
man is not satisfied to be born as the only-begotten Son whom
the Father has eternally born. . ."[16] One is not satisfied to have

this born "within" only. That is, one wants to enter into a complete equality with God—both within *and* without. When this is established, the religious begins to find God "in his path." The Godhead becomes known as the beginning and end of "all your activity." The religious then knows his or her actions as, if you will, shot through with divinity. "Whatever that man performs, God performs." The activities of the powers, which previously had been juxtaposed with the divinity within, become "broken through" by the Divine Light. One begins to live in and through the divinity, through all of one's activities.

> [T]hen He will be the beginning and the end of all your activity, just as His Godhead depends on His being God. To that man who thus in all his actions means and loves nothing but God, God gives His Godhead. Whatever that man performs, God performs,[17] for my humility gives to God His Godhead.[18] . . . God is not only a beginning of *all our acts* and our being, He is *also an end* and a repose to all being.[19] (italics mine)

In the Birth one discovers an expanse within oneself, at the "head of the soul." In the Breakthrough this expanse comes to be seen to pervade even one's powers and actions (and indeed, we will shortly see, even pervade the objects one encounters in the world).

In sum, in this sermon the movement is from the Birth (one remains yet unsatisfied with it) towards the Breakthrough (marked by a new relationship with our actions and all being).

In another sermon depicting the transition, DW 48 = W 60 (no biblical text), Eckhart again begins with what we know as the Birth. One attains oneness and blessedness within, at the soul's spark, he says. The blessedness there discovered is "opposed to all creatures."

> Therefore I say, if a man turns away from self and from all created things, then—to the extent that you do this—you will attain to oneness and blessedness in your soul's spark, which time and place never touched. This spark is opposed to all creatures: it wants nothing but God, naked, just as He is. It is not satisfied with the Father or the Son or the Holy Ghost, or all three Persons so far as they preserve their several properties. I declare in truth, this light would not be satisfied with the unity of the whole fertility of the divine nature.[20]

For this, he continues, would be to discover the simple,

changeless, divine Being which "neither gives nor takes," that is, which has truck with neither actions nor powers. But again, says the Meister, this is not enough. The Soul seeks to fathom this Being even more deeply.

> In fact I will say still more, which sounds even stranger: I declare in all truth, by the eternal and everlasting truth, that this light is not content with the simple changeless divine being which neither gives nor takes . . .[21]

Why is this light not content? Because the soul wants to know more, to get at the ground of the ground, as it were. It wants to know not just the ground of the soul, but that ground's connection with the rest of reality as well. Eckhart continues:

> . . . rather it seeks to know whence this being comes, it wants to get into its simple ground, into the silent desert into which no distinction ever peeped, of Father, Son or Holy Ghost. In the inmost part, where none is at home, there that light finds satisfaction, and there it is more one than it is in itself: for this ground is an impartible stillness, motionless in itself, *and by this immobility all things are moved, and all those receive life that live of themselves, being endowed with reason.*[22] (italics mine)

Here, in the passage which will serve as our benchmark, Eckhart says that this light is not content with this changeless Being "which neither gives nor takes." It seeks to know *whence* this being comes. In other words, one is not satisfied with a Birth which has no truck with the world, which "gives" nothing to the world. Such a silence is of little use in directing one's actions, for it is not even seen as connected with the world. It may give one a sense of joy and stability, but that joy is not connected-in to things. Nor does it "take" anything, i.e., it provides no *telos* for the world. It simply is an expanse, pure Being in itself, within which one finds oneself. But one is not content with this. One seeks to find the even more significant "impartible stillness" which *functions*, i.e., is perceived as the immovable source of all moving things.[23] One seeks until one finds the silence which is also the source.

Passages like these lead me to believe that the Breakthrough crowns and perfects the Birth, not the reverse.[24]

PASSIVE AND ACTIVE

Now I would like to distinguish the Birth from the Break-through. Before I begin, however, I want to say something about the character of the development between these two stages of the mystical journey as I understand them. These are not distinct stages of development with sharp borders. Eckhart suggests instead a process of steady and continuous evolution and slow personal discovery. God's image is revealed in man more and more clearly.[25] Man becomes more and more "like God" and is made more "one with Him."[26] It is "with practice" that the Divine Light moves into one's powers. "In this quiet one can grow and increase without intermission and never come to an end of the increasing."[27] One doesn't "rest content" with the Birth but "quests on" even further. The characteristics I outline as those of the Birth and of the Breakthrough do not come in discrete lumps. The stages Eckhart sketches seem closer to mile-posts than toll booths.

There is a theme in Eckhart's Birth-talk which I have yet to discuss: the passivity of the soul in the Birth.[28] Though I have saved my discussion of this motif until now, it should not seem entirely unanticipated. In preparation for the Birth, you will recall, man gradually released from himself his attachments with the world. What he had cared about he came to neurotically cling to no longer. Sensible objects, one's cares and wants, and even the old sense of the self itself, became as if dead or perhaps "bitter" and "nauseous." The drives which had previously consumed one ceased, leaving a sense of the presence of God, but little else which might motivate one externally. Conversely God (or perhaps the "expanseless expanse") became a new and dominant presence, the unmoving "subject" of all activity. God is active; the soul is passive.

Eckhart employs this motif of God's activity and the soul's passivity both to describe the onset of the Birth and its nature once it is established. He expressed the onset process as man working the preparation, the Father of Lights working the rest: "The soul prepares herself by exercises," he says. "Then she is kindled from above."[29] Preparation means that the individuality is active insofar as he or she *effects* the lessening of attachments, working to discover and release them. One "strives to over-come" one's attachments.[30] I must "strip myself "of attach-ments.[31] This process is accompanied by "pain and strife."[32] Such a self-transformative process takes effort. After discovering my weak points I must mend them myself.

> ... a man might become truly rich in virtues by finding out his weakest points so as to mend them, and diligently striving to overcome them.[33]

Such a "diligent striving" process that I must accomplish myself takes effort.

After such arduous, self-motivated labors, however, the word-less, formless Father of Lights works the rest: He "kindles" the soul from above. Can Eckhart mean by this that the silent expanse is perceived as active in any ordinary sense of the term? Obviously not. The notion of God's "activity" in such passages is clearly being used in an analogical sense. Any ordinary activity would be a mode or a form and God is "mode- and power-transcending."[34] This kind of action is, he says at one point, *secret*, without detectable instrumentality.

> God performs this work in the inmost part of the soul so secretly that neither angels nor saints know of it, and the soul herself can do nothing but suffer it to happen: it is God's province alone.[35]

Such a secret "working" implies that something occurs within but that man has no knowledge of how or where the silent expanse works. Felt as autonomous, it seems to happen *to* one.

> She [the soul] does not know when He comes or when He goes, though she can sense when He is with her. A master says His coming and His going are hidden.[36]

Another way of saying that man works the preparation and God works the rest is that once man has worked the preparation, there is nothing to do but wait: "Just await this birth in you, and you shall experience all good and all comfort, all happiness, all being and all truth."[37]

The passivity of the soul is not only the mark of the Birth's onset, but it is a leitmotif of Eckhart's descriptions of its estab-lished character as well. Once you have abandoned all your attachments to possessions and/or your particular lines of action, then any work or activity is no longer perceived as "yours." Instead you now identify yourself as at One with the divine "expanseless expanse"—and all actions, as it were, now "belong" to it or Him.

> Let me explain. When you have completely stripped yourself of your own self, and all things and every kind of attachment, and have transferred, made over and abandoned yourself to God in utter faith and perfect love, then *whatever* is born in you or touches you, within or without, joyful or sorrowful, sour or sweet, that is no longer yours, it is altogether your God's to whom you have abandoned yourself.[38]

This theme of the passive individual and the active Divinity is seen consistently in Birth passages. God is the "one" who works, the soul merely suffers it to occur or merely watches.[39]

> For just as God is boundless in giving, so too the soul is boundless in receiving or conceiving, and just as God is omnipotent to act, so too the soul is no less profound to suffer, and thus she is trans-formed with God and in God. God *must* act and the soul must suffer, He must know and love Himself in her, she must know with His knowledge and love with His love, and thus she is far more with what is His than with her own, and so too her bliss is more dependent on His action than on her own.[40]

God gives, the individual is merely passive.

Eckhart sometimes communicates this theme through his grammatical constructions. For example, God (here the Trinity) is often spoken of as active, while the soul's role is relegated to passivity:

> . . . [T]he grace which the Holy Ghost brings to the soul *is received* without distinction, provided the soul is collected into the single power that knows God [i.e. the soul has worked the preparation]. This grace springs up in the heart of the Father and flows into the Son, and in the union of both it flows out of the wisdom of the Son and pours into the goodness of the Holy Ghost, and *is sent* with the Holy Ghost into the soul. And this grace is a face of God and *is impressed without cooperation* in the soul with the Holy Ghost, and [it] *forms the soul* like God. This work *God performs alone, without cooperation.* . . . *God leads* His bride [the soul] right out of all the virtues and nobility of creaturehood into a desert place in

Himself, and *speaks Himself in her heart*, that is, *He makes her* like Himself in grace.[41] (italics mine)

Without any doing from my side, God enters, speaks, impresses himself and does the work in my Soul. I am passive, He is active.

This is a theme of the Birth. But now as one "quests on to find out what it is that God is in His Godhead and in the Oneness of his own nature,"[42] things change. One element of this drive to seek further that seems key here concerns the dichotomy between the individual's passivity and the divinity's activity, for a divinity which is opposed to something—the creaturely, the inactive individuality—is yet truly One.

Perhaps the first aspect of the person to resolve this dichotomy (and thus become reactivated) are the powers: the intellect (and hence the thought processes), senses, etc. In his typical Birth grammar, you will recall, these are excluded from the Divine Light. But with practice the powers can become receptive. In the following the Birth occurs within and then it runs over or wells over into the powers.

> It is a property of this Birth that it always comes with fresh light. It always brings a great light to the soul, for it is the nature of good to diffuse itself wherever it is. In this Birth God streams into the soul in such abundance of light, so flooding the essence and ground of the soul that it *runs over and floods into the powers and into the outward man.* . . . The superfluity of light in the ground of the soul *wells over into the body* which is filled with radiance.[43]
>
> So he who would see light to discern all truth, let him watch and become aware of this Birth within, in the ground. Then all his powers will be illuminated, and the outer man as well. For as soon as God inwardly stirs the ground with truth, its light *darts into his powers*, and that man knows at times more than anyone could teach him.[44] (italics mine)

The six powers, says Eckhart at one point, must come to take on a "golden ring."[45] The ring on, for example, discrimination (*rationale*) is "the light, so that your discrimination should be always timelessly illuminated by the Divine Light." On the power of memory, one wears the ring of retention, "that you may keep all things within you." Again, how different in tone are such statements from what we have seen before (i.e., the Lord's flowing into the soul's essence "but not into her powers"[46]). Here the powers are raised up to a nearly supreme level. One now discriminates, remembers, and feels only in this light. In short, the religious begins to employ his or her powers, dominated by the Godhead.

Even the body itself comes to be seen as resting on the expanse experienced within. In the sermon *Deus Caritas est* (DW 67 = W 70) Eckhart first discusses the birth as a being taken up into the "essential mind of God," which "neither receives nor gives." In my vocabulary I would say that the "oceanic feeling" has little apparent connection with the worldly and the physical. There in its own ground the soul grasps God, but this remains above all being and activity: the "personal man-God-being [*personliche wesen mensche-got*] outgrows and soars above the outer man altogether."[47] Yet such a soaring "beyond" the outer man is not the "highest" perfection, Eckhart then tells us. Though one receives the internal "influx of grace from the personal being in many infestations of sweetness, comfort and inwardness, and that is God," this "is not the best." The outer man, too, must come to find itself supported "on" the Divinity.

> [T]he inner man, who is spiritual, would have to come out from the ground where he is one, and would have to be directed by the gracious being by which, through grace, he is supported. Therefore the spirit can never be perfect unless body and soul are brought to perfection. Thus just as the inner man, in spiritual wise, loses his own being by his ground becoming one ground, so too *the outer man must be deprived of his own support and rely entirely on the support of the eternal personal being* which is this very personal being.[48] (italics mine)

The formless one, first found only inwardly, must come to be encountered in and through the body as well. The outer man must come to "rest entirely" on the being first encountered within.[49]

Typically Eckhart uses the term *durchbruch* in conjunction with the term Godhead, or when not using this Neo-Platonic term, simply "God" (without speaking of Father, Son and Holy Spirit). What does the use of such terms indicate about the character of the Breakthrough experience?

The Godhead is the *terminus a quo* and *terminus ad quem* of the pendular process Eckhart speaks of as the *exitus* out of the divine silence into the world and the *reditus* of the created soul back into God. In the *exitus* process, as I have noted, the Godhead is pictured as the silent, unmoving, unchanging One which boils up within itself to create the active Trinity and through its agency the world. The *reditus* process essentially retraces those steps. All creatures are called to return back into the Godhead from which they came.[50] The Godhead, towards which all things, especially human souls, are called back is beyond all change, diversity, and multiplicity; beyond even the bare threeness of Father, Son and Holy Spirit. It is "a non-God, a non-spirit, a non-person, a non-image, rather . . . He is a sheer, pure, limpid One, detached from all duality."[51] To encounter the Godhead would be to encounter just such a formless limpid One.

> If [the soul] sees God as He is God, or as He is an image, or as He is three, it is an imperfection in her. But when all images are detached from the soul and she sees nothing but the one alone, than the naked essence of the soul finds the naked, formless essence of divine unity, which is superessential being, passive reposing in itself. O wonder of wonders, what noble suffering that is, that the essence of the soul can suffer nothing but the bare unity of God![52]

Hence as is often emphasized, Eckhart stressed the absolute desert-like silence of the Godhead. It is a Oneness, beyond all trace of duality.

But to say that the soul suffers or is penetrated with the formlessness of an absolute One is not as simple as it might appear. After all, this silence is the starting point of the *exitus* process and the goal towards which all things are moving in *reditus*. Hence this formlessness has the peculiarity of both being silent and also boiling up within itself, emanating into the Father, Son and Holy Spirit and producing the Universe. For example, in the Latin "Commentary on Genesis," Eckhart writes, "In the one and the same time when God was, when He begot his coeternal Son as God equal to himself in all things, He also created the world."[53] Eckhart conceives of this creation of the world in Neo-Platonic emanationist language, whereby the logos serves as the exemplary cause by which the Divinity creates. As such, the Godhead "contains" the effect, the universe, "in a prior and more eminent way" than the thing contains itself. All things have such a "virtual existence" in the Godhead. What is the "really real" in any creature is in God even more than it is here. Eckhart puts this more poetically in the vernacular works. There he says that all things are "in" God, contained in His "plenitude":

"all creatures are in God and are His very Godhead, which means plenitude . . . "[54] "God is all, and is one."[55]

Hence when Eckhart says that the Soul breaks through ordinary boundaries and becomes interpenetrated by the Godhead, not only does he thereby imply a being interpenetrated with the Godhead's silence, but also he may imply that one will break through to a new relationship with a created, multiple reality as well. Does he describe such a new relationship?

In our benchmark passage we read:

> In the inmost part, where none is at home, there that light finds satisfaction, and there it is more one than it is in itself: for this ground is an impartible stillness, motionless in itself, *and by this immobility all things are moved, and all those receive life that live of themselves, being endowed with reason.*[56] (italics mine)

In this I believe we can see the suggestion of a truly novel form of experience. For me to thus Breakthrough to the Godhead means that somehow I must come to share in these facts of the Godhead and go beyond all distinctions: those between the powers and the spark, between creatures and God, and even the subtle distinctions between the Trinity and the Godhead. Most importantly, all creatures must come to be cognized as nondistinguished from the divine expanse which has been (since the Birth) encountered within myself. The peculiar oceanic feeling is hence encountered not only internally but externally. Eckhart is describing a coming to perceive that BY THE VERY IMMOBILITY WITHIN MYSELF "ALL THINGS ARE MOVED."

To Breakthrough to the Godhead is apparently to directly perceive just this: all things are moved by that which I myself am. It is a coming to see and encounter all things as having God at their ontological core.

> God gives to all things equally, and as they flow forth from God they are equal: angels, men and all creatures proceed alike from God in their first emanation. *To take things in* their primal emanation would be to take them all alike. . . . If you could take a fly in God, it is in God far nobler than the highest angel in himself. Now all things are equal in God and are God Himself. Here God delights so in this likeness that He pours out His whole nature and being in this equality in Himself.[57]

To Breakthrough to the Godhead is to perceive that Godhead

giving rise to all things. It is to see that all things are the One by means of the One alone. It is to find oneself amidst the ontological core of the cosmos. It is to confirm the One's nature:

> There is One *in which* the entire multitude participates, through which the multitude is one and is whole, and this One is God. Moreover the multitude is *in it* alone. Therefore *all things are the One* by means of the One alone.[58] (italics mine)

When Eckhart speaks of the Breakthrough in the first person, he suggests that it involves perceiving the unmoved mover which stands at the source of both "myself" and the world. This entails the perception that self and other are One.

> When I flowed forth from God, all creatures declared: "There is a God"; but this cannot make be blessed, for with this I acknowledge myself as a creature. But in my breaking through, where I stand free of my own will, of God's will, of all His works, and of God himself, then I am above all creatures and am neither God nor creature, but I am that which I was and shall remain for evermore. . . . By this imprint I shall gain such wealth that I shall not be content with God inasmuch as He is God, or with all His divine works: for this breaking through guarantees to me that I and God are one. Then I am what I was, then I neither wax nor wane, for *then I am an unmoved cause that moves all things.*[59] (italics mine)

To breakthrough to the Godhead hence carries this weight: one will perceive that things are moved to their ontological core by the Oneness which is both "I" and "God."

Perhaps the clearest statement of the phenomenological characteristics of this state comes in sermon DW 13a = W 24b (no title). After having stated that one must go beyond creatures and thereby "ascend to the highest and purest part" of one's own creatureliness, Eckhart describes St. John's vision. It is a quite remarkable utterance, not only because he rewrites scripture on his own authority, but because of his version of that vision:

> Now John says he saw a lamb standing on the mountain. I say John was himself the mountain on which he saw the lamb. And whoever wants to see the lamb of God must himself be the mountain, and ascend into his highest and purest part.[60]

"John was himself the mountain . . ." Normally I know myself as distinct from other people and the objects around myself. I interact with them, react to them, and distinguish myself from them in various ways. Here Eckhart suggests precisely the opposite. John *is* the mountain. According to Eckhart, John knew himself to *be* the object of perception, to be one with it, or perhaps to be of the same "stuff."

In what sense can someone *be* a mountain? The novel cognitive element in the Birth dichotomy was an expanded reflexive consciousness: "The eye with which I see God is the eye with which God sees me." In the Breakthrough this "reflexivity" takes on a new meaning. Not only am I just aware of myself as an expansion but I come to perceive cognitive objects as also permeated, interpenetrated, by that expanse. Here objects and the internal silence are brought to a unity. The object is known *as* the subject. This is sometimes called the *unio mystica*, in which the subject is in union with the object of perception. In it things are perceived "in" the pure simplicity of one's own awareness.

> Whoever declares that he has "attained to his nature" must find *all things formed in him* in the same purity as they are in God.[61]

Within the soul is the "nameless place" where all things rest.

> When the soul comes to the nameless place, she takes her rest. There where *all things* have been God in God, she rests.[62]

In such a new cognitive structure the normal subject–object dichotomy is "broken through." One perceives all objects as oneself and knows oneself to be the object of perception. Only under such circumstances is the man truly an "experienced man."[63]

To claim that things are known as One and that all is found in the "nameless place in the soul" is to say that I know things in or as *myself*. I know them "in" my own now expanded awareness. I and Thou, to use Buber's language, are a single unified One.

In sum, I define the Breakthrough of the Soul to the Godhead as a third new State of Consciousness. In it all mental content is encountered on the basis of a new cognitive structure in which any and all objects for perception are encountered as part of or permeated by the expanded reflexive awareness previously encountered within the soul.

That object and subject are united into a grand whole, accounts for a common theme seen in many Breakthrough passages, that of the desert. It can be seen in the treatise on *The Nobleman*. After asking who could be nobler than he who straddles "created things" and "on the other side . . . the inmost ground of the divine nature and its desert," Eckhart answers:

> "I", says our Lord through the prophet Osee, "will lead the noble soul out into a desert, and there I will speak to her heart (Os. 2:14), one with One, one from One, one in One, and in One, one everlastingly.[64]

It is a common theme in the vernacular sermons as well.[65]

Why should there be such an absolute desert-like oneness in a mystical state of this sort? I propose the following explanation. If I perceive all things as in union with myself, I will not encounter a world comprised of several things, but rather I will be amidst a unity which overarches both myself and all objects for perception. There can be no two. Were there even two, a God and a Godhead, for example, the experience would not be one of unity. All that is left is a single "something" in the midst of which one finds both oneself and the world. All distinctions would be transparent, as it were, to the unity. "The unity is the distinction, and the distinction is the unity."[66] If the Godhead is a nothingness and the world is "in" it, then there can be no additional thing against which one might juxtapose the pure Being and mark off its attributes. From its interpenetration into the world comes its nature as utterly devoid of qualities: a desert place.

What, then, is the Godhead for such a soul as this? Though I will discuss it in greater detail in the next chapter, for now let me suggest just this: for the broken-through soul *the Godhead is the term which names the absolute, oceanic one in the midst of which the subject finds both him/her self and all objects for perception.* It names the "expanseless expanse" which is, in the end, all that comes to exist for the advanced adept. What was "me" now is that One, the Godhead. What was mountains and tables and other people now is cognized as that same One. The Godhead is the name of that by which the Soul and the world have both become permeated. It is the Ocean in the midst of which the subject perceives himself and all others.

RELATIONSHIP WITH WORLD, SELF, AND ACT

Eckhart speaks of the new form of life in various ways. I will summarize its features in terms of the new relationship with the world, the self, and one's actions as Eckhart describes them.

1. World

If there is indeed a unity which dominates "all things," then not only a mountain but *every* object seen will have the same cognitive structure: unification with the subject. The entire world will be sensed as in unity with my self. This will overcome all of the world's diversities. Hence Eckhart sometimes speaks of this unity as if it surrounds things. As if immersed in a greater whole, life is "enclosed in Being." Angels know creatures "in God,"[67] things are *"embraced by* the Divine Light."[68] Following his assertion that John was the mountain, Eckhart says,

> God touches all things and remains untouched. God is above all things an instanding in Himself, and this standing in Himself sustains all creatures. . . . What all creatures have God has entire within Him. He is the ground and the encirclement of all creatures.[69]

Sometimes the unity is described as "within" things, transforming them at their core or heart. For "an experienced person" things have an "inward divine mode of Being."[70] One notices the unity "in all things and all places."[71] Things seem to "become simply God to you, for in all things you notice only God, just as a man who stares long at the sun sees the sun in whatever he afterwards looks at."[72] Conversely God is seen to emanate into things.[73]

Dominated by unity, things seem to lose their individuality: they are seen as "formed in a simplicity" or as being in some sense "pure." Diversity is perceived as a unity that is perceived amidst diversity. The soul is,

> embraced by unity. . . . The unity is the distinction, and the

distinction is the unity. The greater the distinction the greater the unity, for that is distinction without distinction.[74]

All things that we have outwardly in multiplicity here, is there all inward and one.[75]

2.   Time

If things are perceived as identified with the One, they would not appear at some level to change through time. In an ordinary way they would appear to change, of course, since all created things bear the mark of change on their backs. But it is impossible that any remnant of "change or mutability can get into God."[76] In order for them to be seen in God and as "His very Godhead," they must be recognized as nonchanging.[77] Thus, for "all those who are thus in unity"[78] (again implying that we have here a portrait of experience), time will seem to collapse into one present now. Such a collapse of time Eckhart communicates best with syntax. By flipping back and forth indiscriminately between tenses, he evokes the sense that the present is virtually indistinguishable from the future and the past. To make this evident, in the following passage I shall gloss the tenses he uses.

> There I was myself and knew myself [past] . . . I am my own cause [present] . . . I am unborn [present] . . . and can never die [implied future] . . . In my Birth all things were born, and I was the cause of myself and all things, and if I had so willed it, I would not have been and all things would not have been [past] . . . When I flowed forth [past] . . . But in my breaking through where I stand free [present] . . . then I am above all creatures [present] . . . There I shall receive an imprint [future] . . . then I am what I was [present and past!].[79]

This strange grammar communicates such freedom! One is what one was, things are now what they were as well as what they will be. He moves through time like some people skate over ice. The religious "thus in unity" lives in an eternal now. Because time is experienced thus, Eckhart speaks of the emergence of things as a constant "now." All things are seen as

> new and timeless. Therefore, St. John says in the Apocalypse: "He that sat on the throne said: 'I will make all things new.'"[80]

What one perceives as an emergence now out of the One is presented as *in illo tempore* as well.[81]

In sum, one encounters a unity within the world and between the world and oneself. Because they are unified, changing objects do not seem to change at their depths through time. All things seem "new" and "original."

3.   Oneself

The God found to be at one's essence in the Birth never deserts one. Rather His light "darts" into the powers, as we saw, and permeates them with its brightness. The entire body and personality become infused with God. The subject becomes, in effect, a God–man.

> You should know what a man is like who has come to his: we can well say he is God and man. Observe, he has gained by grace all that Christ had by nature, and that *his body is so fully suffused* with the noble essence of the soul, which she has received from God and the Divine Light, that we may well declare: That is a man divine![82]

This means paradoxically enough, that such a man would perceive the expansion which is himself to be the "source of" his own body as well as the world. This would result in a very peculiar recognition: I am my own source!

> For in that essence of God in which God is above being and distinction, there I was myself and knew myself so as to make this man. Therefore *I am my own cause*, according to my essence which is eternal, and not according to my becoming, which is temporal . . . In my Birth all things were born, and *I was the cause of myself* and all things . . . Then I am what I was, then I neither wax nor wane, for then I am an unmoved cause that moves all things.[83]

> While I yet stood in my first cause, I had no God and *was my own cause* . . . Therefore let us pray to God that we may be free of God that we may gain the truth and enjoy it eternally, there where the highest angel, the fly and the soul are equal, there where I stood and wanted what I was, and was what I wanted.[84]

> But as I said before, the Father of heaven gives you His eternal Word, and in that same Word He gives you at once His own life, His own being and His Godhead . . . then He gives you the power

of begetting with Himself, yourself and all things . . . Then you too are, with the Father, and in the Father's power, unceasingly bearing yourself and all things in the present now. In this light, as I have said, the Father knows no difference between you and Him . . .[85]

After the years of attachments to this or that aspect of myself, one comes, at the end of the long road, to perceive oneself as the expansive "oceanic feeling" and none other. All else has fallen off, and what had once appeared to be the self comes to be seen as, at its ontological core, nothing but the expanseless expanse.

4.   Actions

The picture I have painted so far is basically static. The world is perceived as unified: the religious is One with God; God is the formlessness in man; God indwells in the world, etc. But no man (genuine or otherwise) lives in stasis. One must eat, sleep, build buildings, and save souls. What are the characteristics of action in a life for which "everything is removed, abstracted and peeled off in a single is?"[86]

If everything I perceive is suffused with the divine essence, then every act, from beginning to end, is so suffused as well.[87] The visualized goal, the people I speak to, the words I speak, the food I eat, all are divine. In short God is known in and through all of my activity,[88] the soul "works divinely in God."[89]

This is, however, a strange about-face. Eckhart has developed at some length the idea that a man must become will-less. To claim that here one knows one's acts as divine sounds like one becomes willful, indeed arrogant. "I can do no wrong," one might expect such a man to say. This is clearly not the statement of a "genuine man, who acts from his own ground" that Eckhart had in mind.

But there is no sense of "I" here, we must remind ourselves, not even enough to pray "My will be Thine." "Let my will be Thine" might be the prayer of such a heart. He/she will feel an utter absence of self-interest and will.[90] But even though there is no sense of "I", Eckhart is clear that one does learn to direct one's own actions and be actively participating in life. If we may take a clue from Eckhart's own life, one participates quite effectively!

Why should the actions of such a man be particularly effective? Were I attached to this or that, I might act ineffectively, e.g., think that I "really want" greater wealth, someone's affections, etc. However, by the time one has reached this settled status, such attachments would long since have been sloughed off. If I know *myself* as in essence *thou*, then every word I speak to you will be, paradoxically, perceived as spoken to myself. Naturally I will treat you with the same absolute unquestioned support with which I would treat myself. When I interact with you, inevitably I will uphold what I take to be your greatest interest. Such an affirmation of you would not be out of some intellectualized obligation. It would stem from an altruistic kind of selfishness. For in supporting you, I would be upholding myself.

> If you love yourself, you love all men as yourself. As long as you love a single man less than yourself, you have never truly learnt to love yourself—unless you love all men as yourself, all men in one man, that man being God and man. It is well with that man who loves himself and all men as himself, with him it is very well.[91]

This holds true for each and every one of my actions. Everything I do will be performed out of such a far-sighted selfishness. My goal would be to raise you to what I perceive as the greatest gain, the beingless being. Every act will lead towards that beingless being, for in so doing I am raising what I take to be myself.

> If a man has right intention in all his works, the beginning of that intention is God and the work of that intention is God Himself and is the pure divine nature, and its outcome is in the divine nature in God Himself.[92]

In every act the actor will "mean" only God.

> To that man who thus in all his actions means and loves nothing but God, God gives His Godhead. Whatever that man performs, God performs . . . "[93]

This "meaning God" does not entail some knowledge of or thinking about the uplifting of someone. Rather, since everywhere one looks one sees the unity of all things in a *reditus* back towards God, each and every action will be, from that Soul's point of view, a moving from, in and towards only the One. This would not be a matter of thinking that this is so. If I understand it correctly, this sense is a direct by-product of the facts of life as one has come to know them firsthand. Acting "from" one's own ground,[94] "according to her primal purity,"[95] "divinely in God," and "God-conformed"[96] would be inevitable, based on the new cognitive structure. Actions in support of those around one would simply result inevitably from perceiving others *as* the self.

The whole tone of Eckhart's portrait of working in this state is entirely different from what we have seen up until now. Previous to this he devalued work. Here work and activity are as if glorified. To this man all creatures will be "subservient, as they were to St. Peter." The sea will close up under his feet and he will walk on the water.[97] To such a man God gives all the fruits, "a thousandfold." Though such a man needs nothing, he does in fact possess everything. He doesn't suffer, no matter what he does, or what befalls him.[98] It must be wonderful! "It is well with that man who loves himself and all men as himself, with him it is very well."[99]

OTHER MYSTICS

Such an experience of perceiving objects as unified with the self must sound unbelievable. I warned you! Yet a similar claim has been thought to stand at the phenomenological heart of many an advanced adept of the religious life. W. T. Stace finds an "inner subjectivity" within things as one of the six distinguishing characteristics of "extrovertive mystical states." He also points to it as one of the critical components of mystical doctrines:

> [T]his fact that the mind, in this experience, is itself what it perceives . . . is spoken of as the Void, or as the unity, or the One, or the Universal Self, or . . . is interpreted as God . . . [100]

Rudolf Otto finds it a key to what he calls the first stage of mysticism from both East and West: "The union which here occurs is . . . that of the self with the object perceived in the unity of the ideal world."[101]

Ramana Maharishi, Plotinus, Maharishi Mahesh Yogi, certain Sufi mystics, and others have all spoken in similar terms. It is especially reminiscent of Plotinus's first Ennead (8:I).

> He who has allowed the beauty of that world to penetrate his soul goes away no longer a mere observer. For the object perceived and the perceiving soul are no longer two things separated from one another, but the perceiving soul has (now) within itself the perceived object.[102]

Among Hindu mystics, Ramana Maharshi says that the enlightened man, the *jnani*, perceives the world to be one's own self. As in Eckhart this is not the ordinary anxiety-bound self, but a "higher Self" known by a man devoid of attachments.

> Ignoring the self, the *ajani* (unenlightened) thinks the world is real, just as ignoring the screen he sees merely the pictures as if they existed apart from it. If one knows that without the Seer there is nothing to be seen, just as there are no pictures without the screen, one is not deluded. The *jnani* knows that the screen, the pictures and the sight thereof are but the Self.[103]

What exists, for such a man as this, says Ramana Maharshi, is the Self alone. All percepts are known as the self.[104]

In his translation of and commentary on The Bhagavad Gita, Maharishi Mahesh Yogi describes several progressive and developmental states of the mystical journey. The most advanced one, which he calls "Unity Consciousness," is, as in Eckhart, permanent.[105] In this state, he says,

> The mind begins to live Unity throughout the whole field of diversity. The whole field of diversity is then appreciated in the light of the inner divine unity.[106]

Everywhere and in everything he "sees everything in terms of God." This God is "one with himself." Such a man perceives all of the world as one with himself. The objects of perception are thus unified with the subject.[107]

We see a similar union between subject and object in the Sufi mystic Mahmud Shabistari (A.D. 1320). He, too, speaks of the unity between subject and object as well as the sense that the actions on the mystical quest lead to the One as their *telos*.

> In God there is no duality. In that Presence "I" and "we" and
> "you" do not exist. "I" and "you" and "we" and "he" become
> one. . . . Since in the unity there is no distinction, the Quest and
> the Way and the Seeker become one.[108]

Finally, Cassian describes something similar.

> Then God shall be all our love, all we desire and seek and follow,
> all we think, all our life and speech and breath. . . . In that union,
> whatever we breathe or think or speak is God. So the end of his
> prayer is attained in us—that they all may be one as we are one: "I
> in them, and thou in me, that they also may be made perfect in
> one": and "Father, those whom thou hast given me, I will that
> where I am, they may also be with me."[109]

Thus, though unusual, even among men and women on the
mystical path, such a *unio mystica* perception of ordinary objects
"as" the self from within which one perceives is not entirely
idiosyncratic to Eckhart. While the experiences pointed to are
similar, Eckhart differs from some of these writers in speaking of
this state in such Neo-Platonic language and in founding on this
experiential cornerstone so much of this thought and philosophy.

THE SIX "TYPES" OF PEOPLE

To summarize, over the last five chapters I have sketched out a
progressive development in the life of the religious, from a
condition of attachment towards a condition of detachment.
Three discrete States of Consciousness result from this condition.
Gezucket is a temporary event in which all mental content ceases
and one becomes enraptured. The Birth is a permanent state in
which an inner, silent, ocean-like expansiveness is maintained
while conducting one's affairs. The Breakthrough is a state in
which the same silence is encountered as the ontological core of
all things.

If the progression is thus, we might expect that Eckhart would
have depicted it in some of the stage portraits he left us. He did.

In chapter three I described a passage in which six types of
people were listed. To the first four "types" of people, the reader

will recall, light came to the Soul in increasingly overwhelming flashes. These, I argued, could not have been truly exclusive types, but had to mark progressive developments. Members of the second "type," for example, had to have once been members of the first "type". The third and fourth "types," who saw a "great flash of lightning, which is bright, and then immediately were in the dark again," were probably once members of the second,[110] etc. Furthermore, it will now be obvious that such transient "flashes" parallel the temporary "flashes" one experiences as *gezucket*. There is a "flash" of contact with the infinite, and then it ceases.

Now the fifth type, Eckhart continues, "are aware of a great light as bright as day, but still as it were through a chink."[111] Light through a chink is permanent. Putting the eye up to the chink, one can see the light clearly and thus know that "my beloved looks at me," and that "His face was comely."

> The fifth are aware of a great light as bright as day, but still as it were through a chink. . . . About this St. Augustine says, 'Lord, thou givest me sometimes such a great sweetness that, if it were perfected in me, if this is not heaven I know not what heaven can be.'[112]

I regard this passage as emblematic of the Birth. The light of both is the true light: both are marked by sweetness; both are constant. Furthermore, the essentially private act of peering up to a chink is quite like the introvertive discovery of finding God within. In both a permanent "relationship" is set up with the light; but neither is "full" nor "complete." Both entail a dichotomy between "light" and "dark." One still longs for a "window," as it were, in which not only is the light itself seen, but the world is also seen, illuminated by the light. Just as in the Birth man "quests on," one longs to connect the light with that which has been in darkness, the rest of the world.

The sixth "type," those who "see God quite clearly," is the very advancement on the fifth that my portrait of the Breakthrough would lead one to expect. In it God is seen "quite clearly," "in act" and "in temporal things." The winds of God[113] "blow through my garden and make my spices to flow." Now God is not only seen, but he "blows" within and throughout the garden of the world, making all its creaturely components, its "spices," flow. He is found everywhere. To this "type" "all things live in the warmth," and all the soul's powers are "perfected."

> Is there then no way of seeing God quite clearly? Yes. In the book of Love the soul says: "My love looked at me through the window"—that is, without hindrances—"and I knew him, he stood by the wall"—that is, by the body, which is perishable . . . "Come wind from the south, blow through my garden and make my spices to flow"—here God bids all perfections to enter the soul.[114]

The beloved, God, here "stands by the wall": the creaturely. His gentle breezes waft throughout the garden. His scent is everywhere.

PART III

The Theological
Investigation

And so we say that when everything is removed,
abstracted and peeled off [from the soul]
so that nothing at all remains but a
simple "is"—that is the proper
characteristic of
His name.

CHAPTER EIGHT

Theology and Experience

> "An angel was sent from God."
> . . . he purifies her from stains . . .
> he purges her from matter
> and makes her collected, and thirdly,
> he purifies her from ignorance.[1]

In the last five chapters I have attempted to give a careful and detailed presentation of the various experiences Meister Eckhart portrays throughout his corpus. This has been by no means a thoroughgoing presentation of either his doctrine as a whole or his doctrine of God. It is now time to make such a presentation. In part this will serve as a summary and review of some of the material we have outlined. But the goal here is to show the place of mystical experience within his theological system as a whole. Then I shall describe the place of the particular experiences in that system. Finally, I will analyze the relationships between Eckhart's theological doctrine and the experiences we have portrayed.

DEUS EST ESSE

Deus est esse. "God is being." In this simple utterance we find the central assertion of Eckhart's theology. The first and most important thing we can say of God is that He is, He exists. Perhaps Eckhart's favorite benchmark texts are the Old Testament's Ex. 3:14, "I am that I am," and Moses's assertion, "I am hath sent me." "I am," says Eckhart in his commentary on this passage, signifies the pure and naked existence of God, His pure substance with neither accident nor quality. It signifies his existence modified by neither form nor "this or that." He is one and simple, a pure one, pure existence in itself, *esse simpliciter*. He simply is. The pronoun *I* of this proposition signifies this pure substance:

> ... pure, I say, without any accident, without anything alien, substance without quality, without this or that form, without this or that. Now this properly describes God and him alone, who is above accident, above species, above genus.[2]

The verb *am* in this expression asserts a similar nature. It "signifies pure and naked existence in the subject and regarding the subject, and that it is the subject, in other words the essence of the subject."[3] God is the only such entity whose existence is identical with his essence, his whatness the same as his existence.[4] He is the only entity whose "existence [is] his very essence."[5] He alone "exists absolutely and purely and simply, with no additions."[6]

> And so we say that when everything is removed, abstracted and peeled off so that nothing at all remains but a simple "is"—*that* is the proper characteristic of His name.[7]

That God is fundamentally and primarily mere existence Eckhart emphasizes by turning this phrase around in his *Opus Tripartum: Esse est deus*, Being is God. This statement is orthodox scholastic doctrine. St. Thomas had asserted the intimacy of Being. Eckhart is emphasizing this by asserting that God is absolutely and purely being. He is attempting to raise God above all distinctions and to assert the purity of His mere existence, His "naked being."[8] Such naked being translates (especially in the German sermons) into the purity of the Godhead, the God beyond all characteristics, the divinity in his "robing room" (i.e., before he puts on the attributes that clothe him).[9]

Because God's Being is pure, He is absolutely one. A man or a creature, for example, is a composite being, composed of body and spirit. Unlike these, God is a simple one, without even attributes. To call Him One is to assert our inability to name Him, i.e. distinguish Him by his particularizing attributes. He is that to which nothing is added, not even in thought. He is not even goodness or truth first, for example, for they would add something in thought.

> St. Paul says: "One God." One is something purer than goodness or truth. Goodness and truth do not add anything, but they add in thought, and when it is thought, something is added.[10]

He is one and simple, one and indivisible, without mode or property. "One thing, than which nothing is more simple."[11] In God there are no distinctions; He has relation neither to number nor to plurality. "We say God is One in opposition to number"[12] and "beyond number."[13] He is purely one, without even the notion of duality. He is not even one as distinct from two, for that would involve notions of plurality. He is the unity "before" or "behind" plurality, for He is "the One in which there is no number."[14] He is oneness itself, "not unity which is the principle of number."[15] "Unity is not itself countable."[16] God is the highest purity.[17] He is divested of whatever is accidental:

> He is an indwelling in His own pure essence where there is nothing that is contingent. He is a pure presence in Himself, where there is neither this nor that.[18]

Eckhart sometimes articulates God's unity with greater linguistic finesse: God is the *negatio negationis*, the negation of negations.[19] Why this? If A is asserted to be not B, A is limited in some way. In so asserting, we assert a plurality, an A and the B which God is not. But God is not limited; nor are there two. There is neither "not God" nor "other thing." Thus Eckhart denies negation of Him altogether. The negation of all negations is thus, paradoxically, the strongest affirmation we can make of His unity.

> The negation of negation is the quintessence, purity, and doubling of affirmed being. Exodus 3:14: "I am who am." Hence it is aptly said: "Show us the Father" (that is, the One) "and it is enough for us."[20]

Here the negation of negation, God's unity, is explicitly identified with the purity and unity of his being, his nature as "I am who am." We see this identification elsewhere.[21]

Considering the purity and unity of God's mere existence, it would appear surprising to find Eckhart adding anything to it. But Eckhart does overlay something onto this essentially Neo-Platonic notion: the Scholastic and Christian doctrine of God as the Trinity. Two factors make this overlay reasonable. The first is man. Owing to the limitations of the human mind, we think of God as possessing qualities: wisdom, goodness, mercy, etc. Such divisions are not in God Himself—as he exists for Himself—but are applied to Him from our side. His distinctions are God's characteristics as He exists for us. Man might take God as the beginning of creatures, or take Him as He is related to creatures. We attribute characteristics to God.[22] Considered in Himself, God is absolute unity, a pure, unchanging Oneness, without motion or distinctions. Generally Eckhart uses the term *God* or the expression *Father, Son, and Holy Spirit* to indicate the Divinity as he exists from our vantage point, and uses *Godhead* to signify Him as He exists from his own vantage point.[23]

The second factor that makes it reasonable to characterize the unitary divinity as trinitarian is built into the nature of the relationship between the Trinity and the Unity. Eckhart speaks of a relationship that is internal within God.[24] God's fullness of inner being is said to "boil up" (*bullitio*) into the three in its preparation to create the world, as I said in chapter five. The most famous "*bullitio*" passage is the one I quoted there from Eckhart's Exodus commentary on "I am that I am." Let us delve into this in greater detail. Eckhart says there that the "am" of this phrase indicates:

> a certain turning back and reversion of His being into and upon itself and its indwelling or inherence in itself: not only this but also a boiling up, as it were, or a process of giving birth to itself—inwardly seething, melting and boiling in itself and into itself, light in light and into light wholly interpenetrating itself, wholly and from every side turned and reflected upon itself. As the wise man says: "Monad begets—or begot—monad and reflected its love or ardour upon itself." For this reason it is said in the first chapter of John's Gospel: "In Him was life." For life denotes a sort of outpouring, whereby a thing, swelling up inwardly, completely floods itself, each part of it interpenetrating the rest, until at last it spills and boils over.[25]

Let us examine this image. Water remains water even though it boils up into activity. This particular melting, boiling and seething reemphasizes that this "something," though active, remains itself: its activity is "inward." The boiling mass "interpenetrates itself" and from every side is "turned and reflected on itself." Through an "outpouring" it "completely floods itself," each part again "interpenetrates" every other. The upshot: even though the three take on distinctions of their own which are different from the substance which composes them, they yet retain its same nature. Eckhart could work no harder to suggest their unity with what underlies them. Characterizations of them—e.g., the "good Good"—though having apparent distinguishability, "signify the unmixed and highest good which is grounded in itself, rests on nothing, and returns full circle upon itself."[26]

The significant point of this passage—and of the trinitarian doctrine in general—is that *all* of the unitary nature of God's pure Oneness, his *esse simpliciter*, is retained in these Persons. The fundamental and bare Oneness is the primary nature of the Three.

> What does the Lord Jesus say? He says he is He who is.[27] What is he then? He is a Word of the Father. In this same word the Father speaks Himself, *all* the divine nature and *all* that God is just as He knows it, and he knows it as it is. (italics mine)

"These three persons are One," a traditional and orthodox teaching, is perhaps the most fundamental tenet of Eckhart's teaching on the Trinity. "These three are the one undivided God."[29] "On account of [the One] in itself there is neither number nor multitude. On account of it the three Persons are not many but one God."[30] Inasmuch as the Three are One, their one-ness stands above their three-ness, for they are not in actuality different. The One which stands at the core of the Father and Son is "among divine things not only the same in species, just as among creatures, but it is even the same being in number."[31] The three Persons are non-one and one.

Though employing both the Christian trinitarian and the Neo-Platonic oneness doctrines, Eckhart leans heavily towards the latter. He emphasizes that their oneness is primary. In the following passage from the Book of Divine Consolation, for example, we see that the distinctions of the Trinity that are "our" attributions but barely cover the essential oneness of God's Being:

> We attribute likeness in the divinity to the Son, heat and love to

the Holy Spirit. Likeness in all things, but *more so and first of all* in the divine nature, is the birth of the One and the likeness of the One, in the One and with the One; it is the beginning and origin of flowering, fiery love. The One is the beginning without any beginning.[32] (italics mine)

The outflowing of the One into the Father, Son, and Holy Spirit, Eckhart repeatedly emphasizes, is an outflowing which retains its essential nature as pure existence and as the One.

In the formal emanation the producing thing [the One] and the produced thing [the Trinity] are one in substance simply, in being in living, in thinking and in operation.[33]

The three are in effect transparent deities. I think of them as like an etched one-way mirror. From one side they seem to be distinguished and substantial. They look like they really are Power and Wisdom and Love. Yet when the light is moved to behind the mirror, illuminating the Trinity from behind, or when one walks behind the mirror (into the dark side), then the three are found to be transparent to pure Being beyond them and nothing substantial in themselves.[34]

IMAGO DEI

The real thrust of Eckhart's teaching on the unity of the trinitarian God concerns the Son. As a spiritual advisor, Eckhart cares more about the transformation of his disciples than about abstract speculation in itself.[35] And it is, of course, the Son who is born within the Soul. Now, who or what is the Son? In his teaching on the relationship between the persons, Eckhart follows the orthodox doctrine. The Son was not "created" but "begotten." What is "created" is unlike its creator, whereas what is "begotten" retains a similarity with its begetter. "When the Father begets the Son. He gives him all that He has of essence and nature."[36] Only the begotten "knows" the begetter since only like can know like: no one "knows" the Father except the Son, who retains his similarity with Him. This is not true of even a second generation of begetting, e.g. the Holy Spirit, who is not the first begotten issue but the second: He proceeds from the generation of the Son.[37] Because only the Son is the first issue of begetting, only he is properly called the "image" of the Father.[38] The Son is the *Imago Dei*.[39]

What is an "image of God?" The nature of an image is important in Eckhart, for it stands as the theoretical connecting link between the unity and the plurality of God. Since man, too, is called an image of God, as we will see shortly, it also is a key term in understanding Eckhart's mystical anthropology.

The relationship between an image and its archetype is particularly well developed in Sermon DW 16b = W 14b. "An image is similar (*similis*)."[40] An image however is more than merely similar, for two things can be like one another without being images of each other. Two eggs, for example, are similar, but are not images of each other.

> Two eggs are equally white, but one is not the image of the other, for that which is the image of another must have come from its nature and be born of it and be like it.[41]

If B and C are both derived from A, B may resemble C, but it is not the image of C. Only if B "flows out of" A, is an expression of A, can B be legitimately said to be A's image. For something to be an image of its archetype it must "come from its nature and be born of it and be like it."[42] It is one with its archetype despite alterations.

Because it is an outflow of the archetype, Eckhart says, it does not exist of itself but "takes its being solely from that of which it is the image without means, has one essence with it and is the same essence."[43] In itself it has no being, it exists from within another; it is not "of itself or for itself, it is solely that thing's whose image it is and all that it is belongs to that."[44] Its essence is not in the image but "more truly in that which it proceeds from."[45]

Perhaps this will become clearer if we look at the nature of one of Eckhart's favorite paradigms, that of an image in a mirror.[46] The mirror image doesn't exist in itself. Take the archetype away and the image goes. Rather it takes its existence from the archetype. This is viewed from the vantage point of the archetype, if you will. From the vantage point of the witness of the image, it *does* have an apparent reality. It is, to the witness, an expression of the archetype: it is the outflowing of appearance from the archetype. One does, in fact, see the archetype, though its location may be skewed. The archetype, from this vantage point, "pours out" into the image.[47] Eckhart puts this elsewhere that the archetype "strives out" into what is inherently unlike: e.g., the image of the divine nature "is always striving against whatever is ungodly."[48] The image is thus both other than the archetype in appearance as well as identical with its being and essence. Once again we find ourselves dealing with something which has, from our vantage point, an appearance but which is *from another perspective* transparent to what is beyond it. An image takes its being and essence from what it images: in itself it disappears.

> For the image in so far as it is an image receives nothing of itself from the subject [e.g. the mirror] of which it is, but receives its own entire being from the object [e.g. the archetype] whose image it is . . . It receives its own being from that alone.[49]

"The Son is the image of the Father." The Father we have seen is that which is in Being and essence purely One, Pure Being.[50] *Ergo* the Son takes his essence from the sole entity whose essence is identical with its being. This "image" is the image of the Oneness, if you will, i.e. has as its essence the unity of the One Pure Being. It is God's oneness which in this case "pours out into His image, while yet remaining intact within itself."[51] Though apparently distinguishable, in essence the Son is transparent. Were a man to somehow discover that he was the Son, he would discover that he was in actuality the Being of another, i.e. of God. The soul would then know itself to be: "not of itself or for itself, but really belongs to that of which it is the image, is its property, takes its being therefrom and is the same being."[52]

One of the virtues of this theology is that it solves the thorny scholastic problem of how a pure, unified God could have attributes. Though Thomas, for example, concentrated on the *via negativa* as the principal manner of asserting God's nature, some positive assertions were inevitable. Otherwise one is led towards an agnosticism.[53] But how is one to assert something, e.g. wisdom, of God? According to Thomas's account of human knowledge, we have an idea of wisdom from knowledge of human wisdom. Were this applicable to God, it would anthropomorphize Him, making Him into a kind of superman.[54] Yet if

God's wisdom is so transcendent as to be entirely unlike human wisdom, what applicable meaning might the term then have?[55]

I would suggest that the critical factor standing at the heart of Eckhart's solution to this paradox can be summed up in the word *perspective*. From one perspective God is unitary, beyond attributes. From this perspective there is no naming, and thus no problem of how to name the *nomen innominabile*. From another perspective, God has attributes; in fact, He is the name which every true attribute names, the *nomen omninominabile*.[56] It is from the vantage point of ordinary man that God has distinctions and marks and is trinitarian. It is from such a man's perspective that the Son is substantial. From another perspective he is so transparent that he disappears altogether, such that He is beyond beings and distinctions altogether.[57]

MYSTICAL ANTHROPOLOGY

This issue of the differences in God's nature from various perspectives is especially relevant for man. Man and man alone is such that he has the possibility of experiencing according to several perspectives. The angels live and have their place in the "divine order where they know by divine wisdom and divine likeness or divine truth, as far as this may be."[58] An angel is a "pure intellectual light, detached from all material things . . . [he] perceives in a light that is beyond time and eternal. He therefore perceives in the eternal."[59] They are blessed with this—but only this—mode of perception. Creatures, on the other hand, though they have God's being at their ontological core, have no possibility of perceiving from the divine perspective.[60] Only humans can both work "in the now of time"[61] and also be "like the angels," returning to God "with the angels and through the angels and by the Divine Light."[62] The noble man is not satisfied with the being that the angels cognize without form and depend on without means—he is satisfied with nothing less than the solitary One."[63] Only man has the capacity to know in the completeness of God's unity, i.e., God in both his atemporal and his temporal modalities. This possibility of knowing God from two perspectives—two modes of knowledge—makes man superior to the angels. Man can know more than in the pure Divine light. Man and man alone can know both without form and with it. Man can know the oneness in its full completion, oneness within the world.[64]

The crux of the claim that God is different according to different perspectives thus is anthropological. It is man who perceives according to these perspectives. It is man who can and must, according to Eckhart, change his vantage points, knowing with a lower and a higher knowledge. The first kind of knowledge is that of the man with "no acquaintance with inward things."[65] He knows God as an external principle, perceives God as if with the eyes with which he sees color. He sees God as if God were in time.[66] The second sort of knowing, the higher knowing, is from within the Divine, as it were. This is not external, but internal. It is a being "informed with the essence of wisdom and its nature, being wisdom itself."[67] Here one knows God "by His own taste and in his own ground."[68] This is not a looking at God but a dwelling "in God" and a having God dwell "in him."[69] This change in perspective can occur in this life: it is a "perfection of the spirit to which man can attain spiritually in this life."[70]

Man's perspectives on God are developed at some length in DW 83 = W 96. The first perspective is to view God as separate. This is taking God as one takes an image: from without. The soul sees God "as He is God or as He is an image [i.e. an image from an exterior vantage point] or as He is three."[71] To see God thus is to see Him as separate from oneself. But Eckhart says this is an "imperfection" in the soul. By so saying he implies that it is perfectible, i.e., one can encounter God differently. This different way of encountering God is to go beyond Him as an image in the sense of something external and separate and to become one with God: "the naked essence of the soul finds the naked, formless essence of divine unity."[72] Man has the capacity to perceive and understand and live with God FROM WITHIN HIM. "You should," he says, implying that you can.

> You should wholly sink away from your youness and dissolve into His Hisness, and your "yours" and His "His" should become so completely one "mine" that with Him you understand His unbecome Isness and His nameless Nothingness.[73]
>
> But if I am to know God without means then I must really

become He and He I . . . so fully one that this "he" and "I"
become and are one "is," and in that "isness" work one work
eternally . . .[74]

Unlike other creatures, man has the capacity to encounter God
from various angles. Eckhart has Christ, here an archetype of the
God-knowing man, say:

> . . . [A]ll that my Father knows I know, and all that I know you
> know, for I and my Father have one spirit. Now the man who
> knows all that God knows is a God-knowing man. That man
> apprehends God in His own selfhood and in his own unity and in
> His own presence and in His own truth: with that man all is well.[75]

The nature of the two perspectives which may be experienced by
man may be seen in the two distinct ways one interacts with
images (*bilde*). One can interact with an image in two ways: first
as one interacts with ordinary images, i.e., by perceiving them as
external to oneself. When I see, for example, a candle, its image
comes from afar through the air and strikes my retina. I perceive
its image by means of my knowing intellect. I become *eigenschaft*
with such an image, attached to it, and identify myself in relationship to it. Because I am attached to such images, my attention
is typically directed outwards, towards these "creaturely"
images.

The second way of interacting with images is the way a reborn
man or woman might interact with the image of God. Here is
where the developments I outlined in Part II of this book come
into play. The "image of God" is within the Soul.[76] God is "in
the image" and it is "in God." To say that in the heart of the Soul
one is an image of God is to say that at some level a man or a
woman is one being and essence—the very same being, essence,
and oneness—with God. One "interacts" with such an internal
image in a new way. One must separate oneself from creaturely
images and come to realize oneself *as* this new kind of image.
This results from the transformation I sketched out in chapters
four and five. Realizing oneself as this image means that one
discovers the Divinity within and "sees" with His (or Its) eyes,[77]
as I showed in chapters six and seven. This second mode of
interaction with an image differs from the manner in which one
deals with external ones in two ways. First, this image is not "of"
something else. One does not becomes some second something in

the same sense that one sees some other thing. Rather than something else, one realizes that this is one's own self, one's "truest" or the really real within.[78] Participation with this image means that God and man become "one mind."[79] One has a very different perspective on an image one is amidst than on an image which is "out there."

Secondly, this archetype mirrored by the image is not a thing at all, but simple being. One realizes oneself as the pure uniform One devoid of plurality. It contrasts with a perception of a sensory image, in which one retains a sense of many discrete things, unrelated ontologically to one another except in theory. In this spiritual image one metaphorically moves to the other side of the one-way mirror and realizes in experience (rather than in theory alone) the fact of a singleness. One cognizes but one. This occurs in the experience we depicted in chapter seven, the *Durchbruch*.

Theoretically, how is this possible? How is it that man can live and experience according to these various perspectives? Eckhart frequently emphasizes that the divine archetype/image relationship is found not in some speculative and far-off heaven, but in the Soul of man. Not only was Jesus of Nazareth the image of God, but so, too, other men's Souls are "the natural image of God" as well.[80] The "same substance whereby Christ is a person, as the bearer of Christ's eternal humanity, is also the substance of the soul."[81] When God created the Soul He impressed His image on it. He made the Soul such that at its peak it is the image of God in the way we have defined it: the divine Oneness is "patterned" within the peak of the Soul.

> You should know that this simple divine image which is impressed on the soul's inmost nature is received without means. It is the inmost and noblest part of the (divine) nature that is most truly patterned in the image of the soul ... God is here in the image without means, and the image is without means in God.[82]

Because the divine (and transparent) image is *within* the soul, the Soul has the possibility of knowing it from various perspectives. One can know God "as God"—i.e. from without—or one can go beyond this external "looking at" God and "become united with God like a light with light" within oneself.[83] Thus one may, in theory, move within one's own self to a new perspective. In short, man may live and cognize from various perspectives, perceiving God first from without and later from within, i.e. from God's own perspective.

Because man is fashioned thus and can view things from these various vantage points, he has the capacity to take himself from different perspectives. He may "take himself" "according to" the Divine which is within him. That is to say, he may live and understand himself according to various perspectives. How I "take myself" is critical.

> Do away with whatever is an accident in you and take yourselves in the freedom of your impartible human nature.[84] But since this very nature wherein you take yourselves has become the Son of the eternal Father by the assumption of the eternal Word, thus you, with Christ, become the Son of the eternal Father by reason of taking yourselves by that same nature which has there become God. Beware therefore, lest you take yourselves as being either this man or that, but take yourselves according to your free, indivisible human nature.[85]

Taking oneself in the imageless image of God means that one knows oneself not as a discrete someone or something, but knows oneself as the "expanseless expanse" if you will. This is of course the key factor in *gezucket*, *Geburt* and the *Durchbruch*.

We have spoken up until now of one "ordinary" modality of experience and three specifically mystical modalities, four in all. Let us compress these four into three vantage points from within which man can cognize. The first is ordinary perception. Here one perceives oneself as distinct from things and from God; images are perceived as substantial. God is also thought to be substantial, and is perceived as separate from both the world and from oneself. Though one may hear that God is an indwelling principle, or may argue this fact, this is a supposition and not a direct perception.

The second vantage point is that of the transient *gezucket* and the permanent Birth. Because one is "stamped" from the start with the image of God, one can "take" the divine, as it were, from within. One can come to experience that oneness of which One is the image by experiencing oneself, as it were, within the Divine. This is having "one mind" with God. This is to participate in an "expanseless expanse" which one recognizes to be the Self itself.

In *gezucket* this is all that one experiences. In the Birth one experiences this within and encounters the world as opposed to it, separate from things. The interior "oceanic feeling" in effect comes into a dichotomous relationship with worldly things. The experience, if you will, is that "I am that, but there is yet also 'this and that.' " Things remain "away from" this interior discovery that one is an image of God.

The third vantage point is the *Durchbruch*. The change here is in the way one relates with things and the world. In the *Geburt* things are separate from myself and distinguished from each other.[86] Since theoretically God stands at the ontological core of all beings, the substantiality of things can be "broken through" in a manner similar to the breaking through of the "image" of God which was within. Again the critical factor is the change in one's perspective. Now the new perspective has to do with external things.

> This or that thing is not all things, for as long as I am this and that or have this and that, I am not all things and have not all things. Cease to be this and that, and to have this and that, then you are all things and have all things and so being neither here nor there, you are everywhere. Therefore, being neither this nor that, you are everywhere.[87]

This new perspective allows one to experience even ordinary reality from within. Exterior images come to be perceived from a new vantage point, i.e., as transparent to the modelessnes which is at their ontological core.

ECKHART'S MYSTICAL DOCTRINE OF GOD

Now, how do these various vantage points relate to Eckhart's doctrine of God? We have four critical terms here. They are difficult to sort out. I see them as interdependent and in two pairs.

"God" and "Godhead" are theological terms that describe "enti-
ties." *Gezucket* and *Birth* (taken together) and *Breakthrough* are
terms that describe epistemological modalities or cognitive structures.

God is distinguished from Godhead by working and not
working.[88] That God "works" signifies that he stands in a relationship with things, i.e., He is their creator. To ordinary man
God is distinct from things. From God's vantage point this is
false.[89] To God all things are savored as the end of the One. In the
Birth, in which one perceives oneself as within God, one
continues to perceive oneself as being in relationship to substantial things. Though God "does the work" of this man, the world
is still separate, even bitter and nauseous perhaps. God is not "in
the powers." "God," the Divinity who works and is separate
from the world, is thus a term which has relevance for the
perception of an ordinary man and of a man experiencing
gezucket or the *Geburt*.

Such a cognitive dualism and such a Divinity who is separate
from the world is not complete. For though one knows from
within God's knowing, one doesn't know *everything* as the One.
One is therefore "not satisfied" with this God who works.

As one becomes accustomed to functioning in this modeless
awareness, one comes to know the world, too, as God Himself
knows it, i.e., comes to savor creatures as God. In this, one joins
with things in one enormous union. This is the *Durchbruch* in
which things are perceived as a single unity. The "object" within
which one is herein conscious is the Godhead. One has come thus
to know creatures, too, as God knows them, i.e., within one
single expanseless expanse. In this unity one perceives neither
work nor working, for there are no separate creatures. All are
one, a single union with oneself. In this, one comes to recognize
that the perception of God as separate from things—i.e. the
perception in the *Geburt*—was false. God is perceived as "in
actuality" a single unity that is the distinction.

Thus "Godhead" has significance for the perception of one
living in either of these two states (*gezucket* or the *Geburt*) or in
the *Durchbruch*. In the birth, "Godhead" signifies the modelessness within. In the *Durchbruch* it signifies all that is. In both cases
Godhead is characterized as a pure modeless being, empty of
distinctions and silent.

CONCLUSION

In short, the result of the religious transformation is a set of experiences that form the perception of the world as described in the theory. In theory God is interior to man at the deepest level; one experiences that theoretical presence in the Birth. In theory the world emerges from the Divine and is created by the Divinity in his distinguishable form, the Trinity; in the Breakthrough one perceives the world as indeed permeated with divinity. One experiences that *Deus est esse* and that the nature of this *esse* is *esse simpliciter*.

In other words, this system, which relies on the differences in perspectives, itself hinges upon a possibility of personal—in fact, mystical—transformation. Only a transformation that one might undergo "spiritually in this life"[90] will allow one to encounter images differently, cognizing from a new perspective, and making the distinctions between Son, God and Godhead apparent.

> If a man dwelt in a house that was beautifully adorned, another man who had never been inside it might well speak of it: but he who had been inside would *know*.[91]

This new perspective, bought about by the transformation process, is both logically and experientially pivotal. It provides the epistemological shift which accounts for a God who has both attributes and a nature beyond attribution. At the cornerstone of theology stands a phenomenology of mystical experience.

It may also be viewed conversely. That is, the theology may be seen as structured to account for the phenomenological facts of spiritual experience. In fact, it seems to me that this is the more fitting way to approach Eckhart. The facts of spiritual experience are the driving energy behind his theology. His doctrine as a whole is deeply informed by the characteristics of religious experience as he knew them. He builds a theory about God's being known from various perspectives because man has such a capacity to change his vantage point. This he knows because men have in fact come to be aware from within the "expanseless expanse." Eckhart builds a theory about God being interior to man at the deepest level because this is what is recognized in experience by one who releases his or her attachments. He builds a theory about a Son, a Soul and a God who are all transparent because what seemed to be a substantial Soul may be discovered to be transparent when one comes to know oneself as within the divine expanse. He theorizes that God is pure being, *esse simpliciter* because of the simplicity and purity of the divine expanse. He writes that the world has its *terminus a quo* and *terminus ad quem* in the One because the world may be seen to be an outflowing of the One when one "breaks through." These facts are what "instructs" a theoretician like Eckhart.

> Sometimes I declare that in whatever soul God's kingdom dawns, which knows God's kingdom to be near her, is in no need of sermons or teaching: she is instructed by it and is assured of eternal life: for she knows and is aware how near God's kingdom is, and she can say with Jacob: "God is in this place, and I knew it not"—but now I know it.[92]

We have all three cognitive structures accounted for here (four counting *gezucket*). To account for the perception of the ordinary man, Eckhart speaks of a substantial world, a substantial self, and a self which is *eigenschaft* with the world in numerous ways. For him Eckhart offers the notion of the creator God, the Trinitarian God, the God who loves us and who promises salvation.

In order to account for the dichotomous cognitive structure of the *Geburt*, Eckhart speaks of a modelessness of God which stands in some sort of relationship with that world. Inspired by the experience of being "within and without," Eckhart described one who knows himself to be one with the Son, One with God, and who encounters God or the pure Oneness. By way of theory to explain this experience, Eckhart asserts that God "stamped His image" on the human soul and that it can be discovered. To account for the experience of an interior silence and a removal from activity, we have the motif of a passive soul and an active God.

Finally, the unity experienced in the Breakthrough between the interior self, the rest of the self, and the world lead Eckhart to speak of a God who is only One, a One which stands as the emanating source of the world. To account for this form of perception, Eckhart describes a reality principle which "boils and seethes" into the perceived world. For him Eckhart describes the union between man, God, and the world. For his experience, as well as his earlier birth experience, Eckhart speaks of God as being, as all life and as *esse simpliciter*. To account for the transformation which leads to this cognition, Eckhart describes a God who had been encountered as having attributes, but "in actuality" is devoid of those attributes.

In other words, the theoretical system is informed by—and leaves unmistakable room for—the possibility of particular experiences unlike those of the "natural man." It is structured in such a way that if one in the course of the religious transformation has these peculiar experiences, one can gauge the level of one's attainments and feel confident that one is on course. In addition, by hearing of the nature of the modeless expanse, one will hopefully be drawn towards it. As Eckhart describes, catalogues, and theorizes, he evokes. Philosophy accounts for and evokes the variety of cognitive structures described herein by means of a set of theologically laden ontological structures.

To summarize, Eckhart's theological system is a systematic world view in a theological paradigm that is informed by and accounts for the structures of perception that one might undergo in the course of one's religious transformation. Theology is informed by mystical anthropology. The mystic is a theologian.

Appendix A

DIAGRAM OF THE MYSTICAL WAY

Since completing this book I ran across this diagram in a very early manuscript of the autobiographical *Vita* by the Blessed Henry Suso, one of Eckhart's most famous disciples.[1] It is a fascinating diagram, full of detail and implications. While it is not in an Eckhart manuscript proper, like other students I believe that it presents a picture of the mystical way which has been deeply influenced by the Meister. Hence I was gratified to see that it is so congruent with the general outline of the mystical way I have depicted above.

It is introduced as follows:

> These next pictures show the presence of the naked divinity in the Trinity of the Persons, and the flowing out and the flowing back again into all creatures, and it shows the first beginning of a progressing man, and his orderly break-through as he increases, and the supernal superabundance of a perfection which is above being. Thus we can expect to see a map of the mystic's journey.

It reads clockwise, starting from the upper left. The concentric circles represent what I have described as the empty though dynamic abyss of the Godhead.

> This is the abyss without manner of the everlasting divinity, which has neither beginning or any end.

According to Eckhart from this dynamic, self-generative emptiness comes the boiling over into three; a similar picture is here

symbolized by the triptych and of course the actual three Persons Who are represented by three male figures. They are

> ... the Trinity of the Persons in unity of essence, which is the faith of Christians.

Suso stresses, as I did, that they have a "unity of essence": note that in the heart of each are the concentric circles which here symbolize the One Godhead. Their essence is the very Godhead Itself; their equality is shown by their equality of height.

From this Divine upper level the "way" proceeds downward to an angel with wings:

> This figure is the flowing out of the angelic nature.

As I stressed in the last chapter, directly from the deity comes that which is the core of humanity; indeed descending from this nature is humanity, represented by the seated figure:

> This is humanity, created and formed according to the divinity.

As Eckhart tells us, if we humans become attached, we fall towards the realm of the creaturely, which is pure nothingness or death. This is here represented as an angel falling towards a bloated corpse with its scythe. Eckhart calls the problem of attachment (*eigenschaft*) that of clinging or caring too much for self and the creaturely. Suso's figures who are falling under death's power are touching sensuously; they are captioned.

> This is the love of the world, which ends in lamentation.

But the attitude which leads away from such a fallen state is, according to Eckhart, one which seeks not attachments to the world but rather an absence of attachments; thus would one move back towards God. The caption over this figure in prayer is,

> I want to make my return to God, for this life is but short.

For Eckhart attachments must be destroyed in order to progress. One must give up – *gelâzen* – or die to everything of the world. Suso represents this as a female figure (the soul) being shot by arrows and knives – thereby destroying all of its attachments. This in turn leads to the drained figure in the lower left corner, cleansed utterly through this purifying process: *"Gelassenheit"* (which is roughly the equivalent in Eckhart of *abegescheidenheit*, detachment)

> . . . will overpower me; alas it was too much.

One loses, in this self-stripping process, everything to which one was formerly attached as the "person." One is stripped naked, emptied entirely of the old creature.

What then? Eckhart tells us that devoid of all attachments to self and things one leaves behind all "creaturely" powers, and gains contact with the highest power within, the Word at the highest within the soul. This occurs during *Gezucket* and the Birth of the Son of the Soul within. In this diagram of the way we see,

> I have been deprived of my senses, the higher powers have conquered.

Note here that the subject is alone, in a meditative, quiet pose, perhaps with closed eyes. This "deprivation of the senses" is in accord with Eckhart's descriptions of *Gezucket*, as well as the descriptions of the silent aspect of the Birth of the Word.

Eckhart's Birth of the soul into God is similar to Suso's depiction of the next higher stage,

> Here has the spirit entered, and is found in the Trinity of the Persons.

For Eckhart the soul is born into God Who is reflexively born again into the soul. Suso, somewhat less scandalously, suggests that the soul enters into and participates in the Trinity.

The final step, however, is more sharply congruent with Eckhart:

> I have disappeared into God; no-one can find me here

suggests the absolute desert-like quality of the Breakthrough of the Soul to the Godhead. Here, for Eckhart as for Suso, there is a complete loss of individuality: one is utterly lost amidst the Divine oneness.

Finally the line leading to such a loss of the self leads back again to its source. As the mystic loses himself to the Deity in the Breakthrough, s/he rejoins that from which s/he sprang: the Trinity and ultimately the Godhead Itself.

That the soul carries within itself the empty, dynamic Godhead is indicated throughout by the concentric circle on the chest of every figure; this circle becomes especially noticeable in the final stage, in which one perceives little else *but* the Godhead.

The motifs and waystations are unmistakably congruent with those I have identified in Eckhart. First, that there is a mystical "way" at all indicates that Suso, at least, understands that there is a specifiable journey at hand: this counters those who find no mystical journey in Rhineland mysticism. Second, we see an outflow from and a return to the Godhead. The outflow leads into the creaturely attachments, which may be overcome through a process of letting go. Third, there are three advanced stages here, which are reminiscent of the Gezucket, Birth and Breakthrough I have described. Fourth, the personal discovery through the mystic's way leads to something akin to a merging with the Trinity and the Godhead.

In short, this is a striking portrait of that which we have seen in Eckhart. Both his mystical anthropology as well as his mystical itinerary are closely reflected.

Appendix B

ROMAIN ROLLAND'S LETTER TO
SIGMUND FREUD[1]

5 December, 1927

Mr dear respected friend,

Your analysis of religions is just. But I would have liked you to
do an analysis of the spontaneous religious feeling or, more
exactly, the religious sensation which is entirely different from
religions properly so called, and much more durable.

I mean by this: entirely independent of all dogma, of all
Credos, of all organization of the church, of every holy book, of
all hope for a personal survival, etc., the simple and direct fact of
the sensation of the "eternal" (which perhaps is not eternal, but
simply without perceptible limits, and like an ocean.)

This sensation is, in truth, of a subjective nature. But as with
the thousands (millions) of individual nuances, it can be shared by
thousands (millions) of actual living men, it is possible to submit
it to analysis, with an approximate exactitude.

I think that you would class this with the *Zwangsneurosen*. But I
had the opportunity to notice often its rich and beneficent
energy, either in Western religious souls, Christian or Non-
Christian—or these great spirits of Asia, with whom I became
familiar—among them I had friends—and about them I am
going to study in my next book two of the personalities which
are nearly contemporary (the first is in the end of the nineteenth

century [Ramakrishna], the second died in the early years of the twentieth [Vivekenanda]), which have manifested a genius of thought and action terribly regenerative for their country and for the world.

I am myself familiar with this feeling. All my life I have never been without this feeling. I always found in this feeling a source of vital renewal. In this way I can say that I am deeply religious. This constant state (like a sheet of water that I can feel under the bark) does no harm to my critical faculties and my freedom to exercise them, even against the immediacy of this interior experience. Thus I lead at the same time, without discomfort or pain, a "religious" life (in the sense of this prolonged sensation) and a life of critical reason (which is without illusion).

I add that this "oceanic" feeling has nothing to do with my personal aspirations. Personally I aspire to an eternal rest; survival doesn't attract me. But the feeling which I have is imposed upon me like a fact. It is a *contact*. Because I recognized it as identical (with the multiple nuances) in many living souls, it allowed me to understand that here was the veritable underground source of the religious energy; which is then captured, canalized and sucked dry by the churches: up to the point that we could say it is inside the churches (whichever they are) that one finds the least of the true "religious" feeling.

(There is an) eternal confusion of the words, the same words here: [these words] either signify obeisance or faith, to a dogma, a word (or to a tradition); or a free, vital source.

Please believe, dear friend, in my affectionate respect.

Romain Rolland

Bibliography

The following books are referred to in the text. For an exhaustive Eckhart bibliography, see O'Meara et al. For a shorter but excellent annotated Eckhart bibliography, see McGinn and Colledge.

Ancelet-Hustache, Jeanne. *Master Eckhart and the Rhineland Mystics*. Translated by Hilda Graef. New York: Harper, 1957.

Aquinas, Thomas. *Quaestitiones disputatatae de Veritate, Truth*. Volume 4. Edited and translated by J. V. McGlynn. Chicago: H. Regenry Co., 1952–4.

Ashley, Benedict M., O.P. "Three Strands in the Thought of Eckhart, the Scholastic Theologian." *The Thomist* 42 (April, 1978): 226–239.

Barciauskas, Jonas. *The Dynamic of Person in Eckhart's Mysticism and its Relation to the Sunyata Doctrine*. Dissertation, Fordham University Department of Theology, 1983.

Benedict, Saint. *The Rule of St. Benedict. Western Asceticism*. Edited and translated by Owen Chadwick. Philadelphia: The Westminster Press, 1958.

Berger, Peter. *The Sacred Canopy*. New York: Doubleday, 1969.

Bernhardt, Stephen. "Is Pure Consciousness Unmediated: A Response To Katz." Paper delivered to the American Academy of Religion, November 1985. In Robert K. C. Forman, ed., *The Problem of Pure Consciousness*. New York: Oxford University Press, 1990, pp. 220–236.

Blakney, Raymond. *Meister Eckhart: A Modern Translation*. New York: Harper and Row, 1941.

Bucke, Richard M. *Cosmic Consciousness*. New York: Causeway Books, 1900, reprint 1974.

Butler, Dom Cuthbert. *Western Mysticism: The Teachings of St. Augustine, Gregory and Bernard on Contemplation and the Contemplative Life: Neglected Chapters in the History of Religion*. London: Constable and Co., 1922.

Caputo, John D. *The Mystical Element in Heidegger's Thought*. Oberlin: Oberlin Printing Co., 1978.

_____. "Fundamental Themes in Meister Eckhart's Mysticism." *The Thomist* 42 (April 1978): 197–225.

Cassian, John. "The Conferences of Cassian." In *Western Asceticism*. Edited by Owen Chadwick. Philadelphia: The Westminster Press, 1958.

Chadwick, Henry. *The Early Church*. Middlesex: Penguin Books, 1967.

Clark, James M. *Meister Eckhart: An Introduction to the Study of his Works with an Anthology of his Sermons*. Edinburgh: Thomas Nelson and Sons, 1957.

_____. *The Great German Mystics: Eckhart, Tauler and Suso*. Oxford: Blackwells, 1949.

Clark, James M. and John V. Skinner, ed. and trans. *Meister Eckhart: Selected Treatises and Sermons*. London: Faber and Faber, 1958.

The Cloud of Unknowing and the Book of Privy Counselling. Edited by Phyllis Hodson. Early English Text Edition. Oxford: Oxford University Press, 1944, reprint 1958.

Colledge, Edmond, O.S.A. "Meister Eckhart: Studies on his Life and Work." *The Thomist* 42 (April, 1978): 240–258.

Colledge, Edmond and McGinn, Bernard. *Meister Eckhart*. New York: Paulist Press, 1978.

Constable, Giles, "Twelfth-Century Spirituality and the Late Middle Ages." *Medieval and Renaissance Studies* 5 (1969): 27–60.

Copleston, F. C., S.J. *A History of Medieval Philosophy*. New York: Harper, 1972.

_____. *A History of Philosophy, Vol. 2, Part 1: Augustine to Bonaventure*. New York: Image Books, 1962.

_____. *A History of Philosophy, Vol. 2, Part 2: Albert the Great to Duns Scotus*. New York: Image Books, 1962.

Devas, R. P., O.P. "On the History of Mental Prayer in the Order of St. Dominic." *The Irish Ecclesiastical Record*, Ser. 5, Vol. 16 (1920): 179-193.

Diekman, Arthur. "Deautomatization and the Mystic Experience." In *Altered States of Consciousness*, edited by Charles Tart. New York: John Wiley, 1969, pp. 23–44. This is a reprint of an article which first appeared in *Psychiatry* 29 (1966): pp. 329–43.

Dittrich, A. "Studies on Altered States of Consciousness (ASC) in Normals." *Research Report*. Zurich: Psychiatric University Hospital, 1980.

Drane, Augusta Theodosia (Mother Francis Raphael, O.S.D.). *The Spirit of the Dominican Order: Illustrated from the Lives of its Saints*. London: Art and Book Co., 1891.

Eckhart, Meister. All books on Eckhart are listed by editor and or translator.

Farid ud-Din Attar. *Mantiq Ut-Tair (The Conference of the Birds)*. Translated by C. S. Nott. Boulder: Shambhala Press, 1971.

Fingarette, Herbert. *The Self in Transformation: Psychoanalysis, Philosophy, and the Life of the Spirit*. New York: Harper and Row.

Fischer, Heribert, "Zur Frage nach der Mystik in den Werken Eckharts."

In *La Mystique Rhenane, Colloque de Strassbourg*. Paris: Presses Universitaires de France, 1963.

Fischer, Roland. "State Bound Knowledge: I Can't Remember What I Said Last Night but It Must Have Been Good." In R. Woods, ed., *Understanding Mysticism*. Garden City: Image Books, 1980, pp. 306–311.

Forman, Robert. "Mystical Experience in the *Cloud* Literature." In *The Medieval Mystical Tradition in England*, Vol. 4, Cambridge: D. S. Brewer, 1987.

_____. "The Construction of Mystical Experience. In *Faith and Philosophy*, 5, No. 3 (July, 1988): 254–267.

_____. "Pure Consciousness Events and Mysticism." *Sophia*, 25, No. 1 (April, 1986): 49–58.

_____. "Introduction: Mysticism, Constructivism and Forgetting." In *The Problem of Pure Consciousness*. Edited by Robert K. C. Forman. New York: Oxford University Press, 1990, pp. 3–52.

_____. "Constructivism in Modern Constructivists and in Paramārtha: Epistemological Monomorphism and Duomorphism." *Faith and Philosophy* 39, No. 4 (Nov. 1989): 393–418.

Fox, Matthew, O.P. "Meister Eckhart and Karl Marx: The Mystic as Political Theologian." In *Understanding Mysticism*. Edited by Richard Woods, O.P. Garden City, N.Y.: Image Books, 1980, pp. 541–563.

_____. *Breakthrough: Meister Eckhart's Creation Spirituality in New Translation*. New York: Image Books, 1980.

Franklin, R. L. "A Science of Pure Consciousness?" *Religious Studies* 19: 185–204.

Freud, Sigmund. *Civilization and its Discontents*. Translated and edited by James Strachey. New York: W. W. Norton and Co., 1961.

Fromm, Erik. "An Ego-psychological Theory of Altered States of Consciousness." *International Journal of Clinical Experimental Hypnosis* 25 (1977): 372–87.

Garrigou-Lagrange, R., O.P. *The Three Ages of the Interior Life: Prelude of Eternal Life*, Vol. I and II. Translated by Sr. M. Timothea Doyle, O.P. London: Herder, 1948.

Grundmann, Herbert, "Die Geschichtlichen Grundlagen der deutschen Mystik." In *Altdeutsche und Altniederländische Mystik*. Edited by K. Ruh. Darmstadt: Wissenschaftliche Buchgesellschaft, 1964, pp. 72–99.

Haas, Alois M. "Das Verhaltnis von Sprache und Erfahrung in der deutschen Mystik." In *Deutsche Literatur des späten Mittelalters*. Edited by W. Harms and L. P. Johnson, 1975, pp. 240–264.

Hallaq, J. H. "Scaling and Factor Analyzing Peak Experiences." *Journal of Clinical Psychology* 33 (1977): 77–82.

Hinnebusch, William A., O.P. *The History of the Dominican Order: Origins and Growth to 1500*. New York: Alba House, 1966.

_____. "Dominican Spirituality." *New Catholic Encyclopedia*, Vol. 4., pp. 971–974.

Holmes, Urban. *A History of Christian Spirituality*. Minneapolis: The Seabury Press, 1980.

Horne, James R. "Do Mystics Perceive Themselves?" *Religious Studies* 13: 327–33.

Hunt, H. T., and Chefurka, C. M. "A Test of the Psychedelic Model of Altered States of Consciousness." *Archives of General Psychiatry* 33 (1976): 867–76.

James, William. *The Varieties of Religious Experience: A Study in Human Nature.* New York: Penguin Books, 1982.

Jarrett, Bede, O.P. Ed. *Lives of the Brethren of the Order of Preachers.* Translated by Placid Conway, O.P. London: Blackfriars, 1955.

John of the Cross, St. *The Complete Works of Saint John of the Cross.* Edited by E. Allison Peers. London: Burns and Oates, 1943.

Johnston, William. *The Mysticism of the Cloud of Unknowing: A Modern Interpretation.* St. Meinrad, Indiana: Abbey Press, 1975.

Jones, Rufus. *The Flowering of Mysticism: The Friends of God in the Fourteenth Century.* New York: Macmillan, 1939.

Julian of Norwich. *Showings.* Translated and edited by Edmund Colledge and James Walsh. New York: Paulist Press, 1978.

Kapleau, Philip. *The Three Pillars of Zen: Teaching, Practice, and Enlightenment.* Boston: Beacon Press, 1967.

Katz, Steven. "Language, Epistemology and Mysticism." In *Mysticism and Philosophical Analysis.* Edited by Steven Katz. Oxford: Oxford University Press, 1978, pp. 22–74.

_____. ed. *Mysticism and Religious Traditions.* Oxford: Oxford University Press, 1983.

Kelley, Carl Franklin. *Meister Eckhart on Divine Knowledge.* New Haven: Yale University Press, 1977.

Kertz, Karl G., S.J. "Meister Eckhart's Teaching on the Birth of the Divine Word in the Soul." *Traditio* 15 (1959): 327–63.

Kessler, Gary and Prigge, Norman. "Is Mystical Experience Everywhere the Same?" *Sophia* 21 (April, 1982). Reprinted in *The Problem of Pure Consciousness.* Edited by Robert K. C. Forman. New York: Oxford University Press, 1990, pp. 269–287.

Kieckhefer, Richard. "Meister Eckhart's Conception of Union with God." *Harvard Theological Review,* 71 (1978): 203–225.

_____. *Unquiet Souls: Fourteenth Century Saints and their Religious Milieu.* Chicago: University of Chicago Press, 1984.

Koch, Josef, ed. *Meister Eckhart Die lateinische Werke Herausgegeben im Auftrage der Deutschen Forschungsgemeinschaft.* Stuttgart and Berlin: W. Kohlhammer Verlag, 1936.

Lagorio, Valerie. "The Medieval Continental Women Mystics: An Introduction." In *Introduction to the Medieval Mystics of Europe.* Edited by Paul Szernach. Binghamton: SUNY Press, 1984, pp. 163–174.

Landgraf, Margot. *Das St. Trudperter Hohe Lied.* Erlangen Verlag: Palm & Enke, 1935.

Leclercq, Jean, O.S.B. *The Love of Learning and the Desire for God: A Study of Monastic Culture.* New York: Fordham University Press, 1961.

Leclercq, Jean, O.S.B., J.L. François Vandendrouck, and Louis Bouyer.

Histoire de la Spiritualité Chrétienne, Vol. 2: La Spiritualité du Moyen Age. Paris: Aubier, 1961.

Leff, Gordon. *Heresy in The Later Middle Ages: The Relation of Heterodoxy to Dissent c. 1250–c. 1450*, Vol. 1. New York: Barnes and Noble, 1967.

Lehner, Francis C., O.P., ed. *Saint Dominic: Biographical Documents.* Washington D.C.: The Thomist Press.

Lerner, Robert E. *The Heresy of the Free Spirit in the Later Middle Ages.* Berkeley: University of California Press, 1972.

Lossky, V. *Théologie negative et connaissance de Dieu chez Maître Eckhart.* Paris: Vrin, 1960.

Louth, Andrew. *The Origins of the Christian Mystical Tradition: From Plato to Denys.* Oxford: Clarendon Press, 1981.

Ludwig, Arnold. "Altered States of Consciousness." In *Altered States of Consciousness*, edited by Charles Tart. New York: John Wiley and Sons, 1969, pp. 9–22. This is a reprint of an article which first appeared in *Archives of General Psychiatry* 15: 225–34.

Maharishi Mahesh Yogi. *On the Bhagavad-Gita: A New Translation and Commentary.* Baltimore: Penguin, 1972.

Maharshi Ramana. *Spiritual Teachings of Ramana Maharshi.* Boulder: Shambhala Press, 1972.

Mandonnet, Pierre F., O.P. *St. Dominic and His Work.* Translated by Sr. Mary Larkin, O.P. London: Herder, 1944.

Margetts, John. *Die Satzstruktur bei Meister Eckhart.* Stuttgart: W. Kohlhammer, 1969.

Maurer, A. ed. and trans. *Parisian Questions and Prologues.* Toronto: Pontifical Institute of Mediaeval Studies, 1970.

McGinn, Bernard. "Meister Eckhart: An Introduction." In *Introduction to the Medieval Mystics of Europe*, edited by Paul Szernach. Binghamton: SUNY Press, 1984, pp. 237–258.

_____. "The God beyond God: Theology and Mysticism in the Thought of Meister Eckhart." *Journal of Religion* 61 (1981): 1–19.

_____. "St. Bernard and Meister Eckhart." *Citeaux Com. Cist.* 1 (1980): 373–386.

_____. "Eckhart's Trial Reconsidered." *The Thomist* 44 (1980): 390–414.

Mechthilde de Magdeburg. *The Flowing Light of the Godhead.* Translated by Lucy Menzies. London: Longmans and Green, 1953.

Muktananda, Swami. *The Play of Consciousness (Chitshakti Vilas).* 2d ed. San Francisco: Harper and Row, 1978.

Naranjo, Claudio and Ornstein, Robert. *On the Psychology of Meditation.* New York: Penguin, 1972.

Needleman, Jacob. *Lost Christianity.* Garden City, New York: Doubleday, 1980.

Nishitani, Keiji. *Religion and Nothingness.* Berkeley: University of California Press, 1982.

O'Meara, Thomas. "The Presence of Meister Eckhart." *The Thomist* 42 (April, 1978): 171–81.

O'Meara, Thomas, et. al. "An Eckhart Bibliography." *The Thomist* 42 (April, 1978): 313–336.

Ornstein, Robert, ed. *The Nature of Human Consciousness.* San Francisco: W. H. Freeman and Co., 1973.

Otto, Rudolf. *Mysticism East and West: A Comparative Analysis of the Nature of Mysticism.* Translated by Bertha Bracey and Richard Payne. New York: Macmillan, 1960.

Ozment, Stephen. "Eckhart and Luther: German Mysticism and Protestantism." *The Thomist* 42 (April, 1978): 259–80.

Petry, Raymond C. "Social Responsibility and the Late Medieval Mystics." *Church History* 21 (1952): 3–19.

_____. *Late Medieval Mysticism.* Philadelphia: The Westminster Press, 1957.

Pfeiffer, Franz, trans. and ed. *Meister Eckhart.* Göttingen: Vandenhoeck and Ruprecht, 1924.

Phillips, Dayton. *Beguines in Medieval Strassburg.* Stanford University Press, 1941.

Politella, Joseph. "Meister Eckhart and Eastern Wisdom." *Philosophy East and West* 15 (1965): 117–133.

Pseudo-Dionysius Areopagite. *The Divine Names and Mystical Theology.* Translated and edited by John Jones. Milwaukee: Marquette University Press, 1980.

Quint, Josef. *Meister Eckhart: Deutsche Predigen und Traktate.* München: Carl Hanser, 1955.

_____. *Die deutsche Werke Herausgegeben im Auftrage der Deutschen Forschungsgemeinschaft.* Stuttgart and Berlin: W. Kohlhammer Verlag, 1936.

_____. "Textverstandnis und Textkritik in der Meister Eckhart Forschung," in *Festschrift fur Fritz Tschirch,* 1972, pp. 170–186.

Rolland, Romain. Letter to Sigmund Freud. *Choix de Lettres de Romain Rolland, Cahier 17.* Paris: Albin Michel, 1967, pp. 264–6.

Sartre, Jean-Paul. *The Transcendence of the Ego: An Existentialist Theory of Consciousness.* Translated by Forrest Williams and Robert Kirkpatrick. New York: Farrar, Straus and Giroux.

Schaefer, Eduard. *Meister Eckharts Traktat "Von Abegescheidenheit:" Untersuch und Textneuausgabe.* Bonn: Ludwig Rohrscheid Verlag, 1956.

Schurmann, Reiner. *Meister Eckhart: Mystic and Philosopher.* Bloomington, Indiana: Indiana University Press, 1978.

_____. "The Loss of Origin in Soto Zen and Meister Eckhart." *The Thomist* 42 (April, 1978): 281–312.

Schmoldt, Benno. *Die Deutsche Begriffssprache Meisiter Eckharts: Studien zur Philosophischen Terminologie des Mittelhochdeutschen.* Heidelberg: Quelle & Meyer, 1954.

Smart, Ninian. "Mystical Experience." *Sophia* 1 (April, 1982): pp. 19–26.

_____. "Interpretation and Mystical Experience." *Religious Studies* 1: 75–87.

Smith, Margaret. "The Nature and Meaning of Mysticism." In *Under-*

standing Mysticism, edited by Richard Woods, O.P. Garden City, New York: Image Books, 1980, pp. 19–25.

Southern, R. W. *Medieval Humanism and Other Studies*. Oxford: Oxford University Press, 1970.

_____. *Western Society and the Church in the Middle Ages*. New York: Penguin, 1970.

Stace, W. T. *Mysticism and Philosophy*. New York: The Macmillan Press, 1960.

Suso, Henry. *Little Rock of Eternal Wisdom and Little Book of Truth*. London: Faber and Faber, 1953.

Suzuki, D. T. *Mysticism: Christian and Buddhist*. New York: Macmillan, 1957.

Tart, Charles. "Introduction." In *Altered States of Consciousness*. Edited by Charles Tart. New York: John Wiley and Sons, 1969, pp. 1–6.

_____. *States of Consciousness*. New York: E. P. Dutton, 1975.

Tauler, John. *Spiritual Conferences*. Translated by E. Colledge and Sr. M. Jane, O.P. Rockford, Illinois: Tan Books, 1978.

Thapa, Komilla and Murthy, Vinoda. "Experiential Characteristics of Certain Altered States of Consciousness." *The Journal of Transpersonal Psychology* 17 (1985): 77–86.

Thorne, F. C. "The Clinical Use of Peak and Nadir Experiences Reports." *Journal of Clinical Psychology* 19 (1963): 248–55.

Tobin, Frank. "Eckhart's Mystical Use of Language: The Contexts of *eigenschaft*." *Seminar* 8 (1972): 159–68.

_____. *Meister Eckhart*. Philadelphia: University of Pennsylvania Press, 1986.

Tuchman, Barbara. *A Distant Mirror: The Calamitous Fourteenth Century*. New York: Ballantine Books, 1978.

Tugwell, Simon, O.P., ed. *Early Dominicans: Selected Writings*. New York: Paulist Press, 1982.

Ueda, Shizuteru. *Die Gottesgeburt in der Seele und der Durchbruch zur Gottheit: Die mystische Anthropologie Meister Eckharts und ihre Konfrontation mit der Mystische des Zen Buddhismus*. Gutersloher: Gerd Mohn, 1965.

Underhill, Evelyn. *Mysticism: A Study in the Nature and Development of Man's Spiritual Consciousness*. New York: Dutton, 1961.

Vicaire, M. H., O.P. *St. Dominic and His Times*. Translated by Kathleen Pond. London: Darton Longman and Todd, 1964.

Wainwright, William. *Mysticism*. Madison: University of Wisconsin Press, 1983.

Walshe, M. O'C. *Meister Eckhart: German Sermons and Treatises*. 2 vols. London: Watkins, 1979, 1981.

Weber, Richard K. "The Search for Identity and Community in the Fourteenth Century." *The Thomist*, 42 (April 1978): 182–196.

Weithaus, Ulrich. *The Reality of Mystical Experience: Self and World in the Work of Mechthilde of Magdeburg*. Ph.D. dissertation, Temple University Department of Religion, 1986.

Wentzlaff-Eggebert, Friedrich-Wilhelm. Deutsche Mystik zwischen Mitt-elalter und Neuzeit: Einheit und Wandlund ihrer Erscheinungsformen. Berlin, 1969.

Zaehner, R. C. *Zen, Drugs and Mysticism.* New York: Random House, 1973.

Notes

CHAPTER ONE

[1] An excellent annotated bibliography can be found in Colledge and McGinn. For a complete bibliography see O'Meara, et. al., "An Eckhart Bibliography," *The Thomist* 42 (1978): 313–336.

[2] Benedict Ashley, "Three Strands in the Thought of Eckhart, the Scholastic Theologian," *The Thomist* 42 (1978): 226–239.

[3] For example, Bernard McGinn's "The God beyond God: Theology and Mysticism in the Thought of Meister Eckhart," *Journal of Religion* 61 (1982): 1–19.

[4] Karl Kertz, S. J. "Meister Eckhart's Teaching on the Birth of the Divine Word in the Soul," *Traditio* 15 (1959): 327–63.

[5] Carl Kelley, *Meister Eckhart on Divine Knowledge* (New Haven: Yale University Press, 1977).

[6] V. Lossky, *Théologie negative et connaissance de Dieu chez Maître Eckhart* (Paris: Virn, 1960).

[7] R. W. Southern, *Medieval Humanism and Other Studies* (Oxford: Oxford University Press, 1970), p. 20 writes: "At the university of Paris he performed the usual scholastic exercises, and on the great philosophical questions of the day he adopted the views we should expect of a member of his Order. His strictly academic writings attracted no great attention in his own time and were forgotten after his death. They would certainly not occupy us now if he had left nothing else behind him: they contain clear evidence of a powerful mind, one that was not at ease or not fully extended in academic work. The place where Eckhart exerted his full strength was not in the lecture room but in the pulpit, and there, not in his Latin sermons to the learned, but in his vernacular sermons to the unlearned."

[8] W 1:1. See also W 1:80, 81, 83, 84, 127. Also see Clark and Skinner, pp. 101, 163 ff.

[9] W 2:165.

[10] W 2:166.

[11] Cf. Kieckhefer, p. 211–2.

[12] W 2:267.

[13] W 2:166.

[14] W 1:91.

[15] W 2:78.

[16] W 2:101.

[17] The great scholar of Jewish mysticism Moshe Idel recently remarked in a Symposium on Jewish Mysticism held at the Jewish Theological Seminary (1986) that all of the utterances of a mystic should be read in the light of his or her principal emphasis. With this I agree.

[18] This is less true of Caputo 1978b and Kieckhefer. However, these accounts do not provide a clear sense of any experiences, as I will discuss.

[19] As well as all the aforementioned, see also McGinn in Szernach. This is the best brief introduction to date in English.

[20] Clark, pp. 26–98.

[21] Kieckhefer discusses in some detail Eckhart's anthropology in terms of God's ontological relationship to man, p. 212, only following which he discusses the experiences Eckhart describes. McGinn in Szernach answers the anthropological question in terms of the dialectical relation between the particular thing in its particularity as this or that existence (*esse hoc et hoc*) and its existence "in the principle" (*in principio*), the virtual reality it has in God, the universal formal cause of all things, p. 250. Only afterwards does he discuss the experiences Eckhart touches upon.

[22] See for example the articles by Owen, Carman, Ching, and Schimmel in *Mysticism and Religious Traditions*, ed. Steven Katz (Oxford: Oxford University Press, 1983).

[23] Kieckhefer, pp. 203–225. See also Dietmar Mieth, *Die Einheit und Vita activa und contemplativa in den deutschen Predigen und Traktaten Meister Eckharts und bei Johannes Tauler: Untersuchungen zur Struktur des christlichen Lebens* (Regensburg: Friedrich Pustet, 1969), pp. 119–233. See here also Caputo, pp. 197–225.

[24] Swami Muktananda, *The Play of Consciousness*, 2d ed. (San Francisco: Harper and Row, 1978).

[25] St. John of the Cross, *The Complete Works of Saint John of the Cross*, ed. E. Allison Peers (London: Burns and Oates, 1943). *The Cloud of Unknowing and the Book of Privy Counselling*, ed. Phyllis Hodson (Oxford: Oxford University Press, 1944, reprint 1958). This is the Early English Text Society's edition. See my "Mystical Experience in the *Cloud* Literature," *The Medieval Mystical Tradition in England*, Vol. 4 (Cambridge: D. S. Brewer, 1987), pp 177–195.

[26] For the thoughts in this paragraph, I am grateful to a private correspondence from John Caputo, 1983.

[27] W 2:201, 2:210.

[28] W 2:206, n. 12.

[29] Ninian Smart, "Interpretation and Mystical Experience," *Religious Studies* 1: pp. 75–87.

[30] Ibid., p. 79.

[31] Ibid., p. 79.

[32] Ibid., p. 80.

[33] An excellent summary of this notion is in the introduction of Frederick Suppe, ed., *The Structure of Scientific Theories*, 2d ed. (Urbana: University of Illinois Press, 1977).

[34] Quoting Pseudo-Dionysius Areopagite *De mystica theologia* 1. The best English translation is *The Divine Names and Mystical Theology*, trans. and ed. John Jones (Milwaukee: Marquette University Press, 1980).

[35] W 1:8.

[36] Kertz, p. 1, 337.

[37] Friedrich-Wilhelm Wentzlaff-Eggebert, *Deutsche Mystik zwischen Mittelalter und Neuzeit: Einheit und Wandlund ihrer Erscheinungsformen* (Berlin, 1969), p. 95.

[38] Ueda, p. 36.

[39] Caputo, p. 223.

[40] Robert K. C. Forman, "Constructivism in Zen Buddhism, Paramārtha, and in Eckhart," Ph.D. dissertation, Columbia University, 1988. Idem., "The Construction of Mystical Experience," *Faith and Philosophy* 5, No. 3 (1988), pp. 254–267. Idem., "Introduction: Mysticism, Constructivism and Forgetting," in Robert K. C. Forman, editor, *The Problem of Pure Consciousness* (N.Y.: Oxford University Press, 1990), pp. 3–52.

[41] Schurmann, 1978a, p. xii.

[42] Colledge and McGinn, p. 25.

[43] Schurmann, 1978b, p. xii. See also here Caputo, p. 101, and Jonas Barciauskas, *The Dynamic of Person in Eckhart's Mysticism and its Relation to the Sunyata Doctrine* (Dissertation: Fordham University Department of Theology, 1983), pp. 12–13.

[44] The principal journal of this discussion has been the *Journal of Transpersonal Psychology*, which began in 1969. *Altered States of Consciousness* ed. Charles Tart, is a well known book which amplifies this notion from a variety of disciplines, as does Tart's *States of Consciousness*. See also *The Nature of Human Consciousness*, ed. Robert Ornstein (San Francisco: W. H. Freeman and Co., 1973) and *The Psychology of Meditation* by C. Naranjo and R. Ornstein (New York: Penguin, 1972). There has been some debate, largely inspired by Zaehner's *Zen, Drugs and Mysticism* (New York: Random House, 1973) over whether it is legitimate to view mysticism as of a piece with drug experiences. See here Wainwright's rejoinder to Zaehner in *Mysticism* (Madison: University of Wisconsin Press, 1983) Chapter II, and Smart. I will not attempt to adjudicate this difficult issue here except to say that even to Zaehner, who argues that this phenomenological parallel does not denote a philosophical identity, the phenomenological parallels between altered states produced by psychoactive drugs and mystical states of consciousness are at least striking enough that he would see fit to raise the question.

[45] Margaret Smith, "The Nature and Meaning of Mysticism," in *Understanding Mysticism*, ed. Richard Woods, O. P. (Garden City, N.Y.: Image Books, 1980), pp. 19–25.

[46] Smith, p. 20.

[47] Caputo, pp. 203–17; Schurmann (1978b); D. T. Suzuki, *Mysticism: Christian and Buddhist* (New York: Macmillan, 1957) pp. 13–20; Ueda; and Keiji Nishitani, *Religion and Nothingness* (Berkeley: University of California Press, 1982).

[48] Smart, "Mystical Experience," *Sophia* 1 (April, 1962): 20.

[49] Smart, "Interpretation and Mystical Experience," *Religious Studies* 1: 75–87.

[50] Smart, "Interpretation and Mystical Experience," p. 75

[51] The first to make this claim was Heribert Fischer, who in 1960 claimed that the designation of Eckhart as a "mystic" is a mere invention of literary scholars. "Zur Frage nach der Mystik in den Werken Meister Eckharts", *Le Mystique Rhenane, Colloque de Strasbourg* (Paris: Presses Universitaires de . . .). His view was echoed by J. Margetts in *Die Satzstruktur bei Meister Eckhart,* 1969, p. 167. A crushing rejoinder is found in Josef Quint's, "Textverstandnis und Textkritik in der Meister Eckhart Forschung," in *Festschrift für Fritz Tschirch,* 1972, pp. 170–186. See also Alois M. Haas, "Das Verhaltnis von Sprache und Erfahrung in der deutschen Mystik," in *Deutsche Literatur des späten Mittelalters,* ed. W. Harms and L. P. Johnson, 1975, pp. 240–264.

[52] Colledge and McGinn, p. 61. Cf. Reiner Schurmann, 1978b, p. 15; Caputo, Udea. Kelley on pp. 107–8 denies that Eckhart had any interest in experiences whatsoever when he characterizes him as a "pure metaphysician." There his arguments show, however, that by "no interest in experiences" he means rather no interest in special states of experience.

[53] The first three are similar to Ueda, pp. 23–4. Many of the quotations in those sections are also noted by him.

[54] Quint denies that this story is connected with the anecdote of the "pregnant monk" and views this story as illustrative. Walshe, p. 1:161 n. 7, asserts that we have here a record of a personal experience.

[55] W 1:158.

[56] James, William. *The Varieties of Religious Experience: A Study in Human Nature* (New York: Penguin, 1982), p. 422. James, however, spoke of the experience as being authoritative, and Eckhart seems to regard his own utterances as authoritative.

[57] Edited by Kurt Ruh in *Festschrift für Josef Quint,* (Bonn: 1964). See the note in Walshe, Vol 1, p. xxxix.

[58] Ibid.

[59] W 32–33. Edmund Colledge points out that there were two "Meister Eckharts" active during Suso's time, Colledge and McGinn, p. 18–19. It is hard to know what he concludes from this interesting fact, however. On the one hand he seems to conclude with certainty—both against the claims of logic and common sense—that the vision was of "Eckhart the younger," and not our man. At most we might conclude that Suso's vision *may* have been about this other man. On the other hand Colledge concludes that, by means of this vision, Suso has defended his teacher's good name. If it is a vision of Eckhart the younger, it says nothing

about his teacher's name. I would say that given the obvious influence of our Eckhart on Suso as well as the mention of the "wolfish men," it is most likely that this was indeed a vision of our subject.

[60] There is a similar passage by Taular, another of Eckhart's disciples, retold by Colledge and McGinn, p. 16, which leaves a similar impression.

CHAPTER TWO

[1] Jeanne Ancelet-Hustache, *Master Eckhart and the Rhineland Mystics*, trans. Hilda Graef (New York: Harper, 1957), p. 10. This does not necessarily indicate a "feminist" spirituality, as Fox argues anachronistically.

[2] See below. See also Robert E. Lerner, *The Heresy of the Free Spirit in the Later Middle Ages*, (Berkeley: University of California Press, 1972) and Dayton Phillips, *Beguines in Medieval Strasburg* (Stanford: Stanford University Press, 1941).

[3] Richard K. Weber, "The Search for Identity and Community in the Fourteenth Century," *The Thomist* 42 (April 1978): 182–196., esp. p. 183.

[4] Flanders and Northern Italy also witnessed an especially dramatic rise of cities. R. W. Southern, *Western Society and the Church in the Middle Ages* (New York: Penguin, 1970) p. 45.

[5] Southern, p. 322–3.

[6] Southern, p. 21.

[7] Cf. Weber, p. 193.

[8] Peter Berger, *The Sacred Canopy*, (New York: Doubleday, 1969).

[9] An interest in mysticism is not isolated to this day and age. A similar coalescence can be seen in a remarkable number of cases. The Hindu Upanisadic fascination with the personal realization that one's *Atman* was identified with *Brahman* occurred amidst the social transformation from the nomadic and tribal Vedic world to the settled agrarian and urban civilization which was then becoming established in North Western India. See here Romila Thapar, *A History of India, Volume 1*, (Baltimore: Penguin Books, 1966) pp. 33–47. Simultaneously and not unrelated, North East India witnessed similar changes from the old social forms to "the more complex forms of economic and political activity associated with the later phases of the urban revolution and the territorial expansion of new imperial states." See Peter Pardue's excellent *Buddhism*, (New York: The Macmillan Company, 1971). p. 1. It was in such a context that a broad interest in mysticism developed, which was seen not only in Buddhism itself but as well in the broader movements of the Ajivikas, Shravakas, Jains, and idiosyncratic solitary ascetics. In China, although the Buddhist missionaries entered that country as early as the first century A.D., the widespread fascination with the mystically oriented Buddhism began only in the sixth

and seventh centuries, following the loss of the north to the Huns and the collapse of the Chin dynasty and its Confucian-dominated synthesis. See Arthur · Wright, *Buddhism in Chinese History* (Stanford Ca.: Stanford University Press, 1959) pp. 3–65. In the Christian West, Anthony and Pachomius, the desert ascetics, appear early in the fourth century. Their followers became a flood later in the same century, the time when the Roman order was collapsing. See on this Henry Chadwick, *The Early Church* (Middlesex: Penguin Books, 1967), p. 178. A millennium later the great Spanish mystics, St. Teresa and St. John of the Cross, appear during the tumultuous reformation. In our own age, a renewed fascination with mysticism occurs amidst our own social upheavals towards a modern urban polity and increasingly mobile society and its corresponding loss of *communitas*. Cf. Peter Berger, *The Sacred Canopy*, (New York: Doubleday, 1969), p. 105–126. Although such a sweep is bound to be oversimplified, I think it is clear that there is an interesting pattern here.

[10] Barbara W. Tuchman, *A Distant Mirror* (New York: Ballantine Books, 1978), pp. 26–7.

[11] Quoted by Matthew Fox, *Breakthrough: Meister Eckhart's Creation Spirituality in New Translation* (New York: Image Books) p. 13, no reference.

[12] Tuchman, pp. 26–8.

[13] Weber, p. 194.

[14] Ibid.

[15] Ibid.

[16] A similar insight can be found in Weber, p. 195. What he does not point out is that again this is no isolated phenomenon. The collapse of a social and institutional synthesis is frequently accompanied by the loss of credibility and respect for the specialists of the religious system, and with them the system itself. For example, as the authors of the Upanisads moved further and further from the sacrificial system, the priests who administered them came to be seen as old-fashioned and uncreative. A frequent theme seen in the Upanisads is the discomfiture—sometimes even to ridicule—of the sacrificial specialists, the Brahmans. In China the collapse of the Chin dynasty was accompanied by the loss of respect for the Confucians who had maintained the status quo. When the upholders of a belief system—and with them the system they represented—lose their credibility the individual is left devoid of plausible religious leadership and systematic religious belief. The resultant vacuum of meaning sets up a craving for some religious system to "fill the gap"; one that is unaffiliated with the established religious authorities. Mysticism is, of course, well suited for such a role.

[17] McGinn in Szernach, p. 238.

[18] Matthew Fox, "Meister Eckhart and Karl Marx: The Mystic as Political Theologian," in *Understanding Mysticism*, ed. Richard Woods, O.P. (Garden City, N.J.: Image Books, 1980), pp. 541–563.

[19] McGinn's specification of the ecclesiastical pressures at work on Eckhart is making a similar claim, i.e. that though he was not a revolution-

ary, some forces were at work on the development of Eckhart's interest in mysticism.

[20] Urban Holmes, *A History of Christian Spirituality*, (Minneapolis: The Seabury Press, 1980), p. 72 does this, for example.

[21] For an introduction to this tradition, see Valerie Lagorio, "The Medieval Continental Women Mystics: An Introduction," in Paul Szernach, ed., *Introduction to the Medieval Mystics of Europe*, (Binghamton: SUNY Press, 1984), pp. 163–174; Ancelet-Hustache, pp. 8–13.

[22] The socio-political forces outlined above concern a later century than hers. I have enumerated them to account for the widespread interest in mysticism; Hildegard was a somewhat solo figure and I make no claims about the social forces at work on her.

[23] See here Margot Landgraf, *Das St. Trudperter Hohe Lied*, (Erlangen Verlag: Palm & Enke, 1935.)

[24] The Beguines were one of the few significant Christian religious movements to have begun as women's movement. Phillips argues that this is due, among other reasons, both to an increase in the numbers of unmarried females due to frequent wars and to the degrading status of lower class women as the Beguines frequently were. Dayton Phillips, *Beguines in Medieval Strassburg* (Stanford: Stanford University Press, 1941), p. 27 ff.

[25] Mechthilde de Magdeburg, *The Flowing Light of the Godhead*, trans. Lucy Menzies (London: Longmans and Green, 1953).

[26] Matthew Paris, *Chronica Majora*, iv. 278. Quoted in Southern, p. 319.

[27] Ibid., v. 194. Southern, p. 320.

[28] As reported by Southern, pp. 322–325.

[29] By this time, due in large part to the Plague, Cologne had declined to roughly 20,000. Southern, p. 323.

[30] Dayton Phillips, *Beguines in Medieval Strasburg*, (Stanford: Stanford University Press, 1941), p. 227.

[31] Ibid.

[32] As noted by Phillips, p. 227, who said that the Beguines "must have represented a considerable phenomenon in the spiritual life of the town."

[33] Phillips notes that Beguinages were frequently leased at low rates from Dominican and Franciscan priories, p. 70.

[34] Phillips, pp. 70–91

[35] Southern 328, J. Asen, "Die Beginen in Köln," *Annalen des Hist Vereins f. den Niederrhein*, (1927–8) cxi, pp. 81–180; cxii, pp. 2, 71–148; cxiii, pp. 13–96. Here cxi, pp. 90–1.

[36] Fox 1980b, p. 38.

[37] Hinnebusch, pp. 388–93.

[38] Hinnebusch, p. 378.

[39] Ibid.

[40] Ashley, p. 228. Similarly Christopher Kauffman, *Tamers of Death: The History of the Alexian Brothers*, (New York: Seabury Press, 1976) p. 123.

[41] See here Weber, p. 191, and Southern, p. 321.

[42] Phillips, p. 19.

[43] Phillips, p. 27.

[44] Southern, p. 326.

[45] H. Grundmann, "Die geschichtliche Grundlagen der deutschen Mystik," in K. Ruh, ed., *Aldeutsche und Altniederländische Mystik* (Darmstadt, 1964), pp. 72–99. Quoted in McGinn (1984), p. 243.

[46] Grundmann, p. 87–9.

[47] Mechthilde, pp. 174–5.

[48] Mechthilde, pp. 47–8.

[49] Mechthilde, p. 226.

[50] Mechthilde, p. xviii.

[51] Mechthilde, p. 252.

[52] Translated in Ancelet-Hustache, 17–18.

[53] Mechthilde of Magdeburg, *Das fliessend Licht der Gottheit*, ed. P. Gall Morel, 1869 (reprinted 1963), p. 7–8. Quoted in Southern, p. 327.

[54] For a translation of these documents, see Southern p. 329 and 330.

[55] Lerner, pp. 68–80.

[56] Hinnebusch, p. 388–93.

[57] It is striking that we have a letter from Eckhart concerning this convent. Since he lived at the same time as Agnes, he may very well have known her.

[58] Simon Tugwell, O.P., ed., *Early Dominicans: Selected Writings.* (New York: Paulist Press, 1982), p. 420.

[59] Cf. McGinn in Szernach, p. 243–4.

[60] Ibid., p. 243.

[61] Ibid., p. 244.

[62] As Southern does, pp. 274–7.

[63] "I will be obedient to you and your successors until death"; Constitution 1:15. This is found in Francis Lehner, C., O.P. ed., *Saint Dominic: Biographical Documents* (Washington, D.C.: The Thomist Press). Lehner provides a translation of the first constitution of the Dominican order. Taken from manuscripts at the Dominican priory in Rodez France, it was a product of the first chapter (1216) and the second (1220), and assembled in the first General Chapter in 1228.

[64] He shall "neither receive nor carry with [him] any gold, silver, money or gifts, but only food, clothing, books, and other necessary objects;" Constitution 1:31.

[65] He was "to be free from the care of administration of temporalities, so that [he] may more effectively accomplish his spiritual task," that of preaching; Constitution 1:31.

[66] Hinnebusch p. 120. Constitution No. 3.

[67] Paraphrased from Hinnebusch, p. 123.

[68] Hinnebusch, p. 134.

[69] Southern, p. 307. Eckhart nowhere encourages such practices.

[70] Unlike the traditional rule, to break silence regularly became a "grave fault." When Dominic counseled a house of Spanish Nuns to a life of discipline, he mentioned fasts, vigils and obedience; but no fewer than

three times in this short letter he counsels them to maintain the silence and "let not [their] time be wasted in conversation." Lehner, pp. 91–2.

[71] For assurance of this I am grateful to Fr. Hennesy of the Dominican Friars Guild, New York.

[72] For the information in this paragraph see R. P. Devas, O.P., "On the History of Mental Prayer in the Order of St. Dominic." *The Irish Ecclesiastical Record* Ser. 5, Vol. 16. (1920), pp. 177–193; and Hinnebusch, p. 352–3.

[73] Bede Jarrett, O.P. ed., *Lives of the Brethren of the Order of Preachers*, trans. Placid Conway. O.P. (London: Blackfriars, 1955), p. 133.

[74] Jarrett, p. 184.

[75] Jarrett, pp. 133; 142–3; 190–7; 191.

[76] Cf. Richard Kieckhefer, *Unquiet Souls: Fourteenth Century Saints and their Religious Milieu*, (Chicago: University of Chicago Press, 1984).

[77] Hinnebusch, pp. 383–4.

[78] Ibid.

[79] Hinnebusch, p. 124. St. Thom. *Summa* II, II, q. 188, a. 6; q. 182, a. 1.

[80] Either the one near Erfurt or the one near Gotha. Tobin, *Meister Eckhart* (Philadelphia: University of Pennsylvania Press, 1986), chapter one. I have seen only the manuscript; hence I cannot give page references.

[81] He quotes an otherwise unknown saying of Albert, which suggests that he had heard it personally.

[82] DW Vol. 5., pp. 137–376. Colledge and McGinn, pp. 247–284; Clark and Skinner pp. 63–108.

[83] A. Maurer, ed. and trans., *Parisian Questions and Prologues* (Toronto: Pontifical Institute of Mediaeval Studies, 1970).

[84] Phillips, pp. 19, 227, *et passim*.

[85] Blakney, p. 258.

[86] Colledge and McGinn, pp. 10–15, and Tobin, *Meister Eckhart*. Each devote many pages to it. I especially commend McGinn, "Eckhart's Trial Reconsidered." *The Thomist* 44 (1980): 390–414, which investigates whether Eckhart was genuinely heretical and concludes, like most recent studies, for his orthodoxy.

[87] He describes them as having "ignorance and shortness of understanding." Blakney, p. 304.

[88] As noted in the Papal Bull, Colledge and McGinn, p. 81.

[89] Blakney.

[90] Contra Fox, "Meister Eckhart and Karl Marx: The Mystic as Political Theologian," who presents Eckhart as a social radical.

[91] That he was so accompanied and that, as he said in a letter, the trial was perceived as an embarrassment for his entire order indicates that the order regarded him as a son in good standing.

[92] As Tobin remarks in *Meister Eckhart*, the fact that they took propositions from every important work suggests that they were attempting to render a judgment on his work as a whole. Tobin (1986), Chapter One.

[93] Tobin, *Meister Eckhart*.

[94] Clark (1957), p. 99. Carl Kelley, *Meister Eckhart on Divine Knowledge* (New Haven: Yale University Press, 1977), p. 1, writes that Eckhart "must

be ranked on a par with the most profound intellects and spiritual guides of Christendom and indeed of our whole Western Civilization."
    [95] Weber, p. 195.

CHAPTER THREE

    [1] Quotation p. 51 adapted from W 2:119.
    [2] Ancelet-Hustache, p. 59. Perhaps she has in mind LW 3:246, one of the few references to this division. Evelyn Underhill, *Mysticism: A Study in the Nature and Development of Man's Spiritual Consciousness* (New York: Dutton, 1961), pp. 198–452, discusses these phases, and mentions Eckhart frequently.
    [3] Clark, p. 93.
    [4] Ibid.
    [5] Rudolf Otto, *Mysticism East and West: A Comparative Analysis of the Nature of Mysticism*, trans. Bertha Bracey and Richard Payne (New York: Macmillan, 1960), pp. 63–72.
    [6] In what way the third's "real above" is distinguished from the second's "superior and prior to" he doesn't say. Nor does he clearly distinguish "all is one" from "one prior to many." It seems to me that his desire for cross-cultural similarities has led him to glib distinctions.
    [7] Otto, p. 62. It is unclear why he would use a term like *stage* for these distinctions. Furthermore, these distinctions may be mere linguistic niceties, and not denote different aspects of an experience at all.
    [8] It is not at all clear what Eckhart passages he had in mind with his division. The book, at least in its English version, is often marred by its lack of textual support and references.
    [9] Caputo, pp. 197–225.
    [10] Ibid., p. 224.
    [11] Barciauskas, *The Dynamic of Person in Eckhart's Mysticism and its Relation to the Sunyata Doctrine*, and personal correspondence, 1985.
    [12] Kieckhefer, pp. 219–220.
    [13] To be precise he writes that these are steps which lead up to and anticipate the passage about the soul's dying in itself before passing over to God. In their original context, however, they enumerate a progressive and developmental series which includes this "passing over." Hence I view them as more than merely anticipatory.
    [14] Kieckhefer, p. 220.
    [15] Although he cannot, of course, consider all passages in a single article, one has to wonder what he would make of one of the more explicitly mystical stage enumerations, e.g. W 1:83, which explicitly includes references to Paul's rapturous encounter. See below.

16 They are: LW 3:246; LW 4:202; W 1:45, 83–4, 204, 260, 266, 273, 277; W 2:135, 202, 204–5, 245, 259, 283, 328; Clark and Skinner, p. 151. In this list I have selected not only passages in which Eckhart states categorically that he is doing stage "analysis" but also those passages which are clearly progressive and developmental.

17 W 1:83–4, 260, 273; 2:245, 328; LW 3:246.

18 W 1:83–4.

19 W 1:260.

20 LW 3:246.

21 LW 4:202; W 1:277; 2:202, 259.

22 W 2:202–3.

23 W 2:259–60.

24 W 1:277.

25 Clark and Skinner, p. 151.

26 W 1:204.

27 W 2:259, 202.

28 W 1:260, 277.

29 E.g. W 1:83–4.

30 W 1:83–4.

31 E.g. W 1:204.

32 Clark and Skinner, pp. 151–2. This is near to Augustine's *De Vera Religione* c. 26, n. 29.

33 Though speaking often to houses of nuns, Eckhart frequently uses the masculine. Herein I have attempted to follow Eckhart's own genders, which are often determined by German grammar.

34 Augustine mentions a seventh stage; though Eckhart places it outside the scheme, as Clark and Skinner note in a gloss.

35 W 1:273.

36 W 2:135.

37 LW 3:246.

38 W 1:204, W 2:328, respectively. This latter ambiguous passage may be read as the characteristics of some static "darkness" or as a more dynamic series of developmental stages which lead to it. I think that the latter is intended.

39 The following quotations are from W 1:204–5.

40 W 2:135.

41 W 1:205.

42 W 1:204, 260, 266.

43 W 2:260. Is this "eternity" *post mortem*, as Kieckhefer suggests on p. 220, or here on earth, as Walshe suggests in a parenthesis and gloss, p. 2:261 n.15? Eckhart remains perhaps intentionally ambiguous, though Eckhart's use of "here" on earth, as well as the Divine-on-Earth theme of the sermon as a whole suggests to me the latter. The "*surge*," arise, spoken to the girl in Luke 8:54, the passage Eckhart here explicates, is an arising on Earth. Cf. the earthly heaven spoken of in Cassian, p. 202.

44 W 1:260.

45 W 1:273.

[46] W 1:277.

[47] W 2:202.

[48] W 1:83.

[49] W 1:83.

[50] W 2:259.

[51] W 2:202.

[52] Keickhefer, p. 220. Kieckhefer goes to lengths to recast such ecstatic-sounding passages as steps in a strictly moral process. His reading, though inconclusive, is reasonable. About his reinterpretation process he writes that every such passage may easily be read either as hyperbolic (e.g. here, according to him, referring to a moral process) or as literal (in this case referring to an ecstatic moment), p. 217. This is, of course, a two-edged sword. If any passage, e.g. this one, may be reinterpreted as moral, so too it (or another passage) can be reinterpreted in the service of a more mystical reading.

[53] LW 3:246, trans. by Clark and Skinner, pp. 206–7.

[54] St. Thomas, Quaestitiones disputatatae de Veritate, *Truth* Volume 4, ed. and trans. J. V. McGlynn (Chicago: H. Regenry Co. 1952–4), q. 13, a. 2. pp. 189–90.

[55] De Divinis Nominibus, c. 4 No. 13.

[56] Kieckhefer, p. 224.

CHAPTER FOUR

[1] McGinn, p. 96.

[2] W 2:53.

[3] Maurer, p. 143. Comm. John No. 59.

[4] Maurer, p. 108.

[5] Liber XXIV Philosophorum, prop. 1: ed. D Baeumker, Beitrage zur Geschichte der Philosophie des Mittelalters, 25 1/2 (Munster, 1927), p. 208. Reference from Maurer, p. 108, n. 10.

[6] Maurer 108.

[7] For a more technical analysis the interested reader should consult McGinn, Kertz, Kelley.

[8] W 1:249. C.f. W 1:99.

[9] W 2:80–82.

[10] McGinn, p. 98.

[11] Comm. John, n. 342 (LW III, p. 291). Translation McGinn, p. 37. See n. 74.

[12] I am indebted here to Colledge and McGinn, p. 38–9.

[13] McGinn, p. 96.

[14] See for example McGinn pp. 123–6, 145–6, 148–9.

[15] W 2:288.

[16] W 2:63–4.

[17] W 1:xlvii. This is out of the Papal Bull, No. 11. According to McGinn and others, this should be read with a caveat: it is true but only *inquantum*, insofar as, the man is just, etc.

[18] 2:135. This passage was similar to those condemned in the Papal Bull. For a caveat, see the preceding footnote.

[19] W 2:62

[20] Maurer, p. 93.

[21] Comm. Wis., nn. 19–22 (LW II, pp. 339–53.) McGinn.

[22] McGinn, p. 89. This quote from *Confessions* 4:12:18.

[23] W 2:53.

[24] Ibid.

[25] Aquinas, *Sys. Theol.* Ia. 94. 1. McGinn.

[26] Para. Gen 143; McGinn, p. 112. Quote from *Sys. Theol.*, Ia.94.2.

[27] *Para. Gen.*, 144; McGinn, p. 112.

[28] McGinn, p. 140.

[29] McGinn, p. 156.

[30] W 1:i Papal Bull, Proposition No. 26.

[31] To call the nonexistent a "realm" gives it a status Eckhart would deny of it.

[32] Ibid.

[33] *Para. Gen.* 145; McGinn, 112.

[34] W 1:1.

[35] For example, Maurer, p. 101; W 1:76, 77, etc. See DW index on "*daz*".

[36] Because for Eckhart it both is pivotal and subtly nuanced, this term has been commented on numerous times. See Tobin (1972); Schmoldt; Quint (1955); Schurmann (1978a); Caputo (1978b). Tobin's recent and careful analysis is the most relevant for our purposes here. The other important recent study of *Eigenschaft* was by Schmoldt in his *Die Deutsche Begriffessprache Meister Eckharts*. Schmoldt attempted to find Latin equivalents for Eckhart's more fluid and imprecise German. He consigns *Eigenschaft* to the Latin terms *proprietas* and *qualitas*. This equivalence is appropriate when explicating a text like DW 1:131:4 = W 2:244 or DW 1:164:3 = W 2:141, where *Eigenshaft* is used to signify the *proprietates*, relations, by means of which one may distinguish between the divine persons or may understand the divine characteristics. Thus Eckhart's statement that "God's *Eigenschaft* is being" found in DW 1:131:4 = W 2:244 is presenting a *proprietates*. But we are analyzing here the more "creaturely" aspect of the term in order to sense the nature of one's pre-transformation relationship with the world.

[37] Benecke-Muller, 1:416.

[38] DW 1:25:8–9 = W 1:73.

[39] DW 1:29:6–7 = W 1:73.

[40] W 1:73.

[41] W 1:100.

[42] Clark and Skinner, p. 176.

[43] Clark and Skinner, p. 163.

[44] W 1:42.

[45] Clark, pp. 166–7.

[46] Clark and Skinner, p. 176.

[47] W 1:42.

[48] See Chapter 5 below.

[49] W 2:134. That all attachments ultimately come down to the attachment to the self is expressed by *The Cloud of Unknowing*, p. 102.

[50] For this insight I am indebted to Tobin, p. 163.

[51] DW 1:28:8 = 1:72.

[52] DW 1:30:1 = W 1:73.

[53] Tobin, p. 163.

[54] W 1:172.

[55] Ibid.

[56] Ochracter, pp. 166–7.

[57] William Wordworth, "The World is too much with us."

[58] W 2:158.

[59] W 1:142–3.

[60] W 1:80. This is a converse reading of a description of the goal. I think it is appropriate to quote it thus since in describing the goal he suggests the form of life which it is not. See below for its full transcription.

[61] W 2:125.

[62] Schurmann and Caputo, both Heideggerian scholars, overemphasize to the point of absurdity Eckhart's term *gelassenheit*. Though Eckhart used it but once, in DW 5:283:8, each devotes an entire chapter to its explication! Eckhart uses more commonly the terms *lâzen* and its derivative, *gelâzen*, both verbs, though he occasionally uses their adjectival forms. *Lâzen* and *gelâzen* denote this transformation process. They do not, as these two commentators imply, depict a state or an end towards which one progresses. They are right to focus on the state of detachment, *abgescheidenheit*, as something Eckhart advocates. They simply focused on the term which denotes the process which leads towards it, rather than the term which describes the new state. This distinction is important inasmuch as the transition process, though it has much in common with the goal, is distinguished from the goal in significant ways. *Lâzen* and *gelâzen* denote the process, *abgescheidenheit* the goal.

[63] Blakney, p. 238, "Fragment No. 14. Even though these fragments are of unclear origin, the point here is consistent with Eckhart's teaching, as well as that of his order.

[64] W 2:160.

[65] W 2:57.

[66] Clark and Skinner, p. 126.

[67] DW 2:61:5 = W 1:142

[68] Clark and Skinner, p. 65.

[69] W 1:110.

[70] W 1:100.

71 W 2:87.
72 W 2:159.
73 W 2:158.
74 W 2:160.
75 Clark and Skinner, p. 126.
76 Clark and Skinner, p. 126.
77 Ibid. Cf. Caputo, p. 136–7.
78 Colledge and McGinn, p. 280.
79 W 1:46–7.
80 W 1:45.
81 W 1:46.
82 W 1:117.
83 W 1:45–6.
84 DW 5:283:8 = Clark and Skinner, p. 98.
85 Colledge and McGinn, p. 277.
86 DW 5:438–40, n. 1. For a fairly direct usage in this sense, see DW 1:250:7 = W 2:252.
87 DW 3:279:5 = W 2:201.
88 W 2:144.
89 Colledge and McGinn, p. 47.
90 W 1:151.
91 W 2:236.
92 W 1:151.
93 Schurmann, p. 16.
94 W 1:80. This is the passage whose converse was quoted above.
95 W 2:133.
96 W 2:125.
97 DW 1:199–20 = D 2:188.
98 W 2:87.
99 W 2:204.
100 W 2:2.
101 W 2:204.
102 W 2:132.
103 W 1:118.
104 W 2:2–3.
105 Schurmann (1978a, b), Caputo (1978a, b), etc.
106 W 2:132.
107 W 2:132.
108 Clark, Kelley, McGinn (Szernach), etc.
109 Caputo (1978 b), p. 202, 207.
110 Schurmann, p. 14.
111 Schurmann, p. 14.
112 Schurmann (1978 a), p. 17.
113 Fingarette.
114 Clark and Skinner, p. 163.
115 W 2:134.
116 Actually Fingarette distinguishes numerous uses of the slippery term

self:-ego, the self of practical life, self-representations, self-consciousness, ego-feeling. However the critical distinction he draws, pp. 311–2, is between just these two.

117 Fingarette, p. 312.
118 Ibid.
119 Fingarette, p. 312.
120 Fingarette, p. 330.
121 W 2:57.
122 Fingarette, p. 327.
123 Fingarette, p. 314.
124 Fingarette, p. 324.
125 Ibid., p. 298.
126 Clark and Skinner, p. 163.
127 W 1:80.
128 Fingarette, p. 312.
129 W 1:142
130 Clark and Skinner, p. 65.
131 Fingarette, p. 318–9.
132 Fingarette, 319.
133 To mention just one famous example, Farid ud-Din Attar's *Mantiq Ut-Tair* (*The Conference of the Birds*) (Boulder: Shambhala Press, 1971), develops the journey motif at length. The motif also abounds in medieval spiritual literature.
134 Jacob Needleman's *Lost Christianity* (Garden City, N.Y.: Doubleday, 1980), pp. 144–65, makes this point.
135 This is but an impression derived from their reputations and a superficial reading of their respective works, *The Little Book of Eternal Wisdom and the Little Book of Truth* and Tauler's *Spiritual Conferences*. See also James Clark, *The Great German Mystics: Eckhart, Tauler and Suso* (Oxford: Blackwells, 1949).

CHAPTER FIVE

1 W 1:29.
2 DW 3:381:3 = W 2:321.
3 DW 3:487:2 = W 1:84.
4 Contra McGinn, "The God beyond God: Theology and Mysticism in the Thought of Meister Eckhart," *Journal of Religion*, 61, p. 16, who asserts that "a careful search reveals that there are only three treatments of *raptus* or what we could call mystical ecstasy in his voluminous writings." He does not enumerate. The passages I have identified using the term *gezücken* are: DW 1:403:1 = W 2:72; DW 3:36:6 = W 2:213; DW 3:38:2 =

W 2:214; DW 3:381:3 = W 2:321; DW 3:487:2–487:10 = W 1:84; DW 3:483:4–9 = W 1:83; DW 5:411:6 = Clark and Skinner 163; DW 420:10 = Clark and Skinner 166; Pfeiffer 273:30 = W 2:280; LW 4:202; LW 5:93–5 (discussing *ecstasis mentis*).

[5] For example, W 1:7; 1:117; Clark and Skinner, pp. 101, 156. There are others.

[6] E.g. DW 3:486:13.

[7] For help on these terms I am grateful to Eckhard Kuhn-Osius.

[8] W 1:3.

[9] W 1:4.

[10] Ibid.

[11] W 1:20.

[12] Ibid.

[13] W 2:14.

[14] Kelley, throughout *Meister Eckhart on Divine Knowledge*, observes the same thing, though he phrases it in terms of principal knowledge.

[15] *The Conferences of Cassian*, in *Western Asceticism*, trans. and ed. Owen Chadwick (Philadelphia: The Westminster Press, 1958). Eckhart demonstrates his acquaintance by paraphrasing Cassian in DW 3:481:2 ff and 5:279 ff. It should be clear that such an acquaintance is not germane to my argument, since I am using Cassian to describe a common pattern of mental activity, which is, I will argue, universal to time and culture.

[16] Ibid., p. 198.

[17] Ibid. p. 241.

[18] Ibid. pp. 244–5.

[19] Ibid.

[20] See here G. Kessler and N. Prigge, "Is Mystical Everywhere the Same?" *Sophia* 21 (April, 1982). Reprinted in *The Problem of Pure Consciousness*, ed. Robert K. C. Forman (N.Y.: Oxford University Press, 1990), pp 269–287.

[21] W 1:20. Obviously intentionality cannot be equated with Eckhart's "outwards." Eckhart's "outwards" refers to the association of the self with the creaturely world and its image within. "Intentional" refers to the fact that consciousness is conscious of some manifold, be it thought, sensation or object, as its content.

[22] W 1:20.

[23] W 1:7.

[24] Clark and Skinner, p. 101.

[25] W 1:7.

[26] Pfeiffer 7:27.

[27] DW 3:486–487 = W 1:83–84.

[28] W 1:20.

[29] W 2:215.

[30] DW 5:411:6, translation mine.

[31] W 1:8 quoting *De Mystica Theologia* 1, MPG 3, 997 (W 1:13, n. 13).

[32] On the possibility of such a state, see articles in *The Problem of Pure*

Consciousness by Forman, Rothberg, Bernhardt, Perovich, Prigge and Kessler, and Franklin.

[33] W 2:72–73.

[34] W 2:72–3.

[35] As is the case in common language, I equate "awake" with not being unconscious or not being asleep. See here Kessler and Prigge.

[36] W 1:7. On this notion, see Robert K. C. Forman, "The Construction of Mystical Experience, *Faith and Philosophy* 5, No. 3 (1988), pp. 254–267.

[37] W. T. Stace, *Mysticism and Philosophy*, (London: The Macmillan Press Ltd., 1960) pp. 85–86.

[38] Robert K. C. Forman, "Pure Consciousness Events and Mysticism," *Sophia*, 25 no. 1 (April, 1986): pp. 49–58. See also the articles in Part I of *The Problem of Pure Consciousness*.

[39] W 1:3.

[40] Elsewhere Eckhart uses an image of "two": the outward and the inward man. The outward is responsible for both thought and perception. (Clark and Skinner, p. 200.) It observes through the five senses, the intellect, the power of desire, etc. (Clark, p. 58–9) Under this metaphor, the "innermost" man plays the same role as the "inner man" we discuss here.

[41] I owe this image to Clark, p. 60.

[42] W 1:144.

[43] W 1:144.

[44] Clark, p. 61.

[45] W 1:275.

[46] Clark and Skinner, p. 183.

[47] The "spark" was Peter Lombard's expression who, it is said, borrowed it from St. Jerome. The concept itself has had an illustrious history among Christian mystics. To Hugh of St. Victor, it was *acumen mentis*, a high and elevated, subtle element. For Richard of St. Victor it was *summun mentis*, a deep and hidden element. To Teresa it was the center of the soul, the spirit of the soul. It was Eckhart however who made the concept and its expression, "spark of the soul," famous.

[48] W 1:144.

[49] W 1:16.

[50] W 1:148.

[51] W 1:3.

[52] W 1:3.

[53] W 1:274.

[54] W 1:275. C. W 1:144.

[55] I say "virtually" here because generally the ground is spoken of as something one "works out of." Working "out of" this ground is thus an advance on the temporary encounter with it in *gezucket*. Yet the ground always retains the characteristics first located in this experience, and is thus defined in precisely its terms.

[56] W 2:108–9. In this paragraph I have referenced only those passages

applying these characteristics to the ground. How they apply to *gezucket* is self-evident.

[57] W 1:3.

[58] W 1:76.

[59] W 1:76.

[60] W 1:144; 275.

[61] W 1:312.

[62] W 1:3.

[63] W 1:258.

[64] W 1:3.

[65] W 1:7.

[66] W 1:117.

[67] W 2:312–3.

[68] W 1:147.

[69] Clark and Skinner, p. 153. Cf. W 1:183.

[70] W 1:64.

[71] W 1:157–8. Walshe suggests that this passage is probably a record of a personal experience, in which Eckhart uses the third person just as St. Paul does in 2 Cor. 12:2ff. I tend to agree with Walshe, only because Eckhart's expressions here are so original and evocative. One is unlikely to be so creative when presenting others' peak experiences.

[72] W 1:296.

[73] W 2:72.

[74] Ibid.

[75] W 1:83–4.

[76] W 2:53.

[77] W 1:147.

[78] W 2:312–3.

[79] Stace, p. 86.

[80] See here "Is Pure Consciousness Unmediated: A Response to Katz," Paper delivered to the American Academy of Religion, November 1985. See "Introduction" to Robert K. C. Forman, ed., *The Problem of Pure Consciousness*.

[81] Stace, p. 86.

[82] Since the phrase "Altered States of Consciousness" has been developed expressly to include both the states induced by psychoactive drugs and those produced by more traditional ascetic and religious regimens, and since in this book we will not touch upon the states produced by psychoactive drugs, I will use the more traditional phrase, *State of Consciousness*, when appropriate to speak of the interior changes spoken of by Eckhart. In doing so we must beware not to confuse this use of *State of Consciousness* with a more trivialized usage like "He is in an emotional state of consciousness," or "after reading about the Hopi, she is in a Hopi state of consciousness." I shall mark off my term with capitals, "State of Consciousness."

[83] Charles Tart, "Introduction" in *Altered States of Consciousness*, ed. Charles Tart (N.Y.: John Wiley and Sons, 1969) pp. 1–2. Cf. Arnold Ludwig's definition: "Any mental state(s), induced by various physiologi-

cal, psychological or pharmacological maneuvers or agents, which can be recognized subjectively by the individual himself (or by an objective observer of the individual) as representing a sufficient deviation in subjective experience or psychological functioning from certain general norms for that individual during alert, waking consciousness." Arnold Ludwig, "Altered States of Consciousness," in Charles Tart, ed., *Altered States of Consciousness*, (New York: John Wiley and Sons, 1969), pp. 9–10.

[84] Roland Fischer, "State Bound Knowledge: I Can't Remember What I Said Last Night but It Must Have Been Good," in R. Woods, ed., *Understanding Mysticism* (Garden City: Image Books, 1980), pp. 306–311.

[85] Charles Tart, *States of Consciousness*, (N.Y.: E. P. Dutton, 1975), p. 59.

[86] Claudio Naranjo and Robert Ornstein, *On the Psychology of Meditation*, (New York: Penguin, 1972). For an excellent bibliography, see Ludwig, but see here Ulrich Weithaus, *The Reality of Mystical Experience: Self and World in the Work of Mechthilde of Magdeburg*, Ph. D. Dissertation, Temple University Department of Religion, 1986. She finds differences between, e.g. female and male spirituality, and would distinguish between states from different ages. But her use of the term *States of Consciousness* is far wider and more general than is mine. As such, it loses its specificity.

[87] Kieckhefer, p. 224. See also McGinn in Szernach.

[88] Kelley, *Meister Eckhart on Divine Knowledge*, argues that Eckhart is no mystic because he does not advocate passing states. Schurmann, p. 15, denies that Eckhart was interested in an "instantaneous *raptus* or a 'mystique of vision'" (p. 23 Cf. p. 84). I noted that McGinn, "The God Beyond God," found "only three" references to it. Elsewhere he writes that Eckhart shows no real interest in rapture" (McGinn in Szernach, p. 248).

[89] This passage is used to buttress this claim in Colledge and McGinn, p. 57; Kieckhefer, p. 223; etc.

[90] W 1:126–7.

[91] Cf. W 1:56.

[92] For instance, in W 1:172 he chastises those who are "bound with attachment" to such.

[93] W 1:117–8.

[94] W 1:72, another popular passage among the antimystics.

[95] W 1:9.

[96] W 1:7.

[97] W 1:84.

[98] W 1:144.

[99] W 1:7.

[100] W 1:82–3.

[101] W 1:138–9.

[102] Cf. Kieckhefer, 1978, p. 224.

[103] Clark and Skinner, p. 101.

[104] DW 5:291 = Clark and Skinner, p. 102.

[105] Clark and Skinner, pp. 156–7.

[106] Ibid.

[107] Clark and Skinner, p. 157.

[108] Clark and Skinner, p. 158.

[109] Clark and Skinner, p. 161 n. 2.

[110] DW 5:420:2–10.

[111] DW 1:91:4 = W 1:117. Cf. also a similar usage in DW 5:262:9 = Clark and Skinner, p. 91.

[112] DW 5:291:3–7 = Clark and Skinner 102.

[113] Colledge and McGinn, p. 254. Clark's translation here is unclear.

[114] DW 5:207 = Clark and Skinner, p. 70.

[115] DW 1:359:8 = W 2:338.

[116] DW 5:276:8 = Clark and Skinner, p. 195.

[117] DW Sermon 86 = W Sermon 9.

[118] Raymond Petry, "Social Responsibility and the Late Medieval Mystics," *Church History*, 21 (1952), p. 4. Dom Cuthbert Butler, *Western Mysticism: The Teachings of St. Augustine, Gregory and Bernard on Contemplation and the Contemplative Life: Neglected Chapters in the History of Religion*, (London: Constable and Co., 1922), pp. 200 ff.

[119] In this reading he follows Aquinas's emphasis on the mixed life. Aquinas, too, had advocated a life of action performed as the fruits of contemplation, though without Ekhart's mystical tenor.

[120] W 1:82–3.

[121] W 1:87.

[122] W 1:88–9.

[123] W 1:80.

[124] W 1:80–1.

[125] W 1:81.

[126] Clark and Skinner, p. 76, Cf. W 1:10, where what "gleams and flashes before my soul" is said to "lure the soul and draw her toward itself."

[127] Clark and Skinner, p. 105–6.

[128] Clark and Skinner, p. 83.

[129] Wentzlaff-Eggebert, pp. 88 and 99 observes a similar compensatory tendency on Eckhart's part, though he does not recognize the interior necessity of this change of emphasis.

[130] DW 5:411, translation mine. The connection between detachment and rapture is here stated explicitly. It is also stated in Clark and Skinner, p. 166, where the inward man is said to be enlivened through a process of detachment; if one gives ones powers over through detachment *entirely* to the inward man, one becomes enraptured. What is the nature of the connection between detachment and *raptus*? There is an intuitive connection between the characteristic Eckhart calls *abegescheiden*, which carries largely psychological and moral overtones, and *gezucket*, but Eckhart does not amplify. I would suggest that the following might be a logical place for research. I start with the obvious truth that the psychology must be involved in the thinking process. There must be a reason that the mind is led to think about this or that, and that reason must in some way have to do with psychologically determined needs and desires. Were someone to

be absolutely fully detached, having absolutely no emotional investment in any objects or lines of action, no conflicting desires would draw him/her outwards. Nothing would therefore lead him/her in any particular direction, and he or she will be left alone and in silence. Hence rapture would result from the absence of attachments. But an amplification and verification of this hypothesis will have to be left to the psychologists.

[131] Clark and Skinner, p. 168.

CHAPTER SIX

[1] W 2:291.

[2] To set them of as distinctive States of Consciousness, I will capitalize these terms.

[3] W 1:68.

[4] W 1:68.

[5] W 2:181. For an explanation of this expression, see 2:185 n. 9. Italics mine.

[6] W 2:230.

[7] W 1:35.

[8] Trans., adapted from W 1:74.

[9] W 1:74.

[10] W 1:67.

[11] W 1:68.

[12] Fingarette, pp. 294, 327.

[13] His sometimes use of *inquantum* (in so far as) would suggest that he means that the Birth develops in proportion to the decrease of attachments. This makes a great deal of sense and it is the route he took in the defense. However, in nearly all of his sermons he asserted that he seeks a complete detachment, "if you grieve in your heart for *anything. . .*" I think we should take such utterances, which form the bulk of his assertions concerning the Birth, quite seriously. He clearly had a complete detachment in mind as his goal.

[14] Though the Birth is the most famous image, it is not the only image he employs. Among others, the new state is a seeing Sion (W 1:66); it makes one a "genuine man" (W 1:118); it is an enlightened or illumined man (W 1:212); or one encounters the fully risen Lord (W 1:248). Though twice he uses the simile of a kiss (Clark and Skinner, pp. 203, 242; W 2:51) and occasionally the term *marriage* (LW 3:244), this conservative Dominican tends to shun the phraseology of human love as he describes this state. Possibly this was in response to the erotic imagery of the frenetic Beguines, as seen for example in a Mechthilde of Magdeburg. The permanent transformation was like a castle which, once prepared, can hold the divine

guest (Clark and Skinner, p. 86). Sometimes the transformed soul is described as like a mirror, in which the sun (e.g. God) is always reflected; or described as like a log which becomes permanently vaporized by fire (W 2:159). While my analysis could be extended to some or all of these images, in the interests of space I will largely restrict myself to Eckhart's favorites.

[15] W 1:67. Cf. 2:157.

[16] Cf. McGinn in Szernach, p. 248.

[17] DW 5:262–84.

[18] For example, DW 20 a, b = W 32 a, b.

[19] Trans. Clark 188. W 2:135 is too compact here.

[20] W 2:136. For this paragraph I am indebted to Caputo, *The Mystical element in Heidegger's Thought*, (Oberlin: Oberlin Printing Co., 1978), p. 114.

[21] W 2:135.

[22] These are from the Bull, articles 10 and 11. W 1:xlviii.

[23] W 1:231.

[24] W 1:231.

[25] Clark and Skinner, p. 154.

[26] For someone who has undergone the Breakthrough of the Soul to the Godhead, and can verify the theory in daily experience, it is descriptive of just that experience. But I am getting ahead of myself. See chapters seven and eight.

[27] W 1:1.

[28] W 2:157.

[29] W 1:157–8.

[30] Jean Leclercq, *The Love of Learning and the Desire for God: A Study of Monastic Culture*, (New York: Fordham University Press, 1961), p. 65. Cf. p. 316.

[31] W 1:74.

[32] W 1:17–18.

[33] W 2:157.

[34] W 2:32.

[35] W 1:117.

[36] W 2:136.

[37] W 2:281; Clark and Skinner, p. 85, LW 3:242.

[38] W 2:157.

[39] W 141–2.

[40] Condemned in Article 12 of the Bull.

[41] W 2:291, *et passim*.

[42] For a history of the notion of the power or spark, see Schurmann, pp. 43–7 and Ancelet-Hustache pp. 65–6. Eckhart's addition of the Birth of the word within is a modification of Augustine who said that "the word of man, by the likeness of which the word of God may be somehow seen as in an enigma." Eckhart's stress on the clarity of this presence is original. See Schurmann, p. 20.

[43] If the experience is dualistic, it may be so because the inherited

linguistic patterns were themselves dualistic, as Professor Katz would presumably argue. Steven Katz, "Language, Epistemology, and Mysticism," in *Mysticism and Philosophical Analysis*, (Oxford: Oxford University Press, 1978, pp. 22–74.) This is no place to argue out a case for or against linguistic prefiguration. But see here my "Introduction: Mysticism, Constructivism and Forgetting" in *The Problem of Pure Consciousness*.

[44] Though this is a term of logic, I intend it more in terms of a physical analogy with the "dichotomy" as used in astronomy. "Dichotomous" is used to describe the moon or a planet, whose surface appears half-illuminated and half-dark. I consider this an excellent analogy with the state of affairs we have here, in which the human awareness is aware of both a "darkness" and "light" simultaneously. Interestingly, this can be taken in two ways; e.g. Eckhart sometimes analogizes "darkness" to the divine nothingness and sometimes to the nonlight of the creaturely world. Being cognizant of something *vis-à-vis* a silent emptiness is the hallmark of this state.

[45] Clark and Skinner, p. 167. See below for an explication of the material which follows.

[46] Clark and Skinner, p. 163.

[47] W 2:125.

[48] W 2:167.

[49] Ibid. The usually insightful Walshe calls the phrase an "obscure remark" in a gloss. I think he is being too literalistic. Eckhart here is at his most poetically evocative.

[50] W 2:125.

[51] W 2:126.

[52] W 2:126.

[53] In the Hindu tradition see Maharishi Mahesh Yogi's *On the Bhagavad Gita* (Baltimore: Penguin, 1969) and Swami Muktananda's *Play of Consciousness (Chitshakti Vilas)* (San Francisco: Harper and Row, 1978). In Buddhism see the experiential portraits in Phillip Kapleau's *The Three Pillars of Zen* (Boston: Beacon Press, 1965). For a modern instance, see Bernadette Roberts' *The Experience of No Self* (Boulder: Shambhala Press, 1982).

[54] Romain, Rolland, *Choix de lettres de Romain Rolland, Cahier 17* (Paris: Albin Michel, 1967), pp. 264–6. This letter was sent to Sigmund Freud, and is discussed in his *Civilization and Its Discontents*, trans. James Strachey, (New York: W. W. Norton and Co. 1961), pp. 11–13 *et passim*. The entire letter is translated into English for the first time in Appendix I.

[55] Rolland, p. 265.

[56] Clark, p. 84.

[57] Schurmann, p. 63; Caputo, p. 199–202.

[58] McGinn in Szernach, p. 254.

[59] Kieckhefer, pp. 208–214; Tobin, p. 167.

[60] W 2:124.

[61] Clark and Skinner, p. 78.

[62] See for example W 1:93.

[63] Cf. St. Thomas, *Summa Theol.* I, Q. 21 A. 4. Cf. also L W IV, 122.

[64] W 2:231–2.

[65] W 2:233. Cf. W 1:124, in which the image of God, which is found in the power, "precedes the will and the will follows the image."

[66] W 1:128.

[67] See below.

[68] Clark and Skinner, p. 168.

[69] W 2:319.

[70] If it is in fact a new State of Consciousness, something identical should be seen cross-culturally. While further research is needed here, the case of Romain Rolland begins to suggests that it is.

[71] W 2:136.

[72] Clark, pp. 144–5.

[73] Clark, p. 146.

[74] Colledge and McGinn, p. 129.

[75] I am indebted here to John Caputo, *The Mystical Element in Heidegger's Thought*, (Oberlin: Oberlin Printing Co., 1978), p. 116.

[76] W 1:83.

[77] W 1:84–5.

[78] A parallel formulation is found in R. L. Franklin, "A Science of Pure Consciousness?", *Religious Studies* 19:193, speaking of the "transcendental consciousness" achieved during Transcendental Meditation. Benedict M. Ashley, O. P., "Three Strands in the Thought of Eckhart, the Scholastic Theologian," *The Thomist*, 42, 1978: 238, calls the goal Eckhart seeks "pure consciousness."

[79] DW 2:275 = W 2:118.

[80] W 2:87.

[81] W 1:60, 63; 2:118.

[82] W 1:138; 2:83.

[83] Clearly Eckhart does not mean the physical optical or auditory mechanisms, the eyeball, optic nerve, etc. These organs bring visual and auditory images (*bilde*) only, and images are eliminated. "If I were to see God with my eyes, these eyes with which I see color, that would be all wrong, being temporal." (W 2:143–4).

[84] W 1:216.

[85] W 2:189.

[86] W 2:115.

[87] Luke 11:28.

[88] Clark and Skinner, p. 201.

[89] W 2:323.

[90] W 2:21. Cf. William James' parallel example: "A presence, I might say, yet that is too suggestive of personality, and the moments of which I speak did not hold the consciousness of a personality, but something in myself made me feel myself a part of something bigger than I . . . (James, *Varieties*, p. 394 n.)

[91] W 1:51.

[92] W 2:159.

93 Perhaps it is like an autochthonous sensation, pins and needles.
94 James, pp. 424–425.
95 James, p. 515.
96 James, p. 508.
97 W 2:87.
98 W 1:63.
99 W 1:60–1.
100 A reflexivity of awareness was a common concern of scholastics. See Thomas, *Sys. Theol.* 1:87:C. Eckhart uses this theme to express a mystical form of awareness in which the subject and the object coalesce.
101 David Hume, *A Treatise of Human Nature*, ed. L A. Selby-Bigge (Oxford: Clarendon Press, 1888), p. 252. Reference from James R. Horne, "Do Mystics Perceive Themselves?" *Religious Studies*, 13:327.
102 W 1:126.
103 Jean-Paul Sartre, *The Transcendence of the Ego*, Trans. Forrest Williams and Robert Kirkpatrick (New York: Farrar, Straus and Giroux, n.d.), p. 44.
104 W 1:139.
105 Ludwig, Arnold, "Altered States of Consciousness," in Charles Tart, ed., *Altered States of Consciousness* (New York: John Wiley and Sons, 1969), pp. 9–22. This is a reprint of an article which first appeared in *Archives of General Psychiatry*, 15 (1966): 225–34.
106 Ludwig, pp. 13–18. Where the characteristics are unexpected, I have given a few instances of these characteristics in the footnotes.
107 Ludwig calls this changes in "Body Image." This is too narrow a term for what he describes.
108 W 1:216.
109 W 1:208.
110 W 2:189.
111 W 1:41.
112 DW 3:151 = W 2:169.
113 W 2:317.
114 W 2:236. Cf. Ancelet-Hustache p. 54, etc.
115 W 2:236.
116 W 1:15. Cf. W 1:127.
117 W 1:216.
118 W 2:144.
119 W 2:142.
120 W 2:157 Cf. W 1:216; 2:314; Note the juxtaposition here of atemporality with "in time." This is the paradoxical dichotomy of this Birth.
121 W 1:203. Cf. W 2:142, 144, 236.
122 See Arthur Diekman "Deautomatization and the Mystic Experience," in Charles Tart, ed., *Altered States of Consciousness* (New York: John Wiley and Sons, 1969), p. 33.
123 Julian of Norwich, *Showings*, trans. and ed. Edmund Colledge and James Walshe (New York: Paulist Press, 1978), exemplifies such visual imagery.

[124] See St. John's *The Dark Night of the Soul* in *The Complete Works of Saint John of the Cross*, ed. E. Allison Peers (London: Burns and Oates, 1943).

[125] W 1:88.

[126] W 1:92.

[127] W 1:143.

[128] Mechthilde of Magdeburg, *The Flowing Light of the Godhead*, trans. Lucy Menzies (London: Longmans and Green, 1953).

[129] As seen in Teresa of Avila's ecstasies, St. John's Dark Night, etc.

[130] W 1:128. See also W 2:133, 125; Clark and Skinner, p. 163.

[131] Richard M. Bucke, *Cosmic Consciousness*, (New York: Causeway Books, 1900, reprint 1974) pp. 8–9.

[132] W 1:61. Cf. Pfeiffer, p. 332:22.

[133] Clark and Skinner, p. 102.

[134] W 2:308. Cf. Aug *Conf*. X 40, n. 65 (Quint), and *Conf*. 1:1. (Walshe).

[135] W 2:308.

[136] W 2:194–5.

[137] See here Roland Fischer, "State-Bound Knowledge: I Can't Remember What I said Last Night, but It Must have been Good," in *Understanding Mysticism*, ed. Woods (Garden City, N.Y.: Doubleday, 1980) pp. 306–11.

[138] W 1:237.

[139] W 2:72.

[140] W 2:115.

[141] James, p. 422.

[142] Ludwig discounts this feeling as bearing little relationship to the objective "truth" of the content of this experience. But this discounting is of the insights during LSD experiences, and is ill-applied, it seems to me, to mystical insights which may stand as the basis for a mature religion such as Buddhism or some sects of Hinduism.

[143] See for example Eckhart's Commentaries on John, number 106, 115, 117, 123, Colledge and McGinn, pp. 162, 167–8, 170. (P. 310, n. 215.)

[144] That a mystical experience may plausibly be thought to be without intentional truths, see my dissertation, "Contructivism in to Zen Buddhism, Paramatha and in Eckhart', (Columbia University, 1988), Chapter 2.

[145] Cf. Colledge and McGinn, p. 51–2.

[146] W 2:136.

[147] W 2:135–6. Cf. 2:333.

[148] W 2:182–3.

[149] W 2:118.

[150] Colledge and McGinn, p. 134.

[151] Of course, these are still *attributes*. But they are attributes in the simplest sense of the term, like sensations, which incorporate a minimum sort of judgment.

[152] W 1:1.

[153] This light is in the darkness image is taken from John 1:5, "The light shines in the darkness, and the darkness has not overcome it." Eckhart

transforms this passage into a statement of anthropology rather than theology.

[154] On being an image, see below.

[155] Colledge and McGinn, p. 243. Clark here is opaque.

[156] "Slough off" is his expression, see W 1:94.

[157] W 1:258–9. That the indwelling of the Word become Flesh, or Truth, is synonymous with becoming the Son of God, see Clark and Skinner, p. 85, 164; LW 3:241: and W No. 35.

[158] Except the relatively trivial fact that it is not X.

[159] See below, on timelessness in this experience.

[160] W 2:144–5. Cf. W 2:142.

[161] W 1:67.

[162] W 1:51.

[163] W 1:60–1.

[164] W 2:118.

[165] W 1:183–4. Clark and Skinner, p. 153.

[166] W 1:231.

CHAPTER SEVEN

[1] W 1:205.

[2] W 2:105.

[3] Ueda, pp. 99–140; Caputo, p. 215–6; Schurmann, pp. 67–74, 159–65; Colledge and McGinn, pp. 55–6, D. T. Suzuki, *Mysticism: Christian and Buddhist*, (New York: Macmillan, 1957), pp. 13–20.

[4] As noted by Schurmann, p. 67–8.

[5] DW 2:473:5 = W 2:252.

[6] DW 5:207:8 = Clark and Skinner, p. 70.

[7] DW 3:181 = W 1:299.

[8] DW 2:448–9 = W 2:295.

[9] DW 2:579:2 = W 1:252.

[10] The parallel with the Cartesian "ghost in the machine" notion is unmistakable. Eckhart's direct influence is unlikely however; let us say that both inherited the same (biblical) tradition.

[11] DW 2:198:4 = W 1:277.

[12] DW 2:198 = W 1:277.

[13] DW 5:208:12 = Clark and Skinner, p. 71.

[14] DW 2:76:3 = W 1:136.

[15] W 2:45–6.

[16] W 2:46.

[17] "God performs" conjecturally by Quint.

[18] That is, the discovery of the Godhead throughout all actions is based on my humility.

[19] W 2:47. I have changed Walshe's "he" to "He".

[20] W 2:105.

[21] Ibid.

[22] W 2:105. In this interpretation of the Breakthrough to the Godhead, I realize I am inverting the standard Eckhart interpretation which has the Godhead as the One *beyond* God, without properties. See below and the next chapter.

[23] Clearly a reference to Aristotle's and Thomas's unmoved mover, though given a mystical slant.

[24] Caputo and Barciauskas, *The Dynamic of Person in Eckhart's Mysticism and its Relation to the Sunyata Doctrine* (Dissertation, Fordham University Department of Theology, 1983) both maintain that both the Birth and the Breakthrough are part of an existential process of withdrawal from and reinvolvement with the world. They go on to say that the Birth is the "outcome or developmental complement to the Breakthrough: the word is spoken by the Father in the stillness of the desert." (Barciauskas, Personal Communication, 1984. Cf. Caputo, p. 224.) While I agree that these two states are part of such an existential process as they both suggest, it is passages like the above which convince me that they have the order reversed. I agree here more with McGinn in Colledge and McGinn, p. 55, that the Breakthrough is the more ultimate of the two.

The problem with Caputo's and Barciauskas's account is that the multivalent term "Godhead" marks both the silent desert "within" the soul and also the desert discovered in the Breakthrough to the Godhead (see chapter 8). Breakthrough-talk consistently entails a discovery of the divine relationship *with objects*, whereas many "Godhead" passages (not in a Breakthrough context) refer to the silent oneness within the soul only. It is true that the Birth is an advancement on the discovery of a silent oneness at the depths, as I have shown in chapter six. However, that discovery of the Godhead within is not *equivalent* to breaking through to the Godhead. The proof texts which Caputo uses to establish that the Birth is the development outcome of the Breakthrough actually never contain the term *durchbruch*.

[25] W 2:118.

[26] W 2:119.

[27] Clark and Skinner, p. 101.

[28] This motif is developed at some length in Ueda, pp. 87–9.

[29] W 1:239.

[30] W 2:57.

[31] W 1:32.

[32] Clark and Skinner, p. 126.

[33] W 2:57.

[34] W 1:77.

[35] W 2:32. Cf. 2:236 "Where understanding and desire end . . ."

[36] W 2:267. Eckhart goes on to say "His presence is not concealed, for

He is a light, and light is by nature revelation." That is, the coming is unknown to one's individuality, but the presence is known, though again not to one's individuality. Rather, one is aware "in" that presence. This is not a knowledge of it, but a being it.

[37] W 1:15.

[38] W 1:32.

[39] W 1:15; 2:32.

[40] W 1:22.

[41] W 2:125–6.

[42] W 2:145.

[43] W 1:16.

[44] W 1:17–18.

[45] W 2:333.

[46] W 2:157.

[47] DW 3:134:9 = W 2:175.

[48] W 2:176.

[49] This is a very difficult passage. One problem is that when he says of the Birth that "this is the highest perfection of the spirit to which man can attain spiritually in this life," he may imply that what follows can only occur at the day of judgment. I think that this would not be a correct reading, however. In general Eckhart demonstrates very little interest in the afterlife. Here the context suggests that for man to attain the latter stage he must be entirely rid of the last vestiges of "me" and "mine," and that this may (and indeed must) occur in this life. That is in fact the point of the passage. And hence he states that "this is not the highest perfection: that which we will possess for ever *with body and soul*."

[50] W 1:179.

[51] W 2:335.

[52] W 2:331.

[53] Colledge and McGinn, p. 78. This is the third article of the Bull of condemnation. From the "Commentary on John," Colledge and McGinn, p. 127. Cf LW 4:380, Colledge and McGinn, pp. 238–9, 290.

[54] W 2:339.

[55] W 2:341. For this paragraph, I am indebted to McGinn in Colledge and McGinn, pp. 40–41.

[56] W 2:105.

[57] W 2:86.

[58] LW 4, Sermon n. 377. Quoted in Ueda, p. 100. Translation mine.

[59] W 2:275.

[60] W 1:193.

[61] W 1:173. This, Eckhart tells us, is the natural perfection of the soul when the soul becomes in herself a "rational world," (*ein vernünfitgiu werit*) or, as Schurmann translates it, an "intelligible world" (p. 50). Such a term would seem to suggest that Eckhart is speaking of a strictly logical process. But we are speaking here of the "rational" world which is discovered within oneself at this most advanced state of mystical development. Eckhart uses the same term at the end of DW 48 = W 60. There he speaks of

the experience in which the ground within one is perceived to be the "immobility" by which "all things are moved." He prays there that we "may thus live rationally."

Clearly it is a higher "rationality" than we are accustomed to. Cf. also DW 2:421 = W 2:105, where a *vernünfticliche leben* is again associated with the most advanced state of mystical experience: the discovery that "by this immobility all things are moved."

62   W 1:274.

63   This term, in German *geuebeten menschen*, is translated thus in Clark and Skinner, p. 95. Eckhart often loosely distinguishes the Birth from the Breakthrough with such appellations: one in whom the Birth has "truly" occurred, the "fully" illumined man, etc.

64   Colledge and McGinn, p. 247.

65   E.g. DW sermons 10, 12, 29, 60, 81, and 86. In the Latin works we also see it, i.e. in Parables of Genesis, n. 149 (Colledge and McGinn, p. 114.) Colledge and McGinn, 310 n. 228.

66   W 2:145. Though this refers here to the unity of the Godhead and the distinctions of the Trinity, the inherent unity is applicable to the distinctions of the world as well.

67   W 2:145.

68   W 1:263.

69   W 1:193.

70   Clark and Skinner, p. 95.

71   W 2:167. Cf. W 1:45.

72   W 1:45. Here he is speaking within a Birth context. I quote it here because he distinguishes it from the early stages of the Birth by saying "once this Birth has *really* occurred." (Ibid.) In certain sermons he distinguishes the two layers of illumination only vaguely.

73   W 2:275.

74   W 2:145.

75   W 2:250.

76   W 2:337.

77   W 2:337–9.

78   W 2:226.

79   W 2:275.

80   W 2:259.

81   W 2:63.

82   W 1:269.

83   W 2:275.

84   W 2:271.

85   W 2:289.

86   W 1:227.

87   W 2:141.

88   W 2:46–7.

89   W 2:114.

90   Cf. W 1:275.

91   W 2:84.

[92] W 2:141.

[93] W 2:47.

[94] W 1:118.

[95] W 2:264.

[96] Ibid.

[97] W 2:71.

[98] W 2:85.

[99] W 2:84.

[100] W. T. Stace, *Mysticism and Philosophy* (New York: The Macmillan Press, 1960), p. 109.

[101] Rudolf Otto, *Mysticism East and West*, trans. Bertha Bracey and Richard Payne, (New York: Macmillan, 1960), p. 67.

[102] Quoted in Otto, p. 67. Otto glosses that the "perceiving soul" is here simply the perceiver himself.

[103] Ramana Maharshi, *Spiritual Teachings of Ramana Maharshi* (Boulder: Shambhala Press, 1972) p. 98.

[104] Ramana Maharshi, p. 10.

[105] Maharishi Mahesh Yogi, *On the Bhagavad-Gita: A New Translation and Commentary* (Baltimore: Penguin, 1972), p. 442.

[106] Ibid.

[107] Maharishi Mahesh Yogi, p. 448.

[108] Quoted by Stace, p. 106.

[109] John Cassian, "The Conferences of Cassian," in *Western Asceticism*, ed. Owen Chadwick (Philadelphia: The Westminster Press, 1958), p. 237.

[110] W 1:204.

[111] W 1:204.

[112] W 1:204.

[113] Perhaps here a reference to *ruach*, the breath of God, with which he breathed life into Adam, Gen. 2:7, and blew over the waters to create the world (Gen. 1:1).

[114] W 1:205.

CHAPTER EIGHT

[1] W 1:212. Quote on previous page: W 1:227.

[2] Maurer, p. 107.

[3] Maurer, p. 108.

[4] Ibid.

[5] Maurer, p. 91, *Opus Tripartum*, Gen. Prologue.

[6] Maurer, p. 93.

[7] W 2:227.

[8] DW 182:10. The usually correct Walshe has mistranslated here simply "own being." Clark, p. 220, is correct here.

[9] W 2:160. Cf. 2:53.

[10] W 2:339.

[11] LW 3:113. Quoted by Ueda, p. 100.

[12] LW 2:116.

[13] *Rechtfertigungsschrift*, n. 57. Ueda, p. 101.

[14] LW 2:57. Quoted in Ueda, p. 34.

[15] Serm. 105. Ueda, p. 101.

[16] Sap. 151. Ueda, p. 101.

[17] W 1:199.

[18] Ibid.

[19] LW 1:175.

[20] Maurer, p. 33.

[21] W 2:53.

[22] Colledge and McGinn, p. 221. Cf. W 2:274.

[23] Cf. Caputo, p. 211.

[24] This is, strictly speaking illogical, of course. An absolute unity could have neither plurality nor internal relationship. Here we must excuse Eckhart since God is said to be a mystery. See below for the point of this inconsistent doctrine.

[25] Clark and Skinner, p. 226.

[26] Ibid.

[27] Walshe has "He says what he is." Though grammatically plausible, Kelley's translation is more telling and in this context appropriate.

[28] W 1:59.

[29] Schurmann, p. 16.

[30] LW 2:112. Quoted in Ueda, p. 34.

[31] LW 4:363. Quoted in Ueda, p. 32.

[32] Colledge and McGinn, p. 221.

[33] John, n. 343. Quoted in Ueda, p. 32.

[34] This one-way mirror is, of course, my own analogy. Eckhart was fond of an analogy between God and his image in a mirror, as we will see shortly, but he knew nothing of one-way mirrors. He does speak, however, of the darkness of the Godhead, and going beyond the Trinity to that darkness (e.g. W 2:145, 175 & 275). I can only hope that this analogy illuminates more than it obfuscates.

[35] Matthew Fox observes this same fact though interpreting what Eckhart preached from a quite different vantage point.

[36] W 2:158.

[37] W 2:158; 1:124.

[38] W 1:124.

[39] I owe the point of this paragraph to Clark, p. 37.

[40] LW 4:509. Quoted in Ueda, p. 59.

[41] W 1:124.

[42] Ibid.

[43] W. 1:126.

[44] Ibid.

[45] W 2:154.

[46] W 1:124; 2:154.

[47] W 1:124.

[48] W 1:238.

[49] John, n. 23. Quoted in Ueda, p. 60.

[50] Sometimes Eckhart uses the term *God* for that which is one, sometimes *Father*, and sometimes *Godhead*. This is merely one of the maddening pitfalls confronting the poor Eckhart scholar.

[51] W 1:124.

[52] W 1:125.

[53] "Unless the human intellect knew something positively about God it could not deny anything of Him." *De Potentia* 7:5, quoted by F. C. Copleston, S. J. *A History of Medieval Philosophy* (New York: Harper, 1972), p. 196.

[54] Here I am indebted to Copleston, p. 196.

[55] Thomas attempted to solve this paradox with his use of the term *analogy*: when *wisdom* is predicated of God it is neither used univocally nor equivocally but analogically.

[56] For a thorough analysis of the *nomen omninominabile* and the *nomen innominabile*, see Victor Lossky, *Théologie negative et Connaissance de Dieu chez Maître Eckhart* (Paris, Vrin, 1960), chapters 1 and 2.

[57] W 2:275. Cf. Caputo p. 211. Kelley also points out something of this sort in his book, *Meister Eckhart on Divine Knowledge* (New Haven: Yale University Press, 1977). He says that Eckhart's key notion is a "principal understanding:" one must consider everything "as it were from there within the Godhead." (p. 26).

> The *principial* mode of knowledge is the consideration of all things and all manifestation as it were from within the Godhead, the unconditioned Principle . . . It is the consideration of all reality from the standpoint of the full actualization of the *intellectus possibilis*, a consideration made feasible by the communication of the eternal Word of God (p. 250, n. 4.).

Participating in such a new perspective, one may come to understand differently. One will perceive from a new perspective. From this intellectual perspective, one would see differently.

Kelley says of this new perspective that it "cannot be mentally beheld, looked at or conceived, and any attempt to do so as though it were 'out there somewhere or in here somewhere' is illusory" (p. 26). One must instead "participate in" this new principle, he says rightly. Such a "participation in" and a "realizing of truest identity" with it, however, is difficult to reconcile with what he says a few lines later and what dominates the book: that we may "understand" our identity with it. This emphasis on understanding is overly simplistic and intellectualistic. Eckhart repeatedly says this is beyond both understanding and will. Rather one *participates in* the new perspective, "sees" with those eyes, "knows" as God knows

(W 2:142–3). This is not an understanding of one's identity. Rather, it is best understood as a living it, a being identical with it.

58 W 2:32.

59 W 2:37.

60 W 1:15, 284.

61 W 2:37.

62 W 2:12.

63 W 2:53. Cf. 2:275.

64 See below.

65 W 2:141.

66 W 2:143–4.

67 W 2:141.

68 W 2:142.

69 W 2:143.

70 W 2:175.

71 W 2:331. Cf. 2:335.

72 W 2:331.

73 W 2:333.

74 W 2:334. Here the point is that one must work with God. This work requires that one "be" one with God. All of life is therefore required to be uniform with God. To work in total "onement" with God is to be at "onement" with God.

75 W 2:141.

76 W 2:118.

77 W 2:87.

78 Cf. Kelley, p. 61–9.

79 W 2:333.

80 W 1:15.

81 W 2:176.

82 W 1:124.

83 W 2:57.

84 This was defined as the "imageless" image of God on the preceding page.

85 W 2:28.

86 W 2:37.

87 W 2:37.

88 W 2:80.

89 This can be known by one in the *Durchbruch*, who perceives everything from God's vantage point. This falsity parallels Huston Smith's notion of "subration." This he expresses as a series of progressively larger stacked one-way mirror boxes. From outside of each, the truth and errors of the preceding perceptions become obvious. (Unpublished Lecture to the American Academy of Religion, Buffalo, N.Y., 1982).

90 W 2:175.

91 W 2:169.

92 W 2:166. Cf. 2:155.

APPENDIX A

[1] See Edmund Colledge, O.S.A. and J. C. Marler, "Mystical" Pictures in the Suso "Exemplar", MS Strasbourg 2929, *Archivum Fratrum Praedicatorum*, 54 (1984), pp. 293–354. All translations are theirs. I am grateful to Frank Tobin for his help in finding both this picture, translation, and commentary.

APPENDIX B

[1] Rolland pp. 264–266.

Index